"Drawing from his extensive teaching experience, cross-cultural immersion in contexts of poverty, and specialized knowledge in both biblical interpretation and the hermeneutics of mission, Michael Barram is just the person to provide this much-needed resource. *Missional Economics: Biblical Justice and Christian Formation* will help readers think deeply about the ways in which discipleship may and must address economic realities of the twenty-first century."

— JOHN T. CARROLL
Union Presbyterian Seminary

"Here is the scriptural depth necessary for truly biblical reflection on economics. Barram's analysis is enhanced by questions and dialogue-starters that will serve equally well in undergraduate classrooms and in church discussion groups."

— MARK GLANVILLE
Grandview Calvary Church, Vancouver

"Barram invites us to approach concrete economic issues with the 'economic reasoning' that arises from an ever-deepening range of biblical texts. He is the right person to guide us on such a journey, as he brings to bear his immersion in biblical exegesis and interpretation, in missional hermeneutics, and in the perspectives of numerous underside communities in Central and North America."

— GEORGE HUNSBERGER
Western Theological Seminary

THE GOSPEL AND OUR CULTURE SERIES

A series to foster the missional encounter of the gospel
with North American culture

John R. Franke
Series Editor

. .

Recently Published

Craig Van Gelder and Dwight J. Zscheile, *Participating in God's Mission:
A Theological Missiology for the Church in America*

Michael W. Goheen, ed., *Reading the Bible Missionally*

Stefan Paas, *Church Planting in the Secular West:
Learning from the European Experience*

Darrell L. Guder, *Called to Witness: Doing Missional Theology*

Michael J. Gorman, *Becoming the Gospel: Paul, Participation, and Mission*

George R. Hunsberger, *The Story That Chooses Us:
A Tapestry of Missional Vision*

For a complete list of published volumes in this series, see the back of the book.

MISSIONAL ECONOMICS

Biblical Justice and Christian Formation

Michael Barram

WILLIAM B. EERDMANS PUBLISHING COMPANY

GRAND RAPIDS, MICHIGAN

Wm. B. Eerdmans Publishing Co.
2140 Oak Industrial Drive N.E., Grand Rapids, Michigan 49505
www.eerdmans.com

ISBN   978-0-8028-7507-5

Library of Congress Cataloging-in-Publication Data

Names: Barram, Michael D., 1966- author.
Title: Missional economics : biblical justice and Christian formation /
    Michael Barram.
Description: Grand Rapids, Michigan : William B. Eerdmans Publishing Company,
    [2018] | Series: The Gospel and our culture series |
    Includes bibliographical references and index.
Identifiers: LCCN 2017048810 | ISBN 9780802875075 (pbk. : alk. paper)
Subjects: LCSH: Economics—Religious aspects—Christianity. | Economics—
    Biblical teaching. | United States—Economic aspects. | Missions.
Classification: LCC BR115.E3 B345 2018 | DDC 261.8/5—dc23
    LC record available at https://lccn.loc.gov/2017048810

Dedicated to
my students at Saint Mary's College of California
and to my friends in Emmaus Community 3
at First Presbyterian Church, Berkeley, California

Contents

CONTENTS

Foreword

In this important and compelling book Michael Barram aims at nothing less than a shift of lens through which we read Scripture. He sees the inadequacy of both a reductionist confessional reading and a historical-critical reading that works too hard to go "behind the text." His intent is to have us focus on the text that is in front of us or, better, the text that we are in front of—the text that addresses us. And when the text addresses us with contemporary urgency, it is unavoidable that economic issues come to us front and center. The two rejected ways of reading (confessional and historical-critical) have protected us from such urgency economics, narcoticized us, and permitted us not to notice or to care much.

Barram's phrase "missional hermeneutics" is just right. The hermeneutics he proposes and practices means that there is hard interpretive work to be done in order to see how this ancient text comes to us with provocative contemporaneity. But "hermeneutics" is profoundly modified by "missional"—the recognition that the God who indwells the biblical text is on a mission to bring the creation to well-being. That well-being naturally focuses on economic justice because as long as there are beneficiaries and as long as there are victims of a predatory economy, there will be no shalom. While the mission that modifies and characterizes hermeneutics is singularly the mission of God, our reading of the Bible recruits us as participants in God's mission of well-being. This recruitment, Barram makes clear, brings with it immediate and inconvenient requirements to act differently concerning the political economy. Before he begins his survey of specific biblical texts, Barram offers probing questions (pp. 36–37) that may teach us how to read differently, what to ask, and how to notice. These probing questions invite honest interpretive activity around hard issues, such as justice and evangelism, kenotic humility and triumphal confidence, and discipleship and conspicuous consumption. When we have the honesty and courage required to respond to Barram's questions, we will perceive the Bible differently and, with equal clarity, perceive differently our world and our discipleship in it.

What follows in the book is a quick, compelling commentary on texts concerning economic justice. Barram reads the Beatitudes as Jesus's invitation to his disciples to see as he sees—a way of seeing that is very different from our conventional domesticated sight. Such a way of seeing contradicts our usual lack of discernment.

Barram's exposition of the Exodus and covenant in the Old Testament is a sturdy, steady read of the core narrative that grounds both Jewish and Christian imagination. Particularly, he contrasts the horizon of the Exodus with the "American Dream." The American Dream has been greatly celebrated since Martin Luther King Jr.'s "I Have a Dream" speech, which offered a vision of freedom for all. But Barram rightly notices that the dream has a shadow side, readily granting privilege to some at the expense of others. He is acutely aware that the implantation of the dream makes a mockery of our creed of "liberty and justice for all."

Barram's hints in this regard are specified and made concrete by Ta-Nehisi Coates (*Between the World and Me*), who sees that the American Dream is a white dream of luxurious well-being that depends on the cheap labor of nonwhites. Contrasted to this is the Exodus, which narrates the prospect of life outside Pharaoh's predatory economy. That alternative life is ordered, Barram shows, according to the regulations of the Ten Commandments and the several law codes of ancient Israel that aim to preclude exploitation and enact genuine neighborliness in concrete ways. Barram sees how this alternative vision of political economy culminates in the provision and practice of Jubilee so that forgiveness is not simply an act of graciousness and piety but is the rearrangement of social power by the cancellation of debts.

Given the centrality of the Exodus and covenant for the tradition, it is not a surprise that the remainder of Barram's discussion shows the acting out of this vision in Israel's prophets and in the creation tradition. It is not a far leap, then, to the New Testament. The final part of the book concerns Jesus's Sermon on the Mount and the Epistle of James, which affirms that the "true religion" is to "care for orphans and widows"; that is, to place on our horizon those outside ourselves and our own ilk. Martin Luther did indeed famously depreciate the Epistle of James in his accent on free grace. But Luther also declared, "God does not need our good works, but our neighbor does." Barram shows that the sweep of the Bible is about neighbor love, which, among other things, takes the form of public policy and public practice.

I regard this book as uncommonly urgent. The prospect of unemployment growing due to new technologies; the prospect of a natural environment further diminishing due to our addiction to fossil fuels; and the fact of public policy being controlled by an oligarchy that cares not at all for the public good—all these together make the mission of economic justice especially urgent. Barram's compelling study is a wake-up call, summoning away from the pseudogospel of self-indulgence that carves its existence at the expense of the more vulnerable in the neighborhood.

WALTER BRUEGGEMANN
Columbia Theological Seminary
author of *Money and Possessions in the Bible*

Preface

I grew up during the 1970s and early 1980s in a relatively conservative, evangelical Christian environment, in which faith in Jesus and familiarity with the Bible were of paramount importance. As a young person, being a Christian was, for me, mostly a matter of personal piety and moral conduct. Reflections on things like wealth, poverty, economic justice, and human suffering played a limited role in my faith development. In 1985, however, when I was 18, things began to change. That February I had the opportunity to travel with a church group on a two-week trip to Nicaragua. The US-funded war between the Contra rebels and the Sandinista government was still going on, and I discovered poverty there unlike anything I had experienced before. Although I had very few tools, intellectual or otherwise, to make sense of that brief experience, I knew that I wanted to travel outside my normal context again. Then, in 1987, I spent four months traveling in Guatemala, Honduras, Nicaragua, Costa Rica, and Mexico City with a Whitworth College (Spokane, WA) study tour. That trip—which included living for a month in a small, rural town with a Honduran family—and two more over the next three years would change my life. In those days events in Central America were reported on daily in the mainstream news cycle in the United States, and I was there during some of that region's more turbulent times. Questions I could neither fully understand nor ignore—about foreign policy, domestic and international politics, economics, and many related matters—impacted and interrogated my Christian beliefs. Where was God among all of the poverty, suffering, and injustice I experienced? What did it mean to follow Jesus in *this* world? My sincere—albeit simple and naïve—personal faith in Jesus was ill-equipped to make sense of life as I had now experienced it.

A couple of years after completing college, I ended up entering seminary—something I had sworn I would never do—largely as a kind of a spiritual quest. At that point I was struggling to see the relevance of faith as I had known it. I wanted to find out whether the Christian tradition in which I had been raised had anything to offer to the suffering world I had discovered. That initial, half-baked decision to begin theological study led to an entirely unexpected odyssey, from which I emerged, ten long years later, with a doctoral degree in biblical studies, a deep-seated aversion to poverty and economic injustice, and a passion for the purposes of God in the world as reflected in the Bible.

For the past sixteen years, I have taught biblical studies and other justice-oriented courses at Saint Mary's College of California. Particularly influential on my thinking have been the opportunity to teach a regular class on wealth and poverty in the Bible, a year-long sabbatical in Nicaragua (2007-2008), and several travel courses to Central America. This short book represents some reflections on matters of poverty and economic justice that have been percolating within me, in various ways, since the mid-1980s. I hope that the reader will find it to be a helpful guide to reflecting on the Bible and economic matters today.

Acknowledgments

I am grateful, first and foremost, to my wife, Kelli, and to my daughters, Jordan and Devyn, for their admirable patience while I was absent, staring at a computer screen for hours on end. Each of them continues to teach me every day about living life justly and with authenticity. I am also thankful for my parents, Doug and Loretta, who have always supported me in my travels and theological explorations.

I am indebted to my students at Saint Mary's College of California over the years, particularly those in the Wealth and Poverty in the Bible course, many of whom have inspired and sharpened my thinking about the matters that are examined in this book. Likewise, I appreciate the support and encouragement to pursue themes of economic justice in the Bible that I have received from Saint Mary's colleagues, especially in the Department of Theology & Religious Studies. The Faculty Development Fund at Saint Mary's College of California has supported the production of this book in numerous ways, from providing travel funding for conferences to enabling me to enhance my scholarly library for research. I offer my thanks, as well, to Saint Mary's president James Donahue, who facilitated my access to the library resources at his former institution, the Graduate Theological Union, while I was on a sabbatical.

I am deeply thankful for the support I have received over the years from my colleagues who have been on the steering committee of the Gospel and Our Culture Network (GOCN) Forum for Missional Hermeneutics—especially John Franke, George Hunsberger, Darrell Guder, Colin Yuckman, James Brownson, and Mike Gorman. The forum has provided a very helpful laboratory for my converging interests in missional hermeneutics and economic justice. Each of these people has helped to make me a better scholar and person.

Finally, I am extremely thankful to my friends at First Presbyterian Church, Berkeley, which has been my spiritual home for more than fifteen years. Among the many I could mention, I will simply thank former pastor Mark Labberton, Mark Stryker, Jonathan Howard, Clark Sept, and Ryan Pemberton, in particular, for their friendship and advice as I have made this journey. They are the kind of people who help make this life of following Jesus a meaningful and fulfilling adventure. Finally, I appreciate the many folks in Emmaus Community 3 at First Presbyterian Church, who, during my 2014-2015 sabbatical, explored many of the passages in this book with me. The opportunity to write early drafts of many of the sections of this book on a weekly basis—and then to reflect on those passages with them—was exhilarating and memorable. I am thankful to everyone in that group for continuing to shape me and for being willing to undergo transformation together.

Introduction

This is a book of reflections on biblical economic justice and Christian discipleship. More specifically, it contains a series of analytical musings on a range of biblical texts that serve to form their readers—individual and communal, ancient and contemporary—for their mission in the world, particularly with respect to economic matters. Space permits me to treat only a brief—but, I believe, representative—sampling of the many biblical texts that relate to matters of economic justice. My goal here is to whet readers' appetites rather than to provide an exhaustive survey of biblical wisdom on economic matters. And, by design and intention, this book raises more questions than it answers, in order to inspire further reflection and dialogue. In many ways, in fact, that is what the Bible itself does.

Some readers view the Bible as a kind of answer book, a collection of facts about God, faith, ethics, salvation, and heaven—among other things. Even though Scripture has, of course, provided answers to innumerable potential questions that readers have brought to it, thinking about the Bible primarily in terms of the answers it can provide may give us the wrong impression of what the Bible is, how it came to be, and how it can help those of us who read it today. The Bible is not primarily an answer book; it is not an encyclopedia of facts, though some do use it, and thus abuse it, that way. Rather, the Bible represents a conversation—or, better, many different conversations—incorporating numerous voices treating diverse topics, all of which are rooted in real-life human experiences and concerns.

I presuppose that the Bible bears authority in the lives of Christian individuals and in their faith communities. It is, in a crucial sense, God's word. At the same time, we will not try to define precisely what it means to talk about the Bible as the "word of God" or about the precise nature of its authority in the life of Christians and the church. One of the sad truths of Christian history is that Christians have often spent far too much time debating how the Bible should be defined and how its authority should be understood, and, by contrast, too little time simply seeking to live lives clearly and concretely informed by biblical teaching.

The definition and demonstration of biblical authority for Christians' lives are ultimately to be found in how the Bible is embodied in concrete behavior. The proof of biblical authority is to be found, as it were, in the pudding of conduct. Arguments about the nature of the Bible and its authority are largely inconsequential if attention to Scripture does not ultimately lead to the kind of reasoning and behavior that it seeks to engender. All too often Christians have engaged in—and sometimes have become fixated on—academic debates about the Bible while their conduct reflects relatively little of the compassion, mercy, justice, and love that characterize the biblical God they claim to serve. Whatever else we may want to say about the Bible and its role in Christian life, to take biblical authority seriously means that the lives of those of us who read and value the Bible will reflect its influence, both in terms of how we reason about life and through our everyday conduct. Anything less risks becoming mere sophistry or, worse, a form of self-serving, delusional idolatry.

My primary purpose in writing this book is to reflect, exegetically and existentially, on some of what the Bible has to say about what we today might call economic matters—keeping the diversity of its dialogical, conversational framework in mind—so as to provide an accessible resource for individual and communal study and reflection. Again, my hope is that this book will introduce readers to some of the discussions in the Bible about economic justice and economic discipleship and thus raise relevant questions for readers, questions that I believe merit extended and ongoing reflection among those who seek to live faithfully as followers of Jesus Christ today.

Most North American Christians are, at best, only vaguely aware of what the Bible has to say about economic issues related to justice and Christian discipleship. Indeed, on the first day of a college course that I taught on this material, it came home to me just how extensively North American Christians tend to be focused on matters other than the kind of economic justice that the Bible discusses—and, as we shall see, seeks to engender in and demand from its readers. The year was 2004, and I was teaching my signature course, "Wealth and Poverty in the Bible," for just the second time at Saint Mary's College of California. The nation was involved in a presidential campaign that fall, and I asked the students what issues Christians in the United States were most concerned about as election day approached. The students enrolled in the class were not theology majors, nor did they seem especially conversant with the sociopolitical dynamics in the country at that time, so I remember being struck by how quickly they responded to my question. Within about ten seconds, three responses to my query were eagerly offered: "Abortion!" "Gay marriage!" "Stem cell research!" Indeed, I had to admit that those did seem to be the things about which many Christians—at least on the political right, whose voices were gaining attention in the national media—were most exercised in the run-up to that election.

I then asked the students to identify which of those three issues is treated in the Bible. The truth is that none of them is directly addressed in the Bible as such. My sense is that most of my students, and perhaps most of the public at large, tend to assume that when it comes to moral behavior, the Bible is especially concerned about sexual and other "bedroom" issues—and that it emphasizes, first and foremost, what people should *not* do.

By contrast, I pointed out to my students that day, biblical texts have much more to say about economic justice and appropriate conduct relative to the poor and marginalized. Indeed, the Bible is not primarily about prohibiting or condemning behavior. Biblically speaking, God's people are *not* to be known primarily for what they are not supposed to do! Unfortunately, the Bible has a reputation—and Christians often do as well—for negativity. But the Bible's primary concern is to foster proactive and positive reasoning and behavior rooted in and reflective of the mercy, compassion, reconciliation, justice, and love of God.

That early class conversation in 2004 reflected what I have now come to believe is a significant blind spot on the part of North American Christians with regard to economic matters in the Bible. Part of the reason for this situation surely has to do with the social location of North American Christians (and their churches), many of whom have relatively limited personal connection to entrenched poverty, economic deprivation, war, and so forth. Most North American Christians are relatively comfortable, at least from a global perspective. Questions about economic justice are rarely at the forefront of the minds of those of us who generally benefit from today's economic status quo.

North American Christians are deeply formed by their economic en-but are often unaware of the extent to which their perspectives are shaped by contemporary economic orthodoxies—more than by biblical and theological reasoning. In this book I attempt to respond to this kind of blind spot by helping to raise awareness among Christians about their own religious texts. Given the repeated and emphatic manner in which the Bible actually deals with issues of economic justice and discipleship, Christians seeking to follow Christ faithfully cannot but reflect carefully, thoughtfully, and concretely on such concerns.

In truth, in this book I am reflecting on something of my own personal and professional odyssey as I have struggled with the implications of biblical materials pertaining to economic justice and related matters of Christian discipleship. Again, I write both to inform and to encourage deep and ongoing conversations in classrooms and churches about what it might look like for the Christian community in North America to embody—increasingly, intentionally, creatively, and faithfully—a biblically informed witness in the world regarding these issues. I invite my readers to think of these brief reflections and musings as a collection of formative conversation starters designed to foster further thought, conversation, and, ultimately, action.

CHAPTER ONE

Transformation for Life

In Romans 12:2, the apostle Paul urges his Roman Christian readers to allow God to transform them and their behavior for the sake of their gospel-oriented mission in the world: "Do not be conformed to this world, but be transformed by the renewing of your minds, so that you may know what is the will of God—what is good and acceptable and perfect."[1] This verse emphasizes "formation" in at least two ways. First, Paul presupposes that the Roman Christians are to some degree already "conformed" to the non-Christian context in which they live, which is apparently a potential barrier to understanding God's will and appropriately discerning how they should live in light of God's perspective. Second, Paul recognizes that his readers will need to "be transformed" in order to move beyond their conformity.

Romans 12:1-2: The Need for Transformation

In the first eleven chapters of his letter to the Romans, the apostle Paul sketches the most influential and compelling account ever composed of the cosmos-transforming gospel of God in Jesus Christ. Then, beginning in chapter 12, he turns to explore the implications of that gospel, especially for the community of those in Rome whose own lives have been forever altered by the good news. As is typical in Greco-Roman letters, Paul follows the main content portions (the "body") of his correspondence with what

---

1. Unless otherwise noted, all biblical quotations are taken from the New Revised Standard Version.

is known in Greek as *paraenesis* (essentially, moral instruction and encouragement). In Paul's letter to the Roman Christians, this paraenetic section begins with Romans 12:1-2. These two verses serve as a critical pivot point in the letter, linking the main theological argument in chapters 1-11 to the moral exhortation that begins in chapter 12.

"Present Your Bodies as a Living Sacrifice"

In Romans 12:1, Paul writes, "I appeal to you therefore, brothers and sisters, by the mercies of God, to present your bodies as a living sacrifice, holy and acceptable to God, which is your spiritual worship." Paul then begins to explore the implications of the gospel for his readers' everyday lives together and within the wider world in light of—and on the basis of ("therefore")—everything he has written in chapters 1-11. When he urges them "to present" their "bodies as a living sacrifice," he uses language that evokes both the Jewish heritage of faith and the potential for suffering and difficulty (cf. Rom. 5:8). Moreover, this phrase calls for concrete, communal witness: he is exhorting individuals—embodied people, in all their humanity and specificity—to come together as a single "living sacrifice." Paul considers this tangible, unified sacrifice on the part of the believing community to be its "spiritual worship." The Greek word translated "spiritual" here in the New Revised Standard Version is *logikos,* from which we get the English word "logical" (the New English Translation renders the word "reasonable"). Paul has in mind a form of worship that makes logical sense in light of the gospel of God. Appropriate worship here is neither a kind of disembodied, otherworldly spirituality nor something that pertains to isolated individuals. Rather, Paul is calling for concrete witness to the gospel lived out within the context of the real stuff of life—a witness that is fundamentally communal in nature. For Paul, this is what "logical" worship looks like, given what God has and is continuing to accomplish in the world.

In summary, Paul seeks in Romans 12:1 to ensure that the individual Roman believers offer themselves "as a living sacrifice" to God, in communal unity, a sacrifice that they offer together as an appropriate response to the good news of God's work in and through Christ on their behalf and on behalf of the entire creation (see, e.g., Rom. 8:18-25).

"Do Not Be Conformed . . . But Be Transformed"

Romans 12:2 then expresses Paul's deep hope for the community's formation: "Do not be conformed to this world, but be transformed by the renewing of your minds, so that you may discern what is the will of God—what is good and acceptable and perfect." This verse in particular provides a fundamental theme for this study, as it presses toward what will be at the heart of this book, namely, the moral *formation* of the Christian community for its mission in the world. Paul is seeking to form the Roman Christians' moral logic and reasoning so that their behavior, both within the community and beyond, will be appropriate in light of the gospel of Jesus Christ, which Paul has been devoted to unpacking throughout the letter.

In Romans 12:2, then, Paul enjoins the Roman Christians *not* to "be conformed to" the world as they know it, but to allow themselves to "be transformed by the renewing of [their] minds." Again, the goal of such transformation is that they "may discern what is the will of God—what is good and acceptable and perfect." Several things in Romans 12:2 are worth noting further, since they relate to the larger approach and purpose of this book. Let us start with the end of Paul's statement and move progressively toward the beginning. Paul wants the Roman Christian community to be able to discern God's will—to be able to figure out and recognize "what is good and acceptable and perfect." Although the will of God cannot be reduced to mere morality, the epistolary context of this statement shows that clarity of moral discernment is the goal of the transformation the apostle hopes to see in the believers.

"Discernment" is not an especially popular word today, but it is a crucial factor for Paul—and for the Bible more broadly—in moral decision-making. Discernment in this context refers to the process of moral reflection by which we decide what behavioral choices we will make in a given situation. Obviously, then, discernment includes the process of selecting, evaluating, and weighing factors that may need to be considered in order to make appropriate decisions. There can be many such factors with which to wrestle: from general moral principles and ethical theories to matters of character and conscience; from norms and laws to the specific circumstances of a particular moral question or dilemma; from mitigating factors to personal experience, and so on.

For the apostle, moral discernment is fundamentally about grasping what God considers appropriate—thus his emphasis on "the will of God" (Rom 12:2). Contrary to what some readers may assume, Paul does not reason primarily on the basis of rules or commands—nor, in fact, does the Bible more generally; instead, Paul thinks through moral situations by seeking to grasp God's "will" within God's larger purposes, often in light of God's actions, past and present—and especially in and through the death and resurrection of Jesus Christ. The context makes it clear that God's perspective ultimately determines what qualifies as "good and acceptable and perfect." In any case, adequate discernment in the context of the Roman Christian community should lead to appropriate and faithful behavior, rooted in the "good," "acceptable," and "perfect."

Paul does not assume that adequate discernment will come easily or naturally to the Christian community. On the contrary, he indicates in Romans 12:2 that believers will need to "be transformed," implying that their lives will need to undergo significant change. The status quo will not suffice. Transformation refers to the radical change that takes place when something in one form takes on another shape or form entirely—such as when a caterpillar becomes, quite remarkably, a gorgeous butterfly. It is not about making minor adjustments or gently tinkering around the edges of something.

For Paul, nothing less than transformation is required in the lives of the Roman Christians in order for them to live out their missional calling in the world faithfully, particularly with respect to the moral choices they make, both inside and outside the community itself. The entire cosmos has been transformed by the death and resurrection of Jesus Christ, and the community—individually and together—needs to experience a similar metamorphosis. As Paul points out in 2 Corinthians 5:17, those who are "in Christ" have indeed become "a new creation." Even so, their moral reasoning and conduct must undergo ongoing transformation so that they increasingly live into the "new creation" that they already are in Christ.

How does such transformation occur? Paul assumes that the Roman Christians' transformation will come about through a "renewing of [their] minds." This is a significant and striking assumption—especially, perhaps, for those of us today who live in a social and cultural environment that valorizes intellect and reason. As heirs of the Enlightenment, we often presuppose the value of reason and the effectiveness of our rational capabilities in order to make decisions and to discern possible options for action. Christians may assume that their reasoned perspectives naturally and readily bring them close to understanding God's will. And yet we have ample evidence that our reasoning does not always lead us to the best choices; indeed, the historical record is replete with examples of times when our human reason has failed us—individually and communally—often with horrific results.

There is a strong sense in the Bible that human reason is limited. By suggesting that the Roman Christians' minds need renewal, Paul indicates that something is wrong with the ways in which they reason about moral issues. Their natural, human logic is not foolproof. They do not automatically discern "what is good and acceptable and perfect." For Paul, a renewed mind thinks and reasons differently than does a traditional "this-worldly" mind. Logical categories and considerations typically relevant in first-century Rome are inadequate for those who are "in Christ." Again, Paul assumes that the resurrection of Jesus Christ has fundamentally altered the state of the cosmos and, whether or not that radical fact is recognized or acknowledged, the state of reality has forever shifted. The kind of moral and spiritual discernment required in this new age necessitates (re)new(ed) minds.

How is such renewal to be accomplished? A second feature of the Greek word for transformation that Paul uses may suggest what he has in mind. The apostle uses a second-person plural imperative: *metamorphous-the* ("be transformed"). Rather than suggesting that such transformation will come about by their own efforts or ingenuity—as if they would be able to grit their teeth and work hard to transform themselves by force of will—Paul uses a passive-voice imperative, which indicates that the transformation of the Roman Christians will be brought about ultimately by God, the real (albeit implicit) subject of the verb. Biblical scholars call this usage of the passive voice in the New Testament the *divine passive*. That is, Paul is urging—indeed, instructing—the Roman Christians to allow themselves to "be transformed" *by God*. Again, the power for transformation will not come from them but from the God whom they serve. In other words, Paul commands his readers to participate willingly and eagerly in the process of their divinely orchestrated transformation. Further, the present tense of the imperative may well imply that the apostle envisions an ongoing and continual need for transformation among the Christians in Rome, not merely a once-for-all change.

Presumably, the same divine presence that effects the transformation in believers is also the operative force behind the "renewing of [their] minds." Paul's language suggests that God is the one who has the ability to change the Roman Christians—to transform them—including their cognitive faculties of reason and logic, if only they will allow themselves to be changed. The apostle's terminology is striking: at one level he is commanding them (the verb is an imperative), but at another level he is acknowledging that they have the capacity to allow God to transform and renew them. God is not forcing transformation and renewal, but Paul is clear that individual and communal faithfulness to God effectively necessitates a willingness to undergo changes brought about by God.

It is incumbent on us now to consider further why transformation is even necessary, according to Paul. Obviously, the words "be transformed" in Romans 12:2 are preceded by the word *but*: in Greek this word has a strongly adversative force (e.g., not this *but* that). The apostle is clearly contrasting what he wants to see, namely, transformation "by the renewing of [their] minds," with something else. And to that we now turn.

The first part of Paul's statement in Romans 12:2, "Do not be conformed to this world," is crucial to our understanding of what he is advocating in the second part of the verse that we have just examined. The apostle is concerned that the Roman Christians may allow "this world"—and presumably its perspectives, values, priorities, logic, rationality, behaviors, and so forth—to shape who they are, how they think, and how they conduct themselves. There is, for Paul, a serious danger inherent in such conformity, because those conformed to "this world" are operating under the terms of an old and vanquished regime—cosmically speaking.

Again, according to the apostle, the resurrection has forever altered the situation in which both believers and nonbelievers find themselves. This means that the reality and implications of the changed situation are not predicated on whether people believe in the risen Christ. Whether or not this world acknowledges the true state of the cosmos, it is now entirely under Christ's lordship.

For Paul, then, ongoing transformation is necessary for the Roman Christians because they are inevitably shaped by—"conformed to"—the characteristics of a world that fails to acknowledge the true state of reality under Christ's cosmic lordship. They must be willing to allow themselves to be changed, reshaped, "transformed" by the power of God's Spirit in their midst. Paul's command not to be conformed (also a Greek imperative) presupposes that formation is an inherent part of human existence. "This world" shapes and forms people; while this is obviously true for nonbelievers, Paul assumes that this world also continues to shape believers.

Each of us is formed by life; not one of us is a blank slate. We are formed by families, experiences, sociocultural and intellectual paradigms—indeed, by myriad factors. The Roman Christians were in the process of being formed by the world in which they lived long before they would become believers. In that sense, it is legitimate to understand Paul's imperative ("do not be conformed") as a reflection of his desire that the Roman believers stop allowing themselves to be conformed to that world. He wants them to turn consciously and definitively toward Christ as the primary shaper of their lives, their perspectives, and their reasoning. They are to be conformed to Christ. That will require, as Paul articulates in the second half of verse 2, a radical process of transformation in which their "minds" will need to be renewed. Being so formed by Christ does not mean that the Roman Christians somehow cease to be human, floating above the everyday phenomena of life. They will continue to be influenced by their families, cultures, experiences, and so forth. Believers do not cease to live in this world; but neither are their lives ultimately to be defined by it.

Families, cultures, experiences, and such factors are not to be the primary shapers of who the Roman Christians are, how they think, or how they conduct themselves. Rather, they are to be formed, first and finally, by Christ. The lordship of Christ in their lives is to trump all other kinds of formation. Paul is aware that such radical change does not come easily or naturally; radical transformation "by the renewing of [their] minds" is necessary. True transformation can be a lengthy process (consider again the caterpillar and the eventual butterfly). The transformation Paul has in mind will presumably involve a lifelong process of change for the Roman Christians—individually and communally. Like the Roman believers, we are always being formed in certain ways, for good or ill. Indeed, we are deeply formed, more than we may often realize, by economic paradigms, worldviews, theories, ideologies, priorities, policies, social norms, and be-haviors, as well as by our experiences with poverty, wealth, money, finance, debt, and the like.

The critical question—for Christians, at least—is whether or not the ways in which our contemporary economic world has and continues to form us are consonant with the economic logic of the gospel and faithful to the perspectives of the God whom we claim to serve in Jesus Christ. As was true of the Roman Christians to whom Paul wrote in the first century, contemporary believers are to be formed, first and finally, by Christ. Every loyalty of the Roman believers was to be transformed by the renewing of their minds. Caesar could not be more important than Christ; the empire could not command more allegiance than God's kingdom did. For the Ro-man believers, all systems and structures, philosophies and worldviews, ideologies and logics had to come under the lordship of Christ. They had already been formed; indeed, as Paul recognizes, they were "conformed" to what they knew. They now had to allow themselves to be transformed. And that transformation would require something radical and, ultimately, divinely empowered—namely, the renewing of their minds. The same is also true, no doubt, for Christians today.

Biblical Economic Formation: Behavior and Reasoning

Paul is, of course, not the only biblical writer who seeks to (re)form both the behavior and the moral reasoning of his readers. Indeed, that dynamic is essentially present throughout the Bible—in different contexts and across various literary genres. As I have noted, my purpose in this book is to offer reflections on the ways certain biblical texts seek to form their readers for economic justice and discipleship in the world—rooted in the assumption that, like the first-century Roman believers, contemporary Christians are in many ways already "conformed to this world," particularly in terms of our economic loyalties, modes of reasoning, and behaviors. Therefore, believers today—individually and communally—are in need of the same kind of transformation that Paul called for in the believers of first-century Rome.

The Bible, properly understood and read, functions in a wide variety of ways as both a tool for and a product of formation, particularly with regard to the individuals and communities that read, value, and seek to be guided by it. On the one hand, biblical documents functioned, at least in part, to form and shape ancient individuals and communities of readers for their lives and vocations as those devoted to God. Biblical documents were individually tools of formation. In a related way, the biblical canon as a whole represents the product of many and varied efforts (through the work of numerous authors and editors) to foster and support individual and communal formation. On the other hand, biblical texts continue to serve as formative documents for those who read them today. And while we will consider some of the ways in which biblical documents served to form and shape the individuals and communities to which they were originally directed, the formative dynamic of these texts for contemporary readers is our primary concern.

The fundamental thesis of this book is that biblical texts form their readers with regard to justice and economic discipleship in two particular ways. First, and most obviously, the Bible seeks, in a wide variety of ways, to form and influence particular kinds of concrete, tangible behaviors among its readers. Many biblical texts seek to engender appropriate economic behavior—which, I will admit, does not look the same for every passage or for every potential context. This particular moral or ethical function of the Bible should come as no surprise—and should not be especially controversial. Although Jesus, for example, is often reported to have said things that may be understood to some extent as hyperbolic in character—and thus he was not always entirely clear about the precise and concrete kinds of behavior he may have expected to see—there can be little doubt that biblical texts generally intend to engender behaviors, economic and otherwise, that would be seen as appropriate in the eyes of God. Indeed, most Christians assume when they read the Bible that it is designed to command, or at least influence, how they behave.

But there is a second—and potentially even more important—aspect of biblical formation, a kind of formation that I believe merits more serious and sustained attention than it usually receives, perhaps especially with respect to issues of justice and economic discipleship. As we think about the potential implications of biblical texts for Christian life and faithfulness, and particularly those whose implications are of a moral or ethical nature, it is important that we as readers discern adequately the extent to which biblical texts often seek not merely to form readers' concrete behavior, but also—and again, no less significantly—their reasoning about why and how they should conduct themselves in the first place. That is, the Bible is not merely interested in commanding or exhorting or even persuading its readers simply to mimic particular behaviors, as if the primary concern were to encourage rote forms of conduct in all situations. Biblical texts go deeper than that in terms of biblical formation.

While there are certainly numerous places in the Bible that call for particular kinds of specific conduct, many readers may be unaware of how often and how emphatically biblical texts seek to form, reform, and, ultimately, transform how readers reflect on and reason through behavioral situations. This is probably due, at least partly, to the tendency within North American Christianity—and certainly within the wider culture—to focus on what we *do*.

Productivity is one of the most deeply engrained values and priorities in North American culture, and, in my experience, that is often no less true in churches. We are workers and doers, and we assume that any problem has a solution if we just work hard enough to solve it. If we discover some kind of injustice, we want to know what we can and should do. Such can-do thinking is usually helpful, and continues to fuel positive change in many contexts. At the same time, we can actually get ourselves into trouble by focusing almost exclusively on what we do. As a society, we understand that our worth and value as human beings is linked to our accomplishments and productivity. Indeed, sometimes it can be difficult for many of us to figure out who we are apart from such things. We tend to be more comfortable with *doing* than with simply *being*. Action, more than reflection, is our bread and butter. It is striking that the Bible seeks to form not merely what we do, but even more, who we are—and how we even perceive and think about the world around us.

Biblical formation never happens in a vacuum. We are always in the process of being formed—through families, cultures, friendships, and so on. We live and develop throughout the course of our lives within incredibly complex webs of influence, and we are affected by these contexts in which we find ourselves. The music we love, the foods we enjoy, the things we consider appropriate and normal—everything is influenced, at least in part, by the formative function of our contextual surroundings.

The same is true regarding our economic thought and behavior. We are already—in truth, continually—being formed in both large and small ways by the economic dynamics within which we live and move. We are influenced by numerous assumptions, values, priorities, and policies that are characteristic of our capitalistic economic system, even if we rarely recognize or acknowledge that influence. We often make sense of our personal experiences in terms of traditional and dominant economic paradigms—again, even when we do not realize that we are doing so. What we think about economic matters—such as poverty and wealth, the stock market and the unemployment rate, personal responsibility and saving, government assistance and taxation—is environmentally shaped in myriad ways. Social and family cultures shape our perspectives, biases, and commitments with regard to economic issues. We do not need to be professional economists to recognize that the ways we think and act economically and financially are rooted, at least in part, in wider sets of contexts, experiences, and influences—from the societal and structural to the personal and behavioral.

According to Catholic economist Charles M.A. Clark, today's economic worldview is rooted in a neoclassical vision of the human being as *homo economicus*—an autonomous, rational chooser.[2] "Economic hu-

---

2. Charles M. A. Clark, "The Challenge of Catholic Social Thought to Economic Theory," *The Journal for Peace and Justice Studies* 12 (2002): 163-77. This paragraph and the three that follow are adapted from my article "'Occupying' Genesis 1-3: Missionally Located Reflections on Biblical Values and Economic Justice," *Missiology* 42 (2014): 390-91.

mans" reckon the value of material goods and services not in terms of labor and creativity (as in, say, classical economics), but rather in terms of market-centric utility. Nearly everything is now subjected to one form or another of consequentialist, cost-benefit analysis. Human beings have little or no intrinsic worth: human value is understood in almost entirely functional terms, calculated in terms of a person's role and utility within the larger market mechanism.

Further, according to Clark, humans are best understood in market terms as isolated, autonomous individuals who occasionally choose, on the basis of self-interest and perceived utility, to come together in the market for one type of exchange or another. In this context, "society" and the "common good" become rather abstract, if not largely meaningless notions.[3] Even human freedom is conceptualized in a relatively narrow way, understood primarily in terms of autonomy, as freedom *from* responsibility to others rather than freedom to live *for* the good of others and the world.[4] In a world of scarce resources—and scarcity is a starting point for neoclassical economic reasoning—human freedom often refers to being unhindered in our attempts to compete with and against others for what we need and want.

In this economic context, humans are understood to have a twofold mission. First, human beings are to participate productively in the competitive market environment, creating goods or services that will be valued by potential consumers. Competitiveness, efficiency, increasing profit margins, and self-reliance become core social values. The implicit, if not explicit, goal is to gain dominion over resources, over competition, over others. Not surprisingly, those who are less productive, or whose contributions are less valued in market terms, struggle to compete. Significantly, human suffering, environmental degradation, and other so-called "externalities" are routinely ignored in market analyses.

Second, humans are expected to consume. Theoretically, we choose what to consume on the basis of self-interest and utility, and market mechanisms tend to treat all choices equally.[5] As long as consumers have the financial resources to make their consuming wishes operational, there is no market mechanism by which to evaluate the appropriateness of such

3. Clark, "Challenge of Catholic Social Thought," 168, 174.

4. E.g., William T. Cavanaugh, *Being Consumed: Economics and Christian Desire* (Grand Rapids: Eerdmans, 2008), 4.

5. Clark, "Challenge of Catholic Social Thought," 166.

choices.[6] Human autonomy and freedom of choice are all-important. Indeed, we assume that we hold the key to our corporate destiny. If we focus on our needs and our wants, we are told that we will effectively contribute to the well-being of humanity as a whole by contributing to wider economic growth. Even if we never completely satiate our desires, faith in the system keeps an eschatological hope in an eventual consumer nirvana alive.[7]

Therefore, when we encounter the formative function of biblical texts, we must remember that they are, in effect, functioning to reform and, ultimately, to transform how we already reason, how we already think, how we already tend to conceive of what is happening—and how we might act in light of such transformation. One of the primary aims of this study will thus be to highlight how biblical texts seek to form the moral and economic reasoning of reading communities, including, for example, their assumptions and presuppositions, their values, their priorities, and, indeed, the conceptual logic or framework within which readers even think about potential behavioral options in a given situation.

For many in North America, Christianity and the gospel have often been understood predominantly in spiritual terms: thus the Bible has been seen as having limited relevance to daily economic concerns. In other words, the good news has been understood primarily in terms of certain anticipated spiritual benefits redounding to believers—especially in terms of a future-oriented salvation in heaven. And though scholars have sometimes emphasized economic issues in the Bible—especially when biblical texts themselves seem to demand such attention—economic concerns, which are in many ways pervasive in the Bible, have seldom received the attention they deserve. But the situation is changing in this regard: interest in economic matters in the Bible is increasing, which is clearly demonstrated by a growing number of publications by theologians and biblical scholars in recent years.

Undoubtedly, this literary output reflects a growing concern about economic dynamics in our contemporary world. Indeed, what we are seeing is a clear indication of the role that social location plays in biblical interpretation. On the one hand, it should not be surprising that economic concerns have tended until recently to receive limited attention. Many

---

6. Michael J. Sandel, *Justice: What's the Right Thing to Do?* (New York: Farrar, Straus and Giroux, 2009), 52–54; Clark, "Challenge of Catholic Social Thought," 174.

7. Similarly, Cavanaugh, *Being Consumed*, 93; Joerg Rieger, *No Rising Tide: Theology, Politics, and the Future* (Minneapolis: Fortress, 2009), 62.

North American Christians and most scholars are privileged in a number of ways—economically and otherwise. Economic distress and poverty are usually theoretical rather than personal issues for those who are relatively comfortable, and those who read the Bible from privileged locations often overlook or fail in other ways to reckon adequately with what Scripture actually says about matters related to economic justice.

On the other hand, we also see the effects of social location when we look at how biblical texts are interpreted by those who *are* marginalized or suffering—economically or otherwise. It is not surprising, for example, that various forms of liberation theology have flourished, especially in deeply poor regions (e.g., Latin America and Asia) that are characterized by extensive wealth inequality. In the mid-twentieth century, biblical scholars and theologians in those contexts began to read biblical texts with "new eyes," as the situation "on the ground" influenced the questions they brought to the Bible—and opened them up to the radical responses they sometimes discovered there.

Questions of an economic nature are now beginning to play a significant role in mainstream biblical interpretation. The 2008 Wall Street crash and its aftermath have negatively affected more people across the economic spectrum and around the world in a deeper way than have previous financial downturns. People who have been solidly middle class in wealthy countries have lost jobs, homes, and life savings. When so many people experience such a radical and decisive shift in their own existential experience—and thus in their social locations—biblical topics that were once perceived to be marginal within the canon are seen as increasingly important by lay readers and scholars alike.

This book grows partly out of a conviction that relatively comfortable Christians have too often failed to pay adequate attention to biblical matters of economic import. We must return to the biblical texts themselves, reading carefully and wrestling thoughtfully with their potential implications from the vantage point of the church's contemporary missional located-ness in the world to which it has been called to bear gospel witness. Our economic reasoning may well need to be transformed.

FOR FURTHER REFLECTION

▶ What might it mean—concretely and tangibly—for communities of faith "to present [their] bodies as a [single, unified] living sacrifice?"

- In what ways are we already conformed to this world? How have contemporary economic thought and practice shaped who you are?

- Reflect on how you discern an appropriate course of action when facing a moral dilemma or a choice with ethical implications.

- How might you need to be willing to allow God to transform you "by the renewing of your mind"?

- Are you open to having your moral reasoning transformed? What concerns do you have?

CHAPTER 2

Biblical Formation in Missional Perspective

The Bible seeks in various ways, across a variety of textual traditions, to form and equip its readers for their communal mission in the world. That is certainly what Paul is doing in Romans 12:2—indeed, throughout the letter—as he urges the believers not to be conformed to this world, but to allow themselves to be transformed by, the renewing of their minds. The goal of such formation is not merely that the Roman Christians will have renewed minds, as if that would be adequate as an end in itself. Rather, Paul encourages transformation in order that the believers "may know what is the will of God—what is good and acceptable and perfect." To know the will of God would involve having some awareness of larger divine purposes, having a sense of what God is doing in and for creation. Moreover, to know the will of God would include recognition that the community of believers has been caught up by and called into those larger divine purposes. For Paul, transformation is not about change for its own sake, change simply for the benefit of the Roman Christians themselves. Instead, the transformation he's writing about is a purposive process, one in which the Roman Christians—and, by extension, believers today—are prepared, empowered, and equipped for their role as witnesses to God's reconciling purposes in the world.

To speak in this way, in terms of a purposive God, is to speak in terms of mission. The God of the Bible, as a purposive God, has a mission—and is *on* a mission, so to speak. The Bible testifies to this *missio Dei*. In fact, God does not merely engage in a mission, but the very nature of the biblical and Trinitarian God is best understood in terms of mission. Insofar as purposive creativity is at the core of God's identity, God is a missional God.

There is another crucial facet of what we mean here by invoking the terminology of mission. The Latin root behind the English word mission (*missio*) connotes the idea of sending. It is appropriate—indeed, theologically necessary—for Christians to describe God in terms of sending. In biblical and Trinitarian terms, the Son and Spirit (and, ultimately, the church) are sent into the world to participate in God's reconciling purposes. Sending and being sent is at the core of who the triune God is. And thus mission involves being sent—for a purpose. So, when I refer to mission in this book, I am, above all, talking about God. That is true whether I invoke the noun "mission," the cognate adjective "missional," or even an adverb, "missionally": they are terms rooted in and relevant for God. Moreover, each of them connotes purposiveness and sending.

Let me be clear. To describe God in terms of mission is to engage in a theologically polemical move in at least two significant ways. First, Christians have traditionally understood mission almost exclusively in terms of human activity. That is, mission has been understood to be something that believers *do*, such as participating in evangelistic outreach among those who do not share the Christian faith. This standard and traditional definition of mission is, however, profoundly reductionist and problematic. If we understand mission primarily in terms of human activity, we effectively place Christian activity and tasks above the theological framework, namely, the purposes of God, within which those activities and tasks make any sense. Mission is not merely, or even primarily, something that human beings do; rather, mission is first and foremost about God. Mission is rooted in the nature, character, and activity of our purposive God. Therefore, whatever else it may be, mission is a theological concern long before it is an anthropological matter.

Second, to understand mission in terms of divine purposiveness and sending offers a major corrective to traditional ways of thinking about mission. Not only is mission typically understood primarily as human activity, but it is almost universally equated with various forms of evangelistic outreach to non-Christians, and thus with one of many potential activities of the Christian community, in addition to worship, education, and so forth. But consider what this perspective implies about God. Does the biblical and triune God do anything that is *not* rooted in divine purposiveness? Is God only sometimes a God of mission? If purposiveness and sending are at the very heart of who God is, the answer to both questions must be No. Divine mission cannot be understood in a partitive manner. Mission terminology must refer holistically to everything that God is and does.

Mission, Divine Purposiveness, and the Church

What does this more holistic understanding of mission mean for the church today? Perhaps most importantly, to envision mission in terms of divine purposiveness and sending is to recognize that the church does not so much *have* a mission as much as it is called to *be* part of God's mission. In other words, the church exists and is sent into the world as a function of and in order to participate in divine purposiveness. The church is thus both a product of and agent within the larger *missio Dei*. Mission is at the core of what the church is no less than it is intrinsic to who God is. Correctly understood, then, the church is missional—sent into the world to participate in divine purposes—or it is nothing. Mission is to be understood primarily in terms of the nature and activity of God: any and all of the church's human activity is derivative of divine mission. Several implications follow, and I will highlight two of them here.

First, in traditional understandings of mission, activities that take place or are oriented to contexts *outside* the Christian community itself, such as evangelistic outreach, work in foreign lands, service trips, and even advocacy for social justice, tend to be the only ones referred to using mission terminology. (Think, for example, of the typical connotations of the following terms: missionary, missions, mission work, mission field, mission trip, mission budget, mission offering, mission pastor, mission committee, mission report.) If we understand mission to be rooted in the holistic purposes of God, however, such terminology appears suspect and inadequate. Do God's purposes only relate to contexts outside the Christian community? Aren't worship, preaching, education, and pastoral care integral to God's reconciling purposes in the world? Don't worship, preaching, education, and pastoral care represent different kinds of formation and equipping for fuller and more faithful participation in the *missio Dei*? Why is mission terminology almost never used with regard to such things? Why do churches tend to define some leadership positions in terms of mission (e.g., "pastor of mission and evangelism") but not others (e.g., "pastor of Christian education")? Such bifurcation reflects a reductionist notion of mission. Again, everything that derives from divine purposes, whether internal or external to the community, is a matter of mission. Everything in the church, including positions, roles, and tasks, should be understood in terms of the church's mission within the larger *missio Dei*.

At this point, some readers may object by saying, as Stephen Neill famously said, "If everything is mission, then nothing is mission." It is important to recognize here that Neill's comment reflects a traditional understanding of mission, conceiving of the term primarily in terms of outreach beyond the Christian community. What Neill means is that if everything is defined as outreach, nothing is, in fact, outreach. He is decrying a tendency to define everything the church engages in as outreach to the wider world, when much of the church's conduct is, in truth, predominantly self-referential and insular. Indeed, that was and is an appropriate warning. But if mission is understood more holistically, along the lines that I have been advocating, we do not stray far from Neill's intent with the following affirmation: Everything that is rooted in and dependent on divine purposiveness and sending *is* mission.

Although traditional understandings of mission have often equated "mission" and "evangelism," they are not synonymous terms. While evangelism—outreach oriented to the conversion of non-Christians—is an important facet of the church's mission, God's purposes are not limited to making new Christians and incorporating them into the community of faith. Ironically, traditional mission terminology implies that activities internal to the faith community itself have nothing to do with mission. Understanding mission in terms of divine purposiveness and sending enables us to avoid such conceptual and semantic bifurcation between internal and external activities. Moreover, this approach provides a theologically useful and necessary framework in which to evaluate the extent to which the church is being faithful to God in its mission.

The activities of a faithful, sent community—both *internal* activities (e.g., worship, preaching, education, pastoral care) and *external* ones (e.g., outreach, evangelism, social justice advocacy)—must be dependent on, formed by, and regularly transformed by the reconciling purposiveness of God. The *missio Dei* must be both the inspiration and the measuring rod for everything the church does. Anything not linked to God's purposes and to what the church is sent to be and do is unnecessary—a distraction at best, a potential idol at worst.

Second, despite their popularity, traditional understandings of mission are actually based on a relatively limited range of biblical evidence. Passages that pertain to sending, outreach, and evangelism among outsiders (e.g., Matt. 28:16–20; 1 Cor. 9:19–23; 2 Cor. 4–5) are readily and commonly associated with mission. But readers have tended not to see evidence of mission in the Bible *unless* a given passage is clearly about such matters. Many Christians have thus assumed that mission is largely absent in the Old Testament, given that so few texts there seem to refer to evangelism and outreach beyond the community of faith. Readers have indeed "found" mission in those New Testament passages that pertain to evangelistic outreach to people beyond the Christian community, but not necessarily elsewhere.

In an earlier book, *Mission and Moral Reflection in Paul,* I observed that, almost without exception, studies of Paul have tended to invoke mission terminology (e.g., "mission," "missionary") only when he is understood to be referring to efforts—either his own or his churches'—to expand the Christian faith through evangelistic outreach in some form.[1] The key point is that mission terminology is almost never used to describe Pauline texts that lack an obvious evangelistic dimension, such as when Paul is writing about matters internal to the community. Thus mission, even in the Pauline Epistles and Acts, has been typically understood as an occasional phenomenon in the Bible, much more common in the New Testament than in the Old Testament. Traditionally, mission terminology has been invoked only when a particular passage seems to demand it (for example, if it relates in some way to sending or to evangelistic outreach); otherwise, mission is not understood to be an intrinsic component of the biblical text. Unsurprisingly, mission has hence not usually been understood as a central concern within biblical scholarship.

This book proceeds from the assumption that attention to God's mission as described in the Bible—understood primarily in terms of divine purposiveness and sending—is a critical interpretive rubric whenever we attempt to make sense of what we encounter in biblical texts. The limited and occasional emphasis on mission in the Bible needs to be rectified. The entire Bible, to the extent that it reflects the purposiveness of God, needs to be understood as a document of mission—both as a *product,* or result, of mission, reflecting divine purposes in the world through God's people, and as a *tool* of mission that forms its readers for the calling they have received from God.

In this book I will use mission as a fundamental and inherently ap-

---

1. Michael Barram, *Mission and Moral Reflection in Paul,* Studies in Biblical Literature 75 (New York: Peter Lang, 2006). For related reflection on mission in Paul and the significance of understanding mission appropriately (as discussed throughout this chapter on "Biblical Formation in Missional Perspective"), see also Michael Barram, "Pauline Mission as Salvific Intentionality: Fostering a Missional Consciousness in 1 Corinthians 9:19-23 and 10:31–11.1," in *Paul as Missionary: Identity, Activity, Theology, and Practice,* ed. Trevor Burke and Brian S. Rosner, Library of New Testament Studies (London: T. & T. Clark International, 2011), 234-46.

propriate interpretive rubric under which to read and understand biblical texts, including ones that pertain to matters of economic justice and economic discipleship. We are not simply, or even primarily, interested in reading "missional texts" in the Bible; rather, we are seeking to engage in "missional readings" of (potentially all) biblical texts. We are not searching for texts in the Bible *about* mission as much as we are reading texts through a missional lens.

Introduction to Missional Hermeneutics

Traditional biblical scholarship has given relatively little attention to mission. Perhaps that is because scholarly attention to mission has been almost entirely restricted to passages in the Bible that seem to incorporate a sending motif or evangelistic outreach. Moreover, commitment to mission as traditionally understood has been especially characteristic of theologically conservative Christian groups, and sustained interest in mission among conservative scholars has rarely extended to wider biblical scholarship. In order to foster greater interest in and attention to mission as an important rubric for biblical interpretation, Christians will find it necessary to demonstrate that mission, understood holistically in terms of purpose and sending, is inherent to the biblical text itself and not merely a fixation of relatively conservative theological presuppositions.[2] To approach biblical texts through a missional lens is to engage them from the vantage point of what is becoming known as *missional hermeneutics*, an emerging subdiscipline of biblical studies—the primary approach, in fact, that inspires this book. Given that some readers may not be familiar with the terms "missional" or "hermeneutics," let us begin by introducing them individually.

The "Missional" in Missional Hermeneutics

The term "missional," an alternative adjective for "missionary," developed initially among those who were moving beyond the traditional mission paradigm. For example, a number of missiologists and other scholars associated with the Gospel and Our Culture Network, convinced that the

---

2. Michael Barram, "The Bible, Mission, and Social Location: Toward a Missional Hermeneutic," *Interpretation* 43 (2007): 42-58.

organizing rubric for theology and ecclesiology must be the *missio Dei*, published an important study of the "missional church."[3] As an adjective, "missional" was fresher and less fraught with historical and conceptual baggage than the adjective "missionary" (which continues to be used almost exclusively as a synonym for terms such as "outreach," "evangelism," etc.). Specifically, using "missional" has enabled scholars to refer adjectivally to the inherently purposive and holistic mission of both God and the church in smooth prose (e.g., a "missional God," a "missional church") and in such a way that mission terminology is not implicitly and narrowly equated with evangelism.

I began to use the term "missional" while in graduate school in the late 1990s. At the time it was a relatively new word, one that some criticized as an unnecessary neologism. Now, nearly twenty years later, the term has arguably become overused. The main problem with the current popularity of the word "missional" is that its use has, to some extent, become a kind of semantic Rorschach test, reflecting as many different meanings as there are people who invoke it. Most problematic, some now use "missional" not in its original, comprehensive, and purposive sense, but rather as just another adjective within the traditional mission-as-outreach paradigm. That is, many have adopted "missional" as an adjectival synonym for the narrower sense of the word "missionary" (e.g., "outreach" and "evangelism"), which does little more than reinforce traditional and reductionist notions of mission.

The rapid rise in the popularity of the term "missional" has led to a situation in which those who use it end up talking past each other. While many persist in using "missional" as an adjectival reference to "evangelistic outreach," some use it more appropriately in the broader sense that I have been advocating in this book: a reference to the church's calling as a community sent into the world to bear witness to God's holistic purposes.

"Missional" can be—and is—a helpful word, but not if it is used uncritically as an extension of the traditional paradigm of mission. If we understand the term "mission" comprehensively as a reference to the purposiveness of God, the term "missional" can and should be used as an appropriate and helpful adjectival form of the noun. Indeed, using "missional" is preferable to the traditional adjective form of mission, "missionary," the overwhelming use of which is entirely rooted in the traditional paradigm. In this book, therefore, I use "missional" in a very specific, in-

3. Darrell L. Guder, ed., *Missional Church* (Grand Rapids: Eerdmans, 1998).

tentional sense: here the word serves as an adjectival form of mission, but only in the comprehensive and holistic sense of purposiveness and sending that I have articulated, and not in the narrow and restricted sense of outreach or evangelism. Perhaps this book will help to encourage a more thoughtful and consistent use of the term "missional" in this holistic, purposive sense.

The "Hermeneutics" in Missional Hermeneutics

A literary text, especially one so large and complex as the Bible, is something like a multifaceted diamond. As we know, the facets of an expertly cut diamond reflect light differently depending on the various angles from which we view it, illuminating aspects of the diamond's style, beauty, clarity, color, and quality. As with viewing a diamond, we can look at texts, including the Bible, from different angles and perspectives—or through various lenses, so to speak—focusing on different facets or aspects of texts. The process and study of such textual interpretation is called *hermeneutics,* from a Greek word referring to the process of interpretation.

Differing hermeneutical approaches can help us see or hear different things in the texts we read. In a very general sense, the lenses through which we focus on texts can be described in one of three ways, each of which reflects different assumptions about texts, interpretation, and the nature of meaning. Perhaps the easiest way to understand these three areas is to think in terms of a spatial relationship between three components: (1) the "background" of the text—that is, what lies "behind" the text we are reading; (2) the text itself; and (3) the readers who read and interpret the text—that is, what lies "in front of" the text we are reading.

Getting behind the Text. The first area of interest to develop extensively in biblical scholarship involves what we might call the background— what is *behind* the biblical texts we read. When we explore this background, we are seeking to learn about the social, cultural, and historical contexts out of which biblical texts arise, as well the historical processes by which those texts developed and came to be in the canon of Scripture. This area of research quickly became so important within biblical scholarship that the discipline has long been understood largely in terms of "historical-critical" concerns, that is, scholarly assumptions and methodologies aimed at historical analysis, broadly understood. Exploring what lies behind a biblical text can be as simple as asking historically oriented questions about how

26

words, statements, concepts, material artifacts, actions, and events would have been understood by people in the Gospel stories themselves—or by the earliest readers of the Gospels.

Two of the most important interpretive methodologies that have developed to explore the actual development of biblical texts have been "source criticism," in which interpreters explore the presence of earlier traditions (e.g., stories, quotations, documents, creeds) reflected in what we read, and "redaction criticism," which examines how and why biblical authors and editors seem to have used those earlier traditions. Those who focus in these areas of research tend to assume that what a biblical text means is closely linked to what the author originally intended to communicate. Interpretation thus necessitates going behind the texts we read in order to understand what they might have meant for the ancient authors and the communities those authors were addressing.

Exploring the Text Itself. The second broad area of scholarly research focuses not on the background behind biblical texts but on the *final form* of the biblical texts themselves—as we read them on the pages of the Bible today. Many scholars began reading biblical texts primarily in terms of the literary characteristics that we can identify about them as they appear on the page, classifying and interpreting them in light of their literary phenomena (genre, setting, character development, plot, etc.) and utilizing particular interpretive methods relevant to a given genre (such as narrative-critical analysis) in order to carefully and fruitfully examine the final form of biblical texts as they are found in the Bible.

The key difference between exploring the *text itself* and *getting behind* the text is that, in the former case, scholars are not concerned with the variety of background issues pertinent to a given document or passage; rather, their goal is to explore the internal dynamics and characteristics of a text and, as far as possible, to understand how such factors may relate to meaning within a text. The narrow focus of study is the text itself and what it suggests internally about its "meaning." Obviously, the notion of meaning here is no longer understood to be limited to what a text would have meant for its original author and readers; rather, meaning is at least potentially multivalent. To illustrate, once a poem is published, the poet cannot control how it is understood.

At the same time, to focus on the biblical text itself does not render interpreters incapable of reflecting on issues of meaning. Awareness of and attention to literary genre are critical in biblical study inasmuch as the character of the information provided in and communicated by a text is in significant part a function of the type of literature within which it appears. The Bible contains numerous literary genres, including, for example, various forms of narrative, legal materials, poetry, philosophical reflection, letters, and apocalyptic literature. Literary genres help readers by providing frameworks for and clues about what they should expect to find within a given piece of writing—and, to some extent, how to make sense of that information. Just as readers do not expect the front page of a major newspaper to provide them with the same kinds of information that the sports pages or the comics do, we should be ready to encounter different kinds of information in various genres of biblical literature—and to interpret that variety accordingly.

Many scholars interested in "the text itself" began to focus, for example, on the narrative characteristics of the Gospels (e.g., the role and style of the voice of the "narrator," the setting, plot, characters, conflict and resolution, etc.). Other scholars focused on exploring the function of biblical texts within the larger literary and theological context of the biblical canon, within the larger "story" told across the Bible as a whole.

Readers in front of the Text. The third and most recent area of study to develop within biblical scholarship emphasizes the role of readers *in front of* the text, as they participate in the process of textual interpretation and the generation of meaning. At a basic level, we witness the role of readers whenever, for example, people discuss and wrestle with the significance and implications that a given text may have for their own lives—theologically, ethically, or otherwise. At a deeper level, readers play a role in the meaning of a text as they read it in light of their own experiences, assumptions, proclivities, and commitments.

Contemporary studies that focus on the role of readers in the process of making meaning tend to embrace the "located-ness" and contextualized perspectives of readers. The concept of social location refers to the readily observable (though not always widely recognized or acknowledged) fact that the experiences, assumptions, values, biases, prejudices, and commitments readers bring to an interpretive moment affect how they understand and interpret what they read. A reader's personal history, memories, experiences, gender, race, ethnicity, religious background and commitments (e.g., Catholic, Protestant, Jewish, Buddhist, atheist, agnostic), theological perspectives, place of residence, education, political views, economic status, beliefs about the world—in fact, anything that may affect how someone views and interprets the world—taken together, "locate" the reader within a wider social web of potential characteristics. No one comes to a text, or any other interpretive task, as a completely blank slate. Each of us has a lifetime of experiences and perspectives that affect what we see and how we make sense of it. Moreover, the social location from which each of us interprets texts (and anything else we might seek to interpret, for that matter) is in constant development as new experiences affect the vantage point, the location relative to other interpreters, from which we view and make sense of the world. Ultimately, the interpretive function of social location can lead in two directions, either helping to illuminate or to obscure various facets of a given text, depending on where readers are socially located.

Traditional, historical-critical scholarship (the first approach discussed above) assumes that what a text *meant* in the past plays a determinative role in establishing what it *means* today—and thus finding the original meaning is understood to be the fundamental task of scholarly interpretation. An emphasis on the role of readers, on the other hand, presupposes that the meaning of a given text is always to some extent contingent on those who interpret it. While historical-critical scholarship assumes that there is, theoretically speaking, a single, valid meaning of a text that will be universally applicable for all readers, scholarship that focuses on the role of readers actually questions whether meaning can be so narrowly restricted and, indeed, assumes that the "universally valid" interpretations proffered by historical-critical scholars mostly reflect the presuppositions, perspectives, and even the prejudices of those readers. Traditional historical-critical scholarship considers the tendency of readers to interpret biblical texts from a particular point of view to be methodologically flawed; but scholarship that acknowledges the role of readers asserts that interpretation from the presumption of a neutral and universally valid standpoint (as in traditional historical-critical scholarship) is essentially impossible. What is a sign of weakness for historical-critical scholarship is considered to be an indication of honesty and authenticity within reader-centered studies.

Focusing on the role of the reader does not mean that interpreters can ignore the text or simply make it say whatever they want it to say. Texts themselves, and their backgrounds, as well as the canonical framework within which texts have been collected, suggest certain parameters for responsible interpretation. The point for scholars working in this third area is that meaning never resides only in texts themselves or in their textual backgrounds; rather, meaning in textual interpretation always has much to do with the interpreters themselves. Given this unavoidable dynamic, scholarship in this area tends to value studies that acknowledge their locatedness from the outset (including various forms of ideological interpretation, e.g., liberationist and feminist) as opposed to feigning a vantage point of neutrality that will supposedly render a universally valid interpretation.

While most studies are oriented within one of the three areas we have examined above, it is not uncommon—particularly for scholars who are interested in matters *in front of* the text—to draw on insights related to all three areas. With the foregoing discussion of the terms "missional" and "hermeneutics" in hand, we are now prepared to discuss the role that "missional hermeneutics" plays in this book.

Missional Hermeneutics in the Present Study

The GOCN Forum on Missional Hermeneutics, sponsored by the Gospel and Our Culture Network (GOCN), provides the primary setting for scholarly discussions of missional hermeneutics. For more than a decade now, the forum has held conference sessions in the context of the annual meetings of the Society of Biblical Literature. Since 2005, I have had the honor of serving as the steering committee chair of the forum, collaborating with an impressive group of biblical scholars, missiologists, theologians, and pastors. Each year, forum sessions are devoted to interpreting biblical texts and reviewing important scholarly books—all from the hermeneutical vantage point of mission. In 2011, George R. Hunsberger published an important review of the early work of the forum (through 2008), "mapping" the contributions of several of its primary participants.[4] Hunsberger suggests that there were at least four different but mutually informing and symbiotic "streams" of emphasis to be discerned in the forum's conversations up to that point, three of which generally correspond to the three hermeneutical areas we have introduced and thus are relevant to the present study.

In the first "stream" identified by Hunsberger, scholarly attention is placed primarily on the shape or "story" of the *missio Dei* that can be discerned across the arc of the biblical narrative and canon—as well as within discrete biblical texts—and thus it corresponds to wider biblical scholarship's concern with "exploring the text itself." This first stream within missional hermeneutics is fundamental to missional hermeneutics, since it provides several key insights through which interpretation from the vantage point of mission becomes possible in the first place.

---

4. George R. Hunsberger, "Proposals for a Missional Hermeneutic: Mapping a Conversation," *Missiology* 39 (2011): 309-21.

As I have already noted, to the extent that God is a missional, sending God, and the church is a community sent by God to participate in the divine purposes, the church does not have a mission of its own; rather, the church is called and sent by God to participate in the mission of God. Moreover, the biblical text that bears witness to God—in whole and in part—is missional literature. Interpreting the Bible faithfully necessitates that we read it within its larger canonical, missional context. Again, this crucial affirmation challenges us as interpreters not to think in restrictive terms about mission as if we already know what it means and entails, and encourages interpreters to move beyond a narrow fixation on passages related to evangelism. In these general ways, the present study draws on the insights of this first stream.

The majority of recent scholarly papers and publications on the Bible and mission, including those not connected to the work of the GOCN Forum on Missional Hermeneutics, have been oriented to this stream of missional hermeneutics. In fact—and from my perspective, quite unfortunately—many seem to equate interest in biblical mission with this single perspective, apparently failing to recognize, or at least acknowledge, the complexity inherent in interpreting the Bible from the perspective of mission. My concern is that this stream, on its own, does not represent a developed hermeneutic as much as it reflects interpretive interest in discrete texts within Scripture—as well as in a perceived narrative arc that runs from Genesis through Revelation—which can be explored from the vantage point of mission, and even from the vantage point of mission understood primarily in terms of divine purposiveness. While such interest is appropriate and salutary, the problem with that approach is that it amounts to a search for texts relating to mission, even if holistically understood, rather than a robust missional hermeneutic. To attend to the apparent "missional" concerns of a putatively "missional text" is not the same thing as reading biblical texts from the interpretive perspective of mission. So, while this first stream does involve readings of missional texts in the Bible, it does not fully emphasize missional readings of biblical texts. There is a significant difference: in the former case, interpreters look for evidence of mission in the Bible, and then reflect on it; in the latter, interpreters read *every* biblical text from a missional perspective, whether or not a given text seems to have anything to do with mission.

My hope is that work on the Bible and mission will increasingly press beyond the broad, metanarrative assumptions and analyses of Hunsberger's first stream and move toward a more thoroughgoing missional hermeneutic.[5] Still, to the extent that we read the biblical text as a means for discerning divine purposiveness and Christian mission, the attention paid in this stream to the narrative of the *missio Dei* has been and continues to be of pivotal importance.

The second stream within missional hermeneutics emphasizes the ways in which biblical texts equipped their reading communities for contextualized participation in the *missio Dei*. Darrell Guder, the primary advocate of this approach, insists that Christian communities today will find themselves better equipped for their life and task as those sent into the world by paying attention to and discerning the ways in which a text apparently prepared its ancient addressees for their corporate missional witness.

Although this stream is not exclusively concerned with the ancient contexts and dynamics of biblical literature, it is nonetheless firmly rooted in the kinds of "behind the text" analysis that characterize traditional historical-critical biblical scholarship. The interpretive movement here is from the historical to the contemporary; that is, the formative and equipping functions of biblical documents within their ancient, sociohistorical contexts is understood to inform—though not necessarily dictate—reflection about the function of those same texts for reading communities in subsequent generations. In other words, the assumption is that, reasoning by way of analogy, contemporary interpreters can learn much about the church's mission—and the ways in which biblical texts function to equip the church for that mission—by exploring how those same texts formed and equipped their original readers for their mission. As in other behind-the-text scholarship, therefore, matters of authorial (and editorial) intention are of particular interest for this stream.

This book, which emphasizes the formative function of biblical texts, draws deeply on this aspect of missional hermeneutics. In the same way that both God and the church can and should be described in terms of purposiveness, biblical texts exist precisely because of their authors' (and editors') purposiveness. Even if we cannot discern precisely what situations and authorial intentions have given rise to certain documents in the Bible, there can be little doubt that biblical texts of all genres function to equip

5. See an updated version of Hunsberger's article, including a similar assessment of the overemphasis by most scholars on this first (as well as the second) stream in George R. Hunsberger, "Mapping the Missional Hermeneutics Conversation," in *Reading the Bible Missionally*, ed. Michael W. Goheen, pp. 45-67 (Grand Rapids: Eerdmans, 2016). Despite Hunsberger's reservations, the book as a whole tends to emphasize these streams.

their readers—individual and communal, ancient and contemporary—for their lives in the world. No one wrote (or edited) the biblical texts that we have today simply because they were unable to think of anything better to do. Biblical texts are inherently missional—that is, understood in terms of purposiveness—to the extent that they were written (and, in many cases, editorially shaped) to form their reading communities for authentic life and mission in the world. Growing in significant part out of the insights of this stream within missional hermeneutics, this book offers reflections on the ways certain biblical passages formed, and continue to form, their readers' economic reasoning and behavior as part of their witness within the larger *missio Dei*.

The third stream within missional hermeneutics, of which I have been the strongest and most vocal advocate, and which most informs the primary orientation for this book, emphasizes the contemporary Christian community as the locus of biblical interpretation. I have argued that missional hermeneutics is best understood in terms of biblical interpretation from the vantage point of the church's concrete social location. Obviously, in terms of the three areas of hermeneutical concern within biblical scholarship, this approach reflects the interpretive function of the reading community "in front of" a text.

Specifically, this stream begins with the affirmation that communities of faith that have been called into the *missio Dei* read biblical texts from a missional social location. Faithful biblical interpretation must reflect the kinds of contextual questions that reading communities bring to biblical texts in light of their missional located-ness, as well as questions that the Bible effectively asks of its readers. As I have written elsewhere, "a missional hermeneutic will self-consciously, intentionally, and persistently bring to the biblical text a range of focused, critical, and 'located' questions regarding the church's purpose in order to discern the faith community's calling and task within the *missio Dei*. Such questions will be inherently contextual: that is, rooted in the fundamental conviction that we read the biblical text as those who have been drawn into the larger purposes of God." Moreover, "to read the Bible from a missional perspective is not an eisegetical enterprise [in the sense of reading into a text something that is not actually there] but merely an honest acknowledgment of our primary interpretive location as we seek to read the Bible more faithfully today."[6]

Studies that proceed from an in-front-of-the-text approach remind

6. Barram, "The Bible, Mission, and Social Location," 58.

us that in the end there is no such thing as an entirely objective interpretation (of anything). No one is entirely neutral. No scholar approaches the biblical text without prior assumptions and commitments. Attempts to conduct biblical interpretation at arm's length can and often do provide critically important insights, of course; but such scholarship never fully comes to terms with the inherently formative nature and function of the documents under examination. Biblical texts expect and require existential engagement and personal investment from their readers, and thus they never submit entirely to attempts at complete critical objectivity—not to mention that claims to such objectivity reflect traditional scholarly pretensions more than actual interpretive possibilities.

We need not despair at what may appear to be a loss of objectivity in this stream. All we have lost is a faulty assumption that we can approach texts with complete neutrality and objectivity. In-front-of-the-text approaches simply remind us to be forthright as we come to the text. As interpreters, we have our own assumptions, proclivities, and allegiances that we bring to the task of interpretation. To affirm from the beginning that a missional hermeneutic proceeds from the perspective of the social location of the church within the *missio Dei* is not to impose an ideological, partisan straitjacket on the Bible that is foreign to its content, but rather to commit ourselves to self-consciously and honestly pursuing biblical interpretation in a way the texts themselves call for. Asking critical and located interpretive questions is an integral part of that process.

Asking Missionally Located Questions

The Bible itself illustrates the importance of questions for understanding the nature and mission of God in the world. Questions punctuate critical turning points in Scripture, in many cases providing the opportunity for a deeper understanding and appropriation of God's purposes and intentions. In the Garden of Eden, the serpent asks Eve, "Did God say, 'You shall not eat from any tree in the garden'?" (Gen. 3:1), twisting God's words so as to create disorientation. After Adam has eaten the forbidden fruit, God confronts him with three questions: "Where are you?" "Who told you that you were naked?" "Have you eaten from the tree of which I commanded you not to eat?" (Gen. 3:9, 11). Cain denies knowing the whereabouts of his brother, asking God, "Am I my brother's keeper?" (Gen. 4:9). Moses asks who he should say has sent him to Egypt, leading to God's self-identification and eventual liberating action on behalf of those enslaved by Pharaoh (Exod. 3:13). At his commissioning, Isaiah hears the voice of the Lord calling out, "Whom shall I send?" (Isa. 6:8). Micah clarifies God's expectations when he asks, "What does the Lord require of you but to do justice, and to love kindness, and to walk humbly with your God?" (Mic. 6:8). Mark's Gospel reaches its climax when Jesus asks the disciples not merely what others say about him but, more importantly, who they say he is (Mark 8:29). On hearing John the Baptist's call for a repentance exemplified by "worthy fruit," the tax collectors and soldiers ask a potentially life-changing question: "What should we do?" (Luke 3:10, 12, 14). Nathaniel asks: "Can anything good come from Nazareth?" (John 1:46). The obvious answer for John's readers is, "Absolutely!" Over and over again, Paul uses a variety of rhetorical questions in his letters to further his primary line of reasoning and to expose erroneous perceptions regarding the implications of his gospel (e.g., Rom. 6:1, 15; 7:7).

In biblical texts, questions regularly lead to crucial insights, refreshed priorities, and more faithful discipleship. Indeed, the Bible suggests that seemingly innocuous, inarticulate, and even half-baked questions can prove to be remarkably important. Consider, for example, the lawyer's surprise in Luke's Gospel upon hearing Jesus's response to his question "Who is my neighbor?" (Luke 10:29). Or how about the confusion and disappointment the apostles must have felt at the beginning of Acts, when they asked, "Lord, is this the time when you will restore the kingdom to Israel?" (Acts 1:6). Jesus's answer demonstrates that human expectations are far less creative and more provincial than anything God has in store, even as he clarifies the apostles' missional calling as witnesses (Acts 1:7-8). Indeed, we could probably discern much of the *missio Dei* simply by exploring biblical texts that feature questions!

At its most basic level, a missional hermeneutic is fundamentally concerned with the articulation of located, missional questions, questions fundamentally about purpose and sending—both God's and ours. Wrestling with such questions will help to guard against our ever-present tendency to define mission in terms of our own presuppositions and proclivities. We read Scripture as a community called and caught up into divine purposes, sent into the world to participate faithfully in that *missio Dei*. Thus we read from a social location characterized by mission. This affirmation, which is at once disarmingly simple and dauntingly comprehensive, provides the requisite missional framework and context for asking critical questions. From this location, every biblical passage becomes a missional text and every interpretive question we ask can become a question of missional hermeneutics.

Allow me to suggest a few missionally located questions worth asking. As *located* questions, they reflect the context or contexts in which I—along with my own community of faith—read the Bible; they may or may not reflect the pressing questions that would relate most directly to communities in other concrete locations. The important point is not that every question is equally applicable to every community, but simply that missionally located questions have inherently located implications for the missional communities who ask them.

- How does our reading of a given text demonstrate humility—recognizing that we see and understand only in part?
- Does our reading of the text challenge or baptize our assumptions and blind spots?
- In what ways are we tempted to "spiritualize" the concrete implications of the gospel as articulated in this text?
- How does the text help to clarify appropriate Christian behavior, not only in terms of conduct but also in terms of intentionality and motive?
- Does our reading emphasize the triumph of Christ's resurrection to the exclusion of the kenotic, cruciform character of his ministry?
- In what ways does this text proclaim good news to the poor and release to the captives, and how might our own social locations make it difficult to hear that news as good?
- Does our reading of the text reflect a tendency to bifurcate evangelism and justice?
- Does our reading of this text acknowledge and confess our complicity and culpability in personal and structural sin?
- In what ways does the text challenge us to rethink our often cozy relationships with power and privilege?
- How does this text expose and challenge our societal and economic tendencies to assign human beings and the rest of creation merely functional—as opposed to inherent—value?
- Does the text in front of us help clarify the call of gospel discipleship in a world of conspicuous consumption, devastating famine, rampant disease, incessant war, and vast economic inequities?
- How does the text clarify what the love of God and neighbor looks like in a particular context?

- How does this text clarify what God is doing in our world, in our nation, in our cities, and in our neighborhoods—and how may we be called to be involved in those purposes?
- Does our reading allow the text the opportunity to define everything about our mission in the world—including our assumptions, processes, terminology—everything?

I do not highlight these particular questions because they are the only important ones to be considered; they are not. I do not call attention to them because they will translate readily into congregational study curricula; they may not. I raise these questions because they are precisely the kinds of crucially important missional questions that my cultural lenses and privileged perspective tempt me to overlook or avoid. As we seek to interpret the Bible faithfully as a missional, sent community, what other located questions do we need to be asking of the text, and what kinds of context-specific questions is the text asking of us? In particular, how might biblical texts, interpreted from the perspective of mission, serve to transform our economic reasoning in ways that may enable us to participate ever more faithfully in the *missio Dei?* These are the fundamental questions that provide the rationale and genesis of this book on biblical economic formation in missional perspective.

FOR FURTHER REFLECTION

▶ This chapter has argued that, while mission is commonly understood in terms of the church's evangelistic outreach, mission—properly understood—is primarily about the nature of God and God's purposes in creation. Does this shift in emphasis affect your thinking about God, the church, and about what mission involves?

▶ If mission is understood to be inclusive of God's purposes both within and beyond the church, as I have explored it in this chapter, how might our understanding of activities such as evangelism, ministry, worship, pastoral work, the kingdom of God, justice, and salvation, be affected?

▶ How might our engagement with the Bible be affected if we were to read and interpret every biblical text from a located missional perspective—that is, from the vantage point of a community called and caught up into the larger purposes of God—as opposed to thinking about mission in the Bible only when passages explicitly invoke some form of evangelism or outreach to outsiders?

► Is it helpful to think about biblical interpretation (hermeneutics) in terms of the three rubrics (behind the text, the text itself, and in front of the text) that I have defined in this chapter? Practice posing questions to the biblical text from each of these approaches.

► As you think about your own contextual "location" as a Christian individual or community, what missional questions might be particularly important and relevant to ask and reflect on?

CHAPTER 3

Jesus's Mission and Divine Blessing

What was Jesus's mission? For Christians, asking about Jesus's mission may be one of the most fundamental interpretive questions that we can ask. If, as I advocated in the preceding chapter, mission is best understood in terms of purposiveness, then inquiring into Jesus's mission begins to take us to the heart of what the Gospel writers understood Jesus to be doing in his ministry; indeed, asking such a missional question points us directly toward the gospel message that Jesus both proclaimed and embodied. Asking about Jesus's mission is thus also of crucial significance for Christian individuals and communities seeking to bear faithful witness to God in Christ in the world today.

Jesus's Mission Statement

In Luke's Gospel, the scene in 4:14–30 serves as the starting point of Jesus's ministry, when he articulates for the first time what his gospel mission is all about. Indeed, this text contains what we might call Jesus's own mission statement. In his hometown synagogue, Jesus rises and reads from the book of Isaiah. Luke's description of what Jesus reads incorporates a quote that combines Isaiah 61:1–2 and 58:6:

> The Spirit of the LORD is upon me,
>   because he has anointed me
>   to bring good news to the poor.
> He has sent me to proclaim release to the captives
>   and recovery of sight to the blind,

39

to let the oppressed go free,
to proclaim the year of the LORD's favor.

According to Luke, after Jesus concluded his reading, he "rolled up the scroll, gave it back to the attendant, and sat down. The eyes of all in the synagogue were fixed on him. Then he said to them, 'Today this scripture has been fulfilled in your hearing'" (Luke 4:18-21).

"Today This Scripture Has Been Fulfilled in Your Hearing"

The synagogue attendees seem to have initially appreciated the beautiful words of hope that Jesus uttered from Isaiah: "All spoke well of him and were amazed at the gracious words that came from his mouth" (v. 22). Again, this passage functions for Jesus as a mission statement, a succinct articulation of his purpose in the world. Note that Jesus is reading from the Hebrew prophet Isaiah, which means that Isaiah is to be understood as the "me" referred to in verses 18-19. The term "anointed" in Greek is the word from which we get the term *Christ* (literally, "the anointed one"; *messiah* is the same word in Hebrew). Leaders of various kinds were anointed to set them apart for their service to God. Therefore, Isaiah was literally "christened . . . to bring good news to the poor . . ." (v. 18).

It is worth noting, though, that when Jesus says, "Today this scripture has been fulfilled in your hearing" (v. 21), he effectively applies the "me" (the "anointed" one) in verses 18-19 to himself. That is, Jesus claims that Isaiah's words are being realized in him ("me"). This Isaiah text is no longer merely a text of hope, according to Jesus; rather, it has now become "fulfilled" (v. 21). Jesus links his purpose, his mission, with the Spirit's work announced through the prophet Isaiah hundreds of years in the past. Isaiah and Jesus participate in parallel missions, with identical statements of purpose. And, given that Jesus acts in the power of the Spirit (4:1, 14), it is clear that his mission (as announced in this passage) is aligned with God's.

The activity of the Spirit described in both Isaiah's and Luke's accounts is purposive to the core: God's Spirit is accomplishing something particular in the process of anointing and sending Isaiah—and now Jesus. This is a purposive God, a God of mission. In Luke 4, we are near the very heart of the *missio Dei*.

"To Bring Good News to the Poor"

How Jesus (and his audience) would have understood each of the references within the quote from Isaiah is not fully clear. Most likely, given the Hebrew background of the Greek text presumably envisioned here, "the poor" incorporates both concretely economic and spiritual neediness. "The captives" would have no doubt included those imprisoned for indebtedness, and their "release" would effectively enact a liberation from debts expected in Leviticus 25.[1] Jesus probably envisioned needing to restore sight to the blind—both literally (see Luke 7:21-22) and figuratively (see Isa. 42:7). Freeing "the oppressed" was an example of the legitimate "fast" that the Lord truly sought from the covenant people (Isa. 58:6-7). "To proclaim the year of the Lord's favor" was to announce that the massive social restructuring of the Jubilee year (see Lev. 25) had finally arrived.[2] Whatever else Jesus may have implied, the mission he articulates here—in view of Isaiah 58 and 61—does not merely refer to what we might call "spiritual" matters. As Jesus demonstrates in his ministry throughout Luke's Gospel, he is eager to pay attention not only to the spiritual but also to the physical and material—including economic—needs of those whom he encounters.

The reaction to Jesus's comments from the synagogue is initially quite positive. Those in attendance speak well of him. But Jesus suddenly seems to turn on the congregation in verse 23, when he says, "Doubtless you will quote to me this proverb, 'Doctor, cure yourself!' And then you will say, 'Do here also in your hometown the things that we have heard you did at Capernaum.'"

Why does the mood change so quickly? Verse 22 may well contain two different reactions to Jesus. At first, they "spoke well of him and were amazed at the gracious words that came from his mouth." But then Luke adds, "They said, 'Is not this Joseph's son?'" Coupled with the positive statement at the beginning of verse 22, this question may sound as though the synagogue congregants are expressing, in an affirmative way, surprise at Jesus's abilities and skills as a reader and interpreter of Scripture. That is, they appear amazed that one of Joseph's sons is so accomplished: "Wow, look at the phenomenal local boy!"

If that positive assessment of Jesus is what is implied by the question

---

1. Bruce J. Malina and Richard L. Rohrbaugh, *Social-Science Commentary on the Synoptic Gospels,* 2nd ed. (Minneapolis: Fortress, 2003), 243.

2. On Leviticus 25, see chap. 6 below.

in verse 22 ("Is not this Joseph's son?"), Jesus's suddenly negative comments beginning in verse 23 seem odd. More likely, Luke's original readers would have recognized that the question in verse 22 is actually where the negativity begins. Bruce Malina and Richard Rohrbaugh indicate that, "in asking if Jesus is Joseph's son, the synagogue participants are probably trying to cut him down to size by questioning how such honorable teaching could come from one born to a lowly artisan. This exchange has often puzzled Western commentators, some of whom fail to understand the magnitude of the insult implied by the question."[3] If the community was beginning to ridicule Jesus for his lack of "standing," his retort beginning in verse 23 makes much more sense.

Jesus gives two examples of the ways in which God did *not* act in a way that God's chosen people would have anticipated. Rather, in some very difficult times for the Israelites, God actually helped Gentiles instead of them. (On the reference to Elijah, see 1 Kings 17:8–16; on the reference to Elisha, see 2 Kings 5:1–14.) At the very least, Jesus seems to be pointing to the fact that God's reign will not necessarily look like what his people assume it will. In fact, it may offend some of their sensibilities and their sense of what God's priorities should be. Jesus effectively raises "the possibility that outsiders ('the nations' other than Israel) are better able to judge the honor of a prophet than those who know him best."[4] At a time when Jesus's people (and Luke's readers as well) were very much under the power of the Roman Empire, Jesus's comments would have been heard as quite an insult. In fact, the people in Jesus's own town drove him out and tried to kill him (Luke 4:28–30). There is a massive irony here, of course: the Spirit of God has sent Jesus, *the* prophet of God, into the midst of God's own people, in order to announce God's truly good news. Jesus's own community then turns on him and, like previously misguided Israelites, tries to oppose and even kill God's prophet. This early public event in Jesus's hometown sets the tone for this Gospel. Luke, more than the other three Gospels, emphasizes the ways in which the reign of God will entail a reversal of the status quo in this world. (See, e.g., how young Mary talks about God in Luke 1:51–55; similar "reversal" echoes can be found throughout Luke.) Jesus attends to the poor, women, and the marginalized more often and explicitly in this Gospel than in any of the others.

In the context of the present book, Luke 4:18–19 represents Jesus's

3. Malina and Rohrbaugh, *Social-Science Commentary*, 243.
4. Malina and Rohrbaugh, *Social-Science Commentary*, 243.

mission statement—and thus, from Luke's perspective, also God's. The Isaiah reading encapsulates the good news Jesus has been anointed to announce (verses 18–19): "Today this scripture has been fulfilled in your hearing" (v. 21). This is what Jesus's mission is about.

It is important to consider the signs that will distinguish this good news. The poor and marginalized will find a new era dawning in Jesus. Note what Jesus says to John the Baptist's disciples when, later in the Gospel narrative, they question whether or not he is the awaited Messiah (Luke 7:22–23): "Go and tell John what you have seen and heard: the blind receive their sight, the lame walk, the lepers are cleansed, the deaf hear, the dead are raised, and the poor have good news brought to them. And blessed is anyone who takes no offense at me."

Good news! How quickly, though, the tables turn when the people question the young prophet in their midst. How quick they are to assume that they know what God's mission is, what God is up to, what God cares about: "God attends to the foreigners when we are suffering? Why not us?"

If Jesus's perspective is correct, those in the synagogue are wrong. And rather than being teachable, they become filled with rage. Jesus does not fit what they believe about God. Although the people in the Nazareth synagogue are on board, intellectually and philosophically, with the good news that Jesus announces—he is reading their Scripture, after all—they are deeply opposed to his claim that everything is occurring through him, and that it may all happen in ways that do not fit their preconceived notions of what God should be doing.

What might this account imply about our understandings of and reactions to what God may be up to through Christ in our own midst? What would it mean for us to focus closely on what the gospel of Jesus really looks like, according to this passage: a gospel in which the poor have good news brought to them, in which captives are released, in which the blind receive sight, the oppressed are freed, and the spirit of the Jubilee year defines the tenor of healthy human relationships with one another and with God?

We will want to be attentive to the themes Jesus has raised in his reading of Isaiah. What we will discover is that these are themes, purposes, and concerns that the Bible indicates God has had all along. Jesus knows his Bible, and he is not reading these things in Isaiah alone. God has always been about bringing good news to the poor, the oppressed, and the marginalized, according to the Bible. In Luke 4, though, we find Jesus summarizing what God is up to and how his own mission intersects with divine purposes. Again, in this passage we come into close contact with the nature and character of the *missio Dei*.

Are we comfortable with God's mission as Jesus reveals it in his mission statement? In what ways might we find Jesus's Nazareth message surprising or disconcerting? Are we ever like the folks in the Nazareth synagogue? How do we see the poor and marginalized? Do we even *see* them? What assumptions do we have about how they came to be in the situations in which they find themselves, and about how God thinks about them? Do we see society's outsiders, like those cited by Jesus, as the direct and expected recipients of the good news? What would it mean for us to see them—and to respond—as God does? What does Jesus's mission statement in Luke 4 mean for us, concretely, today? How might Jesus's words inform, form, and even transform our understandings of what the contemporary church's mission is in the world, particularly given the ways in which our economic paradigms and structures tend to leave the poor and marginalized to fend for themselves? And, ultimately, how might Jesus's statements transform our economic reasoning so that the Christian community may become ever more faithful to God's mission? These are the kinds of missionally located questions I will continue to raise and explore in the remainder of this book as we interact with a wide range of biblical texts.

Again, Jesus understands his own mission in biblical terms drawn from Isaiah: "[T]o bring good news to the poor . . . to proclaim release to the captives and recovery of sight to the blind, to let the oppressed go free, to proclaim the year of the Lord's favor" (Luke 4:18–19). If this is Jesus's purpose, his *mission,* it is worth noting that his quotation from Isaiah does not say much about those who tend to figure most prominently in our contemporary socioeconomic environment, namely, the wealthy, privileged, and comfortable. Using Isaiah's terminology, Jesus describes his mission as having to do with those who suffer marginalization in various ways. Given the extent to which contemporary economic thinking tends to honor those with monetary and financial resources, it is worth reflecting on what Jesus's mission means for those, such as the rich and powerful, who go unmentioned in the quotation from Isaiah. If Jesus's mission is directed to the poor and oppressed, what does that mean for those who have comfort and status in society? Luke 6:17–26 provides some remarkable commentary in this regard, suggesting that our contemporary evaluations of wealth and economic status may not have much in common with God's own perspective.

The Beatitudes

The Luke 6:17–26 passage further illuminates what the good news is from Jesus's perspective. It consists of Luke's version of the Beatitudes (the Latin word for "blessings"). Another version of the Beatitudes—perhaps more familiar and, for many, the more comfortable and appealing version—is found in Matthew 5:1–12. Matthew's version of the Beatitudes introduces Jesus's most famous teaching, the so-called Sermon on the Mount. Luke's version of the Beatitudes introduces his account of Jesus's "sermon" (often called the Sermon on the Plain because Jesus is described as coming down to stand "on a level place" to address his followers and the crowds [Luke 6:17]).

In Matthew, Jesus's sermon is three chapters long (Matt 5–7); in contrast, Luke's version is much shorter (6:17–49). Nevertheless, there is significant overlap between the two texts. Indeed, the content and wording of these passages are so similar as to suggest to most scholars that Matthew and Luke probably had a common written source that they both drew on. It is clear that these sermons are not precise transcripts of Jesus's teaching on two different occasions. Rather, Matthew and Luke have consciously and carefully put together a synopsis—or perhaps even a sort of "greatest hits" compilation—of some of Jesus's most memorable teachings, and they have done so in such a way that each sermon reflects and furthers the individual concerns, themes, and emphases that Matthew and Luke exhibit throughout their respective Gospels.

In his introduction to the Beatitudes, Matthew describes Jesus as going up on a mountain to teach (5:1–2). By framing the passage in this way, Matthew effectively portrays Jesus like Moses, who also went up a mountain and then expounded on God's will. In fact, throughout his Gospel, Matthew highlights connections between Jesus and Moses. Ultimately, though, he portrays Jesus as the preeminent interpreter of the law, who, unlike Moses, teaches "as one who has [his own] authority" (e.g., Matt. 5:21–22, 27–28, 31–32, 33–35, 38–39, 43–45).

By contrast, Luke does not accentuate connections between Moses and Jesus. Instead, he emphasizes that the kingdom of God entails a great reversal of the status quo: Jesus, God's prophet, closely identifies with and comes down "to a level place" to be among those he teaches—at their level, as it were. The description of the massive crowds, inclusive of folks from Tyre and Sidon, suggests that Luke is foreshadowing the fact that the good news will extend even to the Gentiles (see Acts 1:8).

45

"Blessed Are You . . ."

Now let us turn to the Beatitudes themselves. The Greek words in both Matthew and Luke translated as "blessed are" could be translated "congratulations to . . ." or "fortunate are . . ." or even "happy are. . . ." It is striking that Jesus announces blessings on those who would *not* have been considered fortunate or blessed in those days—or now, for that matter! We tend to assume that those with wealth, power, comfort, or fame are happy and blessed, whereas Jesus's comments suggest that true happiness (or "blessing") is linked to very different things.

It is interesting to compare the Matthean and Lukan Beatitudes side by side. Some of the statements in Matthew seem to correspond closely to those in Luke, although not exactly. For example, Jesus says in Luke 6:20: "Blessed are you who are poor, for yours is the kingdom of God." In Matthew 5:3, Jesus says, "Blessed are the poor in spirit, for theirs is the kingdom of heaven." Notice that Matthew's version uses the third person plural ("those," "they," "theirs"), whereas in Luke, Jesus speaks directly to the people in the familiar second person, "you" (in the plural, as in "y'all").

Luke's phrase "you who are poor" may appear to today's readers to be a more direct reference to the experience of poverty per se than what we find in Matthew's version, which refers to "the poor in spirit," apparently invoking those who recognize that before the awesome power and holiness of God everyone is impoverished. That is, Matthew's phrasing suggests that those who humbly recognize their spiritual poverty before God are blessed. In actual fact, each of these references to the "poor" in Luke and Matthew is probably best understood—historically, linguistically, and theologically—as incorporating both spiritual and material marginalization.

Note, further, how Matthew's version reads "kingdom of heaven" at the end of verse 3, whereas Luke's reads "kingdom of God." These are best understood as synonymous phrases: Matthew's specifically Jewish sensibilities (evident throughout his Gospel) lead him to use "heaven" as a circumlocution for "God" in order to avoid referring directly to God. Judeans often used indirect ways of referring to the deity in order to show their respect for God. Note also, for example, Matthew 5:6, which refers to "those who hunger and thirst for righteousness." The Greek word behind the NRSV's "righteousness" (*dikaiosynē*) can also be translated "justice"— and a good case can be made for it as the preferable English translation in this context. In any case, Matthew's version seems, at least at first glance, to have more of an attitudinal connotation (i.e., hungering and thirsting for justice/righteousness) than does the Lukan equivalent, "Blessed are you who are hungry now" (v. 21), which seems to emphasize the immediate and concrete physical hunger of the blessed.

It is noteworthy that, despite what we might assume, there are no imperatives (commands) in any of these blessings, with the exception of two instances: "rejoice" and "leap" (Luke 6:23); "rejoice" and "be glad" (Matthew 5:12). The blessings are thus not to be understood as instructions or directives for getting into the kingdom of God. Rather—and this is crucially important—Jesus is painting a picture, so to speak, of the way reality looks from God's perspective.

Are the poor blessed from a human vantage point? No. Most people in Jesus's day would have assumed that the poor and marginalized did not have God's blessing. By contrast, those who were powerful and wealthy could point to their bounty as evidence of blessing from God. There is an analogous logic today, even in a secular culture in which many question the very existence of God. Those who are considered "blessed" (fortunate, lucky, successful, honorable) tend to be wealthy, powerful, socially connected, or popular. Poor and marginalized people, by contrast, are often invisible, powerless, and disconnected. Moreover, such people are often seen as being at fault for the situations in which they find themselves—undeserving of a better, more "blessed" situation. But Jesus indicates—in a way that is rather counterintuitive for us—that, from God's perspective, the poor and oppressed *are,* in fact, blessed. God sees and honors them even if the rest of us do not.

"Woe to You . . ."

Especially striking in the Lukan Beatitudes are the "woes" (which do not appear in Matthew). In announcing God's judgment on disobedience and unfaithfulness, the biblical prophets sometimes say, "Woe to you, because you have done thus and such." And the language of "woe" also appears in apocalyptic writing (e.g., the book of Revelation), where there was sometimes a notion that the coming of the Messiah would be preceded by a period of "messianic woes" that would point to God's impending judgment.

My basic point is that "woe" is strong language. "Woes" are correlated with God's judgment. Bad things are in store for those under a woe ("you have received your consolation," "you will be hungry")—bad things, significantly, that others have already experienced. The deep irony is that, despite all appearances, those who are *currently* experiencing such bad things are blessed by God. Again, as Luke's Gospel suggests repeatedly, the reign of God will entail major reversals of the status quo.

It bears repeating that the Beatitudes do not represent a blueprint for action in the kingdom of God, nor do they provide a how-to manual for Jesus's followers. In Matthew, Jesus does not say, "Blessed are those who grit their teeth and try really hard to hunger and thirst for justice." Nor does he say, "I command you to start hungering for justice." In Luke, Jesus does not say, "Make yourself poor, and then you'll be blessed," or "Start weeping because then God will be happy with you." The blessings are not commands. Jesus does not articulate what people *must do* in order to be blessed.

"See As I See!"

The Beatitudes are not instructions; they are more like characteristics. Jesus does not say, "Do such-and-such" as much as he says, "See as I see!" He provides a vision of God's way of looking at the world, showing what reality looks like when viewed rightly. In effect, Jesus paints a picture of reality—of God's *economy*, as it were—from a cosmic, divine perspective. It is an image of the way things work and are managed when God is in charge.

These Beatitudes reflect reality from the vantage point of the kingdom of God. The nature of God's reign and the community that will participate in God's kingdom is reflected in certain kinds of characteristics that may well be surprising to us: in Luke's words, the poor, the hungry, the weeping; in Matthew's, the poor in spirit, those who mourn, those who hunger and thirst for justice—as well as the meek, merciful, pure in heart, and peacemakers. The way God sees and evaluates reality is radically different from the ways we do. These passages raise questions about what "reality" really means. The way we see and evaluate the world—in terms of power, wealth, social status, and so forth—can seem to us to be simply "the way things are." But is that true? Not according to Jesus. He assumes that God's perspective reflects what is really real—and it is greatly at odds with our own perspectives.

At first glance, it may seem as though Jesus's announcements of blessing in these passages, particularly in the Lukan version, are designed to placate the poor and hungry with pious rhetoric, encouraging them to be content with their present pain in view of a heavenly respite to come in the future. Let's be honest: the world does not seem to work as Jesus describes it. But the Beatitudes do not, in fact, represent cynical or pious rhetoric.

In fact, Jesus is describing a reality that we cannot see, one that in God's economy is both currently real and will also, eventually, become fully evident. Jesus refuses to paper over concrete suffering and marginalization. Rather, he names what reality is from God's vantage point, which represents a serious reversal of the human status quo, a reversal we can begin to imagine only if we are willing to be formed by—and adopt for ourselves—Jesus's vision of reality from God's perspective. Only then would it make sense to say, "Blessed are you who are poor," and "Woe to you who are rich."

Again, note that Jesus consistently uses second-person plural pronouns throughout the passage. Jesus's message is not primarily an individualistic one, despite our penchant in the West for seeing things in terms of our commitments to radical individualism. Behind Jesus's vision of the kingdom lies a sense of the community's covenantal relationship with God and with one another. The communal context of these blessings is not incidental; rather, it is at the very heart of what it would mean to live as the people of God—and to bear witness to God's kingdom. The community of faith is integrally related to the gospel, and not a mere add-on to an otherwise individualistic search for the reign of God.

What would it mean for us to think about reality, not in terms of how we typically see and understand it, but in terms of how it really is, from God's vantage point? What would have to change about our perspectives, reasoning, and behavior if we really began to see as God sees, and to evaluate reality as God evaluates? Could many of our contemporary markers of blessing, including, perhaps, material comfort and stability, be potential indicators of woe? What kind of community would we become if we were to orient everything about our lives—individually and communally—to the kingdom and its values? What would it look like if we were to be marked by the characteristics of those that Jesus declares are truly blessed?

Many of us in North America find ourselves uncomfortable when confronted by Jesus's statements that poor, hungry, and weeping folks are blessed—and that rich, full, and laughing people are under the specter of "woe." In churches and classrooms, I have heard questions and comments similar to those below in response to this text:

"What does Jesus mean by 'rich' people, and why does he have a problem with them?"

"I'm not really rich. Bill Gates and Warren Buffett are rich!"

"Surely, Jesus can't be referring to us."

Typical North American reactions to this passage, especially to the "woes," suggest that many of us find it difficult to hear Luke 6:17-26 (or Matthew 5:3-12) as "good news." What might such reactions say about us and about our understandings of who God is and what God is up to in the world?

Of course, some readers find great news in this passage. For those who experience poverty and other forms of marginalization, it is certainly good news to hear that God really sees and honors the poor and the outsiders, and that ultimate reality is not what it now seems to be. Again, according to Luke's Gospel, the full flowering of the kingdom of God will entail a great reversal of the status quo. And as we proceed, we will see some of the ways in which Jesus's perspectives in Luke 4:14-30 and 6:17-26 (and Matthew 5:3-12) are rooted in even older biblical texts and themes.

What do the Beatitudes contribute to our understanding of the *missio Dei* and the church's mission? Jesus's statements seem to cut against the grain of our sociocultural and economic presuppositions and experiences, which suggests that we have been formed and shaped more by contemporary perspectives, values, and priorities than by God's purposes and vision of reality. What would the church's missional witness in the world begin to look like if this passage were more fully to form—and thus completely transform—our reasoning and conduct, individually and communally? That is a missionally located question that must be asked by Christian communities in every age and context.

FOR FURTHER REFLECTION

▶ If, as I have suggested, Luke 4:18-19 represents Jesus's "mission statement," then he was anointed (or christened, i.e., "Christ-ed!") "to bring good news to the poor . . . to proclaim release to the captives and recovery of sight to the blind, to let the oppressed go free, and to proclaim the year of the Lord's favor." In what ways does the church today need to reflect on Jesus's mission, as articulated in Luke 4:18-19?

► Are there facets of Jesus's mission that might be challenging—or even upsetting—to us?

► To what extent are we willing to be engaged in Jesus's mission today?

► What might be some contemporary contexts in which the mission described in Luke 4:18-19 might be especially relevant and necessary today?

► How might the church, as the community of Jesus's followers, need to reassess its mission in view of Luke 4:18-19?

► How might our reasoning and behavior need to be transformed in order for us to participate faithfully in that mission?

► The blessings and woes in Luke 6:17-26 (and Matthew 5:1-12) do not provide a to-do list, but rather a vision of reality from God's perspective. Jesus calls us, as a new covenant community, to see as he sees. How might the Beatitudes inform—indeed, transform—our understanding of God's character and mission in the world?

► What might it mean, concretely, to live increasingly into God's vision of reality, in which the poor and hungry are blessed, and the rich and satisfied do not have their current status?

CHAPTER 4

The Exodus: The God of Liberation
Provides a Way Out

Missionally located questions concerning the character and conduct of the God whom we claim to serve are crucial for the community of faith in every age. Seemingly "entry-level" questions, such as "What is God like?" and "How does God act?" are important to ask on a regular basis because humans are so prone to idolatry—which the Bible, of course, prohibits. Although relatively few people today actually worship physical statues or "graven images," there are many potential forms of idolatry. A persistent temptation is the tendency to assume that God conforms to our notions of the divine. Idolatry often involves worshiping *our* god, that is, a god we have fashioned—individually and as social groups—to fit our values and perspectives, rather than the God of the Bible, whom we claim to follow. It is always easier to believe in and serve something of our own creation. As familiar as Christians may be with biblical descriptions of God—all of which, ultimately, are rooted in metaphor and never encompass the totality of God—we regularly fashion God in ways that conform to our own presuppositions, proclivities, and priorities.

Beyond the problem of idolatry per se is the extent to which many of us in the contemporary world elevate matters of cognitive assent to a belief structure over existential engagement in a humble journey of authentic discovery of God in relationship. Enlightenment reductionism has so effectively defined the terms of religious debates—for Christians and non-Christians alike—that the operative question of faith now pertains primarily to the question of God's existence. From a biblical perspective, however, mere belief in the "fact" of God's existence represents little more than a starting point for Christian faith.

Sadly, Christians probably bear significant responsibility for the increasing numbers of those around the world who reject the notion of God. Much of what passes for Christianity today, and perhaps in every generation, tends to be fundamentally at odds with the teachings and conduct of Jesus. It is often difficult to reconcile the God that Jesus knew and proclaimed with the deity envisioned by contemporary "believers" who espouse various forms of religious hatred, social exclusion, and dehumanizing economic policies. It is unlikely that Jesus himself would have believed in the God imagined by many contemporary Christians.

Mere belief in God has never been the primary concern of Christian faith. To be sure, the biblical writings presuppose that God exists. Almost everyone in biblical times believed in one or more gods—or at least in some sort of reality beyond the world that humans experience empirically. The biblical writers assumed belief. What they wanted to see was appropriate *living* in light of that belief. In some quarters, Christianity seems to reflect a nearly idolatrous fixation with "belief in God," in which believers congratulate themselves on their beliefs in a deity whose character and conduct, biblically speaking, have been at least partly overlooked or forgotten. From a missional perspective, perhaps the Christian community would do well to declare a moratorium on most public claims of belief, if only to reemphasize the justice, mercy, and love of the biblical God we claim to worship.

Given our contextual location as a Christian community—generationally, culturally, linguistically, politically, economically, and so on—we regularly need to reflect on and wrestle with the implications of our missional calling within the larger purposes of God as illuminated in the Bible. Mere belief in God is not enough. Plenty of people claim to believe in God and yet live in ways that are manifestly contrary to the nature and character of the God of the Bible. Christians are to live in the contemporary world bearing faithful and concrete witness to who God is and to what God cares about. We are called to be faithful not to the God of our own imaginations, but rather to the God whose character, concerns, and conduct the Bible seeks to reveal. In short, questions such as "What is God like?" and "How does God act?" are missionally located questions of the highest order.

As we reflect on issues of economic justice and discipleship, there may be no better place to begin exploring God's character and conduct than the story of the Exodus. Among the most familiar of all biblical narratives, some of its contemporary implications have nevertheless escaped the notice of many North American Christians.

The Exodus

The Israelite Exodus from slavery in Egypt (esp. Exod. 1:1–17:7) is one of the most important narratives in the Bible, describing in fascinating detail God's victory over the Egyptian pharaoh and his army, who had enslaved a large but otherwise insignificant population soon to be adopted as God's chosen people. The word "exodus" derives from the Greek words *ex* ("out of") and *hodos* ("way" or "road"), so the story is literally about how God provides "a way out of" slavery and oppression. The Exodus represents a classic story of identity and character; it reveals much about God and, for that matter, much about the Israelites as well. Let us reflect on what God's actions in support of the Israelites suggest to us about God and God's relationship to those who suffer from oppression.

As the narrative begins, Moses is in Midian, far from Egypt. He had fled Egypt years ago in fear for his life after killing an Egyptian who had been beating one of Moses's own people. Now married to Zipporah, a Midianite priest's daughter, Moses is taking care of the sheep that belong to his father-in-law. In the wilderness at Mount Horeb (an alternate name for Mount Sinai, which appears in certain strands of biblical tradition), identified as the mountain of God, Moses encounters a bush that is burning but is not being consumed by the flames. God calls to Moses by name from out of the bush, and instructs him to remove his sandals, for he is standing on holy ground (Exod. 3:1–5). God first self-identifies as "the God of your father, the God of Abraham, the God of Isaac, and the God of Jacob" (v. 6), connecting this experience for Moses with the God his ancestors had known.

God has become aware of the oppression suffered by "my people" in Egypt and has "come down to deliver them from the Egyptians, and to bring them up out of that land to a good and broad land, a land flowing with milk and honey . . ." (v. 8). The "cry" of the Israelites has made its way to God, and God has "seen how the Egyptians oppress them" (v. 9). God will send Moses to Pharaoh to announce the liberation of God's people. When Moses asks for God's name, he is provided with a special one—Yahweh (YHWH in consonant-only Hebrew letters)—a name that Moses is to pass on to the Israelites when he explains who has sent him to them. Moses is told that this name is to be God's name forever (3:13–15).

Let us reflect on God's fascinating personal name, YHWH (commonly pronounced "Yahweh"): the Bible apparently views the etymology of the name Yahweh as connected to the Hebrew verb "to be." The Hebrew phrase thus indicates that God says something to Moses like "I am who I am" (or, perhaps better: "I will be who I will be"). In a very real sense, then, God is described in the text as having to do with existence or with being it-self (or even the one who causes everything to exist). Nothing exists—noth-ing *is*—apart from God. At another level, God's character—indeed, God's name—will be clarified by Yahweh's first actions on behalf of his oppressed people. In order to know who God is and what God cares about, we need to look at what God eventually does. Ultimately, Yahweh is and will be a liberator of the oppressed.

Following several dialogues between Moses (and Aaron) and Pha-raoh, and a series of ten incredible plagues, God dramatically rescues the people from the Egyptians, utterly destroying Pharaoh's military (14:10–31). Pharaoh, who originally had no previous knowledge of—or respect for—Yahweh (see 5:1-2), now surely knows Yahweh's name (see 9:16)!

The theological implications of this identity-defining action on God's part are enormous. Who is God? The LORD is to be known largely by his conduct, his actions. According to the book of Exodus, the divine "I Am" is a liberator of slaves. And where does the story imply that God can be found? Yahweh will be found, first and foremost, with those who are op-pressed, enslaved, and suffering—at the bottom of society rather than with the powerful and mighty (such as Pharaoh).

Symbolically, it is worth noting what God the liberator does in the face of injustice. Leslie Hoppe makes three particularly helpful observa-tions in this regard.[1] First, Hoppe suggests that the behavior of the Egyptian monarch illustrates how oppression and injustice are best understood as fundamentally *human* creations.

The Exodus story serves to remind Israelites of subsequent genera-tions—and those of us who read the story today—that oppression and injus-tice do not simply exist or arise in a vacuum, in some kind of inexplicable way. Rather, human actions bring about such suffering.

On one level, the Exodus story implies that injustice is not, at root, an impersonal phenomenon—despite how it can often feel in our globalized context today. Injustice is fundamentally rooted in what one or more hu-man beings (e.g., Pharaoh) do to other human beings (e.g., Israelite slaves). Injustice is rooted, down deep, in interpersonal attitudes and actions. Even when oppression becomes large and systemic—seemingly impersonal and often impenetrable—the story implicitly reminds us of the important fact

---

1. See Leslie Hoppe, *There Shall Be No Poor among You: Poverty in the Bible* (Nash-ville: Abingdon, 2004), 21-34.

that injustice is never *merely* impersonal and systemic. Rather, impersonal and systemic injustice is the result of multiple and often multifaceted layers of *personal* injustices. At another level, the story makes explicit that God did not—and presumably, by implication, does not—create injustice. Humans do. Injustice is not part of the created order, as if God were its source. God is not to be blamed for oppression.

It can be tempting to think, given what we see going on around the world, that injustice is somehow simply part of the fabric of the universe— as if it is somehow part of the primordial order of things. But the Exodus story reflects a significant faith claim here. The LORD is a dramatically powerful, good, and just God who fights for those suffering oppression— and who is *not* the origin of the injustice we experience in the world. In Genesis, God is understood as the Creator, but the Exodus indicates that God does not create injustice. Humans did—and do. God is the one who liberates those who suffer under the pharaohs of the world, regardless of the form in which such oppressors may arise. The story thus informs and forms, for example, how its readers will understand human phenomena such as oppression and injustice.

Israelite writers tend to attribute to God pretty much everything that occurs—from military successes and failures to bountiful crops, devastating famines, premature deaths, regime changes, and so forth. The Exodus story, however, strikingly suggests that God cannot be considered the source of everything, at least when it comes to injustice and oppression. The narrative absolves Yahweh of responsibility for the things done by Pharaoh, disavowing, in effect, that injustice and oppression should be traced back to God.

To be sure, the story assumes that Pharaoh owes his very existence to God, so we might be tempted to say that Yahweh is still ultimately responsible for Pharaoh's injustice—given that God is Pharaoh's creator. This brings us to a second point raised by Hoppe. The Exodus story reminds us that injustice and oppression result from human *choices*. Pharaoh ultimately owes his existence to God, from a biblical perspective. Nevertheless, Pharaoh—and by implication, all humans—have a remarkable ability to make their own choices and do their own things. Human freedom is a fundamental and consistent theme that runs through the Bible. God creates human beings, but allows for human choices.

The biblical conviction is that humans, as creatures, can even choose to turn against the Creator. God is no marionette puppeteer. The Egyptian monarch is not a robot. God grants human beings the freedom to choose what they will do—even to the extent that they may end up opposing God and wreaking havoc on creation. The biblical writers envision the results of God's radical generosity toward human beings in this regard as having been—and often continuing to be—quite devastating. Humans make many bad choices, often with catastrophic results.

Some will certainly question whether human choice is a relevant category for the Exodus story, given that we are told on several occasions that God "hardened" the heart of Pharaoh (Exod. 9:12; 10:1, 20, 27; 11:10), apparently causing the ruler to refuse, again and again, to let the Hebrew people go (see also 14:4, 8, 17). Did Pharaoh really have any choice in the matter? Doesn't God's "hardening" of Pharaoh's heart imply that the Almighty was, in fact, to blame for at least some of the injustice the Israelite slaves experienced?

The references to God's hardening of Pharaoh's heart are not intended to suggest that God the Creator acts as a marionette puppeteer. The Exodus story makes it clear that the initial decision to oppress the Israelites was Pharaoh's own (1:8-14), as was the subsequent decision to increase the slaves' labor and suffering (5:6-18). Moreover, there are several points in the story where Pharaoh seems to be responsible for his own hardened heart (7:13-14, 22; 8:15, 19, 32; 9:34-35). It is probably significant that, except for the comment in Exodus 9:12, the references to God's hardening of Pharaoh's heart appear after those in which Pharaoh hardens his own heart.

No matter how we understand the hardening of Pharaoh's heart by God, perhaps we may imaginatively consider what happens when we find ourselves beginning to harden our hearts toward others, refusing to see them the way God sees them. Perhaps we act selfishly, speak unkindly, or fail to take another person's needs into account. In such moments, we choose to harden our own hearts toward others.

What happens when we make such choices frequently? The more we make hardhearted choices, the more we establish patterns and form habits—and our conduct becomes increasingly ingrained. Eventually, we can become so accustomed to acting with hardened hearts that it can become difficult to break the habitual pattern we have established. Before long, we may become consistently hardhearted.

Readers are told early in the Exodus narrative that God would eventually harden Pharaoh's heart, ultimately intensifying the conflict over Moses's requests to allow the Israelites to leave (Exod. 4:21). Nevertheless, God is not in fact the one who initiates the hardening of hearts. Again, readers are first told in 7:13-14 that the Pharaoh has hardened his own heart. He begins to develop a pattern in this regard (see Exod. 8:15, 32). The Pharaoh's self-hardening becomes habitual until, beginning in 9:12, the Lord becomes the consistent hardener of his heart.

Recall that biblical authors tend to attribute nearly everything to God. If Pharaoh chose to act with a hard heart often enough—habitually enough—it would have become increasingly difficult for him to choose to act in a different way. Indeed, it would begin to seem that he had only one choice, namely, to act with a hard heart. He would have, in effect, lost the ability to make his own choices. Perhaps the description of the Lord hardening Pharaoh's heart can be understood, at least symbolically, not as a cruel manipulation of Pharaoh by God but as a reflection of the sense that, at a certain point, Pharaoh's heart had become so intractable that he was effectively unable to choose a more appropriate response to Moses's requests. In effect, within the narrative world, choice had been taken away from Pharaoh.

Today, we might say that Pharaoh had become a victim of his own choices, even if we are uncomfortable with the notion that God forced him to do something against his own will. It may be best to assume that the narrative is attempting, albeit in a way that is odd and even off-putting to us, to describe how Pharaoh's heart had become intractable—even to the point where he would be unable to change. How else could ancient biblical storytellers explain why Pharaoh remained unwilling to choose a different path, despite continuing to face the horrifying and overwhelming challenges that the plagues represented? Such unbelievable intractability must have meant that God was involved.

In the end, we must acknowledge that the text affirms the hardening of Pharaoh's heart by God. According to the story, the Lord's purposes are furthered through this divine hardening. Pharaoh is not a puppet. While he does not have as much control as he assumes, he does have freedom to choose how he will conduct himself. The Exodus story attributes everything to God—everything, that is, except for what results from hardhearted human choices. Even Pharaoh—at least up to a point—has the ability to choose. And he chooses to pursue oppression and injustice to the extent that he establishes an intractable pattern of behavior.

Leslie Hoppe's third salient point can be highlighted briefly. He reminds us that when God addresses the unjust Egyptian system of slave labor, "there is no attempt to 'reform the system.'"[2] God does not merely

2. Hoppe, *No Poor among You*, 22.

tinker around the edges of the oppression, as if proposing a few tweaks that would fully rectify deep injustice. Rather, God destroys the entire Egyptian system, drowning in the sea the military-industrial complex that ultimately enforced the oppression.

In the Ancient Near East, large bodies of water often symbolized primordial chaos. According to the creation imagery of Genesis 1, God brought order to a preexisting watery chaos. Now, as a consequence of the injustice they have perpetrated, Pharaoh and his army are actually swallowed up by the chaotic waters. Symbolically, Pharaoh caused chaos for the Israelites through oppression; in the end, he and his forces reaped what they had sown, drowning in chaos themselves.

We must not forget Moses in this discussion. Although the Exodus narrative indicates that it is ultimately God who rescues the Israelite slaves, Moses plays an important role in the process of uprooting the injustice and oppression caused by Pharaoh. God sends real, fallible human beings, such as Moses and Aaron—and today, us—to serve as agents in the struggle to undo the damage, including oppression and injustice, that we humans have wrought, and continue to wreak, in the Creator's world.

Social Location and the Exodus

How the Exodus story is interpreted has a lot to do with where the reader is coming from—and thus with whom the reader most closely identifies in the story.[3] The biblical account of the Exodus has been far more important to marginalized and exploited groups than it has been for the comfortable elites of society. The Puritans, for example, read the story of the Exodus as a call to leave Europe in search of religious freedom. They saw the New World as "the promised land" and understood God to be calling them to gospel faithfulness in that new context. Viewing themselves as an oppressed people subject to an unjust kingdom, it did not take much to see themselves in the story of the Israelite move to freedom.

By contrast, for African slaves in the United States—and for many of their descendants—the Exodus became the quintessential narrative of freedom. The story left no doubt that God was the supreme agent of libera-

---

3. I am indebted, in this paragraph and the one that follows, to David W. Kling, *The Bible in History: How the Texts Have Shaped the Times* (New York: Oxford University Press, 2004), 193–230.

.on, fighting on behalf of slaves and those demeaned and abused because of their race. Martin Luther King Jr., in particular, used the language of the Exodus and the sought-after "promised land" to guide a nonviolent revolution against hatred and bigotry in this country.

The Exodus story has also been crucial for Latin American Christian leaders. During the middle to late twentieth century, when heavy-handed military governments—usually funded by the United States—ruthlessly opposed a perceived threat of socialism on the continent, many Latin American theologians and religious leaders saw in the Exodus narrative a paradigmatic story of freedom from oppression. Rejecting the traditional Enlightenment approach to biblical interpretation dominant in Europe and North America, which attempted to view the biblical text at arm's length and with a kind of scientific neutrality, these liberation theologians claimed that the most appropriate way to read the biblical text was actually from the perspective of the poor and marginalized. While they did not entirely reject scholarly, analytical methods of interpretation for unpacking the history and culture of the biblical world, those interpreters argued that the starting point for appropriate biblical interpretation must be the concrete context—the social location—of those on the margins. The Exodus story was told and retold by a people who descended from former slaves rather than from the vantage point of the Pharaonic empire. Ultimately, the social location of the poor and marginalized puts them in a position to help the rest of us understand the text.

These interpreters pointed to God's desire throughout the Bible to liberate humans from all that oppressed and enslaved them—beginning with liberation from physical oppression and slavery in the Exodus and continuing through spiritual alienation from God in the New Testament—as evidence that God was first and foremost a God of liberation. Further, while God did not and does not play favorites, neither does God remain neutral in contexts of injustice and oppression. Indeed, the Bible regularly says that in such situations God sides with those who are marginalized. The Exodus is but the first and most definitive example of this biblical theme.

Contrasting Stories

Biblically speaking, the Exodus was the Israelites' most fundamental and formative story. It provided a vision of who they were as a people, providing them a sense of *identity* (an underdog, albeit chosen, people whom God rescued from the jaws of Egyptian oppression and slavery) and *purpose* (a special, holy people whose ongoing relationship with God was to bear witness among the nations to God's character, faithfulness, power, and holiness). The story thus defined both God and the Israelites in fundamental ways—in the present and into the future.

Stories such as that of the Exodus were not only important for ancient, prescientific societies like Israel. Stories continue to play incredibly important roles in our lives today. They provide a primary way—probably *the* primary way—in which we make sense of ourselves and of the world in which we live. Stories are everywhere—in books, magazines, movies, music, art, history, and in our daily conversations; they guide, form, orient, frame, inspire, remind, and contextualize. Whether we narrate fond memories of our childhood exploits to a new friend, summarize for loved ones how we spent the day, read a beloved bedtime tale to a sleepy child, or describe a work project, stories serve as the warp and woof of our existence. The stories we remember and retell help us to interpret what is happening, to clarify why things are the way they are, and to challenge us to see reality anew.

Some stories, such as the biblical Exodus narrative, are especially significant because they are appreciated and shared by many; such stories can effectively provide the groups who value and retell them with a larger sense of communal identity and purpose, as they understand themselves together in light of those stories. In the United States, the "American Dream" is one of the familiar and fundamental stories that functions this way and retains great social power. While particular narrations of the story may differ in detail, the gist of the plot and its implications remain consistent: the United States is a land of freedom in which everyone has the opportunity to experience the best that life has to offer—socially, materially, and spiritually. Inequalities among individuals may exist in this country, but they function to incentivize effort, personal initiative, and merit. Anyone can achieve success—especially material abundance—through hard work. You can have it all, even if you begin with nothing. In this land of endless opportunity, it all depends on the individual. Get an education, show up on time, work hard, play by the rules, and you can achieve your goals. In short, through personal effort and dedication, any one of us can improve our life—and live the dream.

The American Dream is an incredibly influential story. It shapes our communal identity as a people: we are free, we are hard-working, and we hold the key to our own destinies. We believe that all citizens have a shot to rise above the situation into which they were born. We are all individually responsible for the ways we approach and respond to the opportunities and challenges we encounter in life. The American Dream is a formative story: it forms the intellectual and pragmatic backdrop for life in the United States. We applaud those who are focused on—even single-minded in—their entrepreneurial and moneymaking efforts, and we then honor and champion those who "have arrived."

Of course, the story of the American Dream does not simply shape individual lives; it also influences wider social values, priorities, and policies—from political perspectives and allegiances to housing, social welfare, and taxation. Even if most Americans rarely invoke the story explicitly, it shapes and reinforces how we understand the world in which we live, individually and communally. Indeed, specific stories of individual achievement regularly bolster our sense of trust in the fundamental truth of the larger American Dream story.

There is, however, a shadow side to the American Dream. Since all of us are understood to be individually responsible for our situations, the story essentially teaches us that (1) everyone can "win," and that (2) losers have no one to blame but themselves. Americans often attribute lack of success (e.g., poverty) to personal failure. The story tells us whom to cheer (the successful) and why (because they must have worked hard); but it also tells us whom to scorn (the unsuccessful) and why (because they must not have worked hard enough). Americans downplay social and cultural structures—forces that might hinder opportunities to "achieve the dream"—as factors contributing to success or failure in achieving the dream. Consequently, the American Dream narrative engenders little empathy for the poor and marginalized. It inspires and reinforces a worldview in which there are few, if any, logical incentives to assist and care for others who may not be achieving the dream. In fact, the story implies that assisting the "unsuccessful" creates unhealthy dependency. How will others improve themselves unless they learn to work harder? In a free society of seemingly unlimited opportunity, the comfortable cannot be blamed for the fate of those who are uncomfortable. If you do not achieve the benefits of the "dream," it is your own fault.

This story endures in the United States because of its formative power. It inspires hope. Even those who are struggling to feed their families value the story because it suggests that they, too, may not always be in the same situation. Any of us can eventually find success; the plotlines of our stories are still unfolding.

It is also worth recognizing, however, that the story of the American

Dream benefits those who have power, privilege, and material resources already. Whether or not wealthy people have actually earned, achieved, or deserved their own success, they benefit when this iconic story endures and remains vibrant in the popular imagination. As long as the story provides the basis of our collective identity, relatively few will question whether it is actually possible, in a highly competitive, bottom-line-oriented economy, for everyone to have real opportunities to "win" economically. Moreover, questions about injustice, oppression, and the fairness or unfairness of the system will remain muted because they do not fit easily within the larger social metanarrative.

The key point is that stories matter: they form us, they shape how we understand and make sense of reality, and they affect how we live together. In upcoming chapters, I will explore a variety of biblical laws that focus on fairness and economic justice for those at the bottom of society. It should not surprise us to find such concern for the poor and marginalized in an ancient society whose foundational story recounts divine liberation from oppression and slavery. Neither should it surprise us that in the United States, where we are deeply influenced and shaped by the story of the American Dream, much of our legal framework is oriented toward protecting the property and financial strength of the wealthy, while weaker members of the society—the working poor, minorities, the disabled, and those without permanent housing—often find themselves ignored and ostracized by legal means. Is it any wonder that, in contrast to the liberating Exodus narrative, the story of the American Dream influences the country with a yawning gap between the richest and the poorest? As Christians, we are grafted into the community whose foundational story is the Exodus. It is our story. But have we really heard it?

How might Christian reasoning and conduct pertaining to economic justice need to be reevaluated in light of the biblical story of the Exodus? For many today, falling real wages, shrinking benefits, and decreasing economic security make the US economy feel more like Egypt than the Promised Land. Indeed, the hard reality of economic life—even in the United States—is, for many, more nightmare than American Dream. What happens when we read the Exodus story in that context?

As I have noted, the Exodus reminds us that humans, not God, create oppression and injustice—which suggests that they result from human choices. In what ways do we choose to participate, perhaps unwittingly, in the creation and maintenance of systems and structures that enslave and dehumanize? Are there ways in which our own hardhearted tendencies toward others can, as with the Pharaoh, become nearly intractable patterns and habits, even to the extent that we may find ourselves unable to break out of—or perhaps even recognize—behavioral patterns, including those in the economic sphere, that have in some sense taken us over? When it comes to oppression and injustice, we tend to think small, in terms of reform. Perhaps we need to be more ruthless in dealing with dehumanizing structures and policies than we usually are, given how the Exodus story portrays God as utterly destroying the Pharaoh's unjust system.

In order to become truly faithful to the biblical witness of the Exodus, contemporary Christians will do well to reflect on the nature and purposes of God as the liberator of the oppressed Israelites, and allow ourselves to be transformed by that imagery. We have too often been conformed to the Pharaonic empire and its ways. The Exodus narrative indicates that God is attentive to the needs of those who suffer, and that God does not remain neutral in the face of radical injustice. Missionally speaking, we must reason and conduct ourselves in light of who God actually is: the one who looks out for and is present with those needing liberation. As we saw in Luke 4:14-30 and 6:17-26, Jesus clearly understood God's mission in this way—and sought to form his followers accordingly.

FOR FURTHER REFLECTION

▸ How does the story of the Exodus inform your understanding of who God is and what God cares about?

▸ The God of the Exodus did not stay neutral when a powerful ruler chose to oppress a marginalized people. How might the Exodus influence our understanding of God's mission today? How might the story transform our reasoning and behavior?

▸ Does the Exodus imagery of God as a liberator of the oppressed resonate with you? Why or why not?

▸ Reflect on the so-called American Dream story and compare it with the story of the Exodus. How have we been formed by the story of the American Dream? How might we be challenged to shift our values, priorities, and even policies if we were to increasingly embrace the Exodus story as our foundational narrative for making sense of the world?

CHAPTER 5

Economic Formation in the Decalogue

The Christian tradition affirms that both testaments in the biblical canon—the Jewish or Hebrew scriptures (what Christians traditionally call the Old Testament) and the New Testament—together form Christian Scripture. That is, the Christian Bible includes both collections of sacred writings, and together they are understood to be God's word, bearing witness to God's self-revelation in and through human history. Accordingly, the texts and traditions in the Old Testament help to reveal who God is and what God's purposes are in the world, and are thus of fundamental importance for ongoing Christian formation.

Nevertheless, many Bible readers today assume that most of the laws in the Old Testament no longer serve as specific practical requirements for conduct. It can be difficult to relate much of what we find—particularly in the legal materials in Exodus, Leviticus, and Deuteronomy—to our very different sociohistorical and cultural environments today. Still, the laws in the Old Testament illuminate much about divine purposes, and thus about the missional formation these texts provide for the communities that read them.

Many specific biblical statements cannot be translated directly into our contemporary contexts. The Israelites' economic assumptions, values, priorities, and practices were different from ours. We must reckon seriously with the distances between our thoroughly different social, historical, cultural, political, economic, and religious environments, recognizing that attempts to make easy, one-to-one correlations between the ancient world and our own are fraught with difficulty and may often result in misinterpretation—or worse, misappropriation—of biblical texts.

Despite the great difficulties inherent in appropriating ancient biblical writings for contemporary contexts, however, we need not conclude that seemingly obscure or outdated texts are rendered mute or irrelevant for us. Let us consider one example: We live today in an economic context in which interest is charged on loans; we take this for granted, and we find it difficult to imagine the economy working in any other way. Yet Torah (or the Pentateuch, the first five books of the Bible) specifically prohibits charging interest on loans (Exod. 22:25; Lev. 25:36–37; Deut. 23:19). The conceptual distance between such ancient and contemporary norms is remarkable, and many simply disregard such biblical laws as hopelessly outdated and economically naïve.

While we cannot import biblical laws uncritically into a contemporary context, the distance between the ancient and contemporary worlds does not prohibit us from taking such statements seriously. In fact, faithfulness to God's reign—particularly in our economic environment today—may require that contemporary believers pay increased attention to such passages, including those that seem foreign, outdated, and irrelevant.

Biblical writers used analogies when describing God and God's interactions with the created world. We see the results of such analogical thinking, for example, when we read about God as a *king,* or about God's covenantal relationship with the Israelites described in terms of a *marriage.* Such analogical thinking was important not only for the biblical authors, but also for us as we seek to interpret biblical texts faithfully. Responsible biblical interpretation must be conducted, at least in part, by means of analogy.

Faithful analogical reasoning requires that we focus our attention on the fundamental presuppositions, assumptions, values, and priorities that seem to inspire particular statements in the Bible. Despite the tremendous distance between ancient and contemporary economic thinking, it will not do simply to declare an ancient biblical perspective irrelevant for us. Even as we explore biblical texts using the full range of standard methods and tools for interpretation—illuminating, as much as possible, the contexts and meanings of ancient passages—we must go further, creatively reflecting on what even seemingly obscure or irrelevant laws in the Torah may tell us about what the biblical writers wanted to communicate about God's character and purposes, and what God considers important.

When in a sustained manner we ask such questions of biblical texts that incorporate economic dynamics, we open ourselves up to reflecting on biblical assumptions, values, and divine purposiveness. Why is God portrayed as being against interest charged on loans, and what does that say about the character of the God the Israelites claimed to serve? What are God's assumptions and values, so to speak? If making profit through collecting interest on a loan is not important to God—and, indeed, forbidden within the Israelite community—what *is* important to God? Why is God portrayed as being against charging interest on loans, and how does that fact illuminate for readers the purposes of God—the *missio Dei*? What might a prohibition on charging interest say about human beings and how they are to treat each other—from God's perspective? And how might such texts form contemporary Christian communities in very different economic contexts for their mission in the world today?

God and People in Covenantal Relationship

In order to understand legal reasoning in the Bible concerning economic and social justice, we must pay attention to the covenantal framework within which the Torah's authors and editors conceptualized their relationships with God and each other. Indeed, it is difficult to overstate the importance of the Israelite covenant for understanding biblical justice, particularly within the books of Exodus, Leviticus, and Deuteronomy.

In the Ancient Near East, two or more political entities would come together to establish a treaty relationship. Often, a powerful empire (e.g., Assyria or Babylon) might enter into a treaty relationship with a much less formidable political neighbor (e.g., Israel). A dominant power could effectively dictate the terms of an agreement, and a subordinate one might have few options when faced with a treaty offer. Failure to comply with the terms of the treaty could have disastrous consequences, particularly for the weaker party.

Biblically, God's relationship with the Israelites is sometimes described in terms of this kind of political treaty. Although God was the more powerful participant in the covenantal relationship, the biblical writers understood this divine-human relationship in positive terms. God was not a political bully, as might have often been the case in typical political treaties, but rather the very one who acted decisively to rescue and liberate the oppressed Israelites from Egypt.

The implications of such biblical covenants are wide-ranging and crucial. God is described as choosing to limit divine freedom, entering into a relationship that required unremitting fidelity from both human and divine partners. God is thus not understood in the covenantal tradition to be completely free within that relationship, at least not in terms of the kind of freedom with which we tend to be most familiar. Today we tend to think of freedom in terms of "autonomy," an understanding of freedom that presupposes independence from others and tends to limit our responsibility to others. Such a libertarian notion of freedom has almost no resonance with biblical imagery. The Lord is a God who uses freedom not for independence and autonomy *from* others, but rather *for* the benefit of others through ongoing and faithful relationship.

God's faithfulness to the terms of the covenant established with the people at Sinai is crucial for understanding divine conduct from another perspective as well. Some biblical prophets describe the covenantal relationship between God and people in terms of a marriage. They envision God as a husband and the Israelite community as a wife, and where such marital imagery appears in the Bible, it envisions the Lord as a faithful spouse, one who does not cheat on the Israelite people. By contrast, God's spouse, the community, is often described as stubborn ("stiff-necked") and unfaithful to her covenantal marriage vows. Indeed, when the Israelites acted unfaithfully toward God (e.g., by worshiping other deities), their behavior is often described in terms of cheating on their marital partner (God), often with offensive, sexualized imagery. The point is that marriage, like a covenant, is understood to be a two-way street, even in a very patriarchal, ancient Israelite context. Both parties in a relationship had to stay faithful in order for the marriage to remain healthy. And the biblical writers were clear: God always stays faithful to the terms of the covenant, even though the people do not.

Law, Understood Positively

North Americans tend to be enamored of freedom—again, understood primarily in terms of personal liberty and autonomy. To have freedom today means especially that we, as individuals, can choose what we will do, when we will do it, and with whom. No one can impose anything on us, given that we are free people in a free society. Moreover, we assume that everyone has basic rights that cannot be taken away or disregarded. And the ability to make our own choices seems to be at the very heart of what it means to be human in this world. Such "libertarian" values are deeply ingrained in our contemporary societal ethos.

But there are problems with this largely libertarian understanding of freedom, especially for those who would seek to understand and faithfully embody biblical perspectives. The Bible tends to have a radically different view of freedom and—not incidentally—of law as well. Let us begin with the latter and return to the former.

When I drive to work, I pass through a school zone that prohibits speed in excess of 25 miles per hour. I know that there is an important, community-fostering value embedded in such laws. Speed limit restrictions require that I contribute to the common good, reminding me to help make the world a better place, specifically by ensuring that schoolchildren stay safe. But I don't always regard speed limits positively. I often interpret them as restrictions on my freedom, especially when I am in a hurry. And speed limits do restrict my freedom. Therefore, I often see them in a negative light, as an annoyance, instead of thinking about the positive role they play in fostering the common good. When we understand freedom in terms of a lack of coercion, we naturally experience law in terms of restrictions and limitations.

For centuries, Christians—and especially Protestants—have tended to contrast biblical-law observance with God's grace and mercy brought to us through the death and resurrection of Christ. Law, in this sense, has been understood primarily as the negative foil to the gospel. The preponderance of biblical evidence suggests, however, that law was viewed positively in the Israelite and Jewish traditions, as a sign and means of God's grace and mercy. For those who tend to think of law negatively, such positive biblical imagery merits attention.

To illustrate, let us return to the notion of covenant as a marriage. Today, when two people marry, they usually make vows to one another. For example, they promise to care for one another into old age and they commit to staying faithful to one another. In effect, we might say that these covenantal vows represent "laws" that the two partners make for themselves. Do newlyweds view such marital laws negatively? When my wife and I got married, I vowed to be faithful to her, sexually and otherwise. But I did not view this "law" negatively. Indeed, I submitted to it eagerly and voluntarily: by swearing to be faithful to my wife, I would be getting her all to myself. That was completely positive!

The analogy of marriage is instructive in another way. I did not promise to stay faithful to my wife *in order* to get her to love me, as if by means of obedience to our mutual vows I might earn her favor and affection. On the contrary, my wife and I already loved each other. We did not establish marital "laws" in order to earn each other's love. We made our promises in order to ensure that our relationship, already characterized by deep love and commitment, would develop in a healthy way. Love and commitment came first, not obedience to a "law."

This illustration can be helpful in understanding the covenantal framework of biblical law. In love, God initiates a marital relationship with the people and vows to remain faithful to the people, to be their God and to be with them through thick and thin. Each partner in the relationship, God and people, must uphold its vows in order for the relationship to remain strong and healthy. This self-imposed law is an obligation to which even God freely submits and which God must obey. The legal materials in the Bible represent the vows that the people, as God's spouse, must observe. Obedience does not come first in the relationship, as though the Israelites could convince God to marry and love them through prior legal compliance. On the contrary, God already loved the Israelites and initiated the relationship before they ever obeyed a single biblical law. Divine covenantal love is the context for Israelite obedience, never the reverse.

In biblical imagery, righteousness was fundamentally a covenantal matter. People were understood to be righteous when they were in a right relationship with their covenantal partners, both God *and* neighbors. Picture two perpendicular intersecting axes: the vertical axis would represent the relationship between God (at the top) and the people (at the bottom); the horizontal axis would represent human relationships—Israelites with fellow Israelites. A righteous person is someone who maintains healthy covenantal relationships on both axes. This relational understanding of righteousness is a key for understanding biblical justice as well. In biblical perspective, justice is something that requires and reflects faithful and just relationships. Unfortunately, today we often think of righteousness as having to do with fidelity to a set of static principles, rules, or laws, things that tend to be understood in external and propositional terms. In doing so, we miss much of the covenantal framework of righteousness.

"Choose Life!"

The biblical covenantal tradition suggests that God's law is something entirely positive. For the Israelites, having God's law meant that Yahweh loved and had chosen them, just as marital vows are made by those who love each other and have chosen to be lifelong partners. In a committed and faithful marital relationship, both partners have the opportunity to live to the fullest—sexually and otherwise. By analogy, biblical law thus becomes the means by which God and people can maintain a loving covenantal relationship. Obedience to the terms of the covenant is not a burden but a means to true relationship and freedom, despite how heavy-handed biblical laws may sound to many of us today. In obedience to God's law, the Israelites experience the fullness that life offers, even as they learn to trust that God's love and faithfulness have the power to sustain them. Deuteronomy 30:15-16 articulates this understanding explicitly:

> See, I have set before you today life and prosperity, death and adversity. If you obey the commandments of the LORD your God that I am commanding you today, by loving the LORD your God, walking in his ways, and observing his commandments, decrees, and ordinances, then you shall live and become numerous, and the LORD your God will bless you in the land you are entering to possess.

In other words, "If you stay faithful to our covenantal vows, obedient to my law, our relationship will stay healthy and you will truly have the freedom to flourish." After warning the people about the negative ramifications of potential unfaithfulness, Moses emphatically urges them to "choose life" (30:19-20). Law is good. Faithful obedience enables the people to live in true freedom. Readers are presented with a choice: those who choose obedience are effectively making a choice in favor of life at its fullest and best.

Just as in marriages, of course, things did not always go smoothly for the Israelites in their relationship with God. The people were often unfaithful, and in those moments God is described as becoming angry and jealous. Nevertheless, God's grace and mercy always have the final say. The sacrificial system established by God as part of the covenantal framework provided a gracious means of atoning for sin and restoring the divine-human relationship following episodes of unfaithfulness. Bearing in mind such fundamental, biblical themes, assumptions, and values—love, obedience, faithfulness, freedom, mercy, and grace—we are better prepared to explore in more depth and specificity a range of especially significant texts and themes in the Torah, beginning with the Decalogue, or as it is most widely known, the Ten Commandments.

Introduction to the Ten Commandments

The Decalogue, or the Ten Commandments (literally, "ten words"), is understood as being especially characteristic of the Jewish and Christian traditions—by people both inside and outside of those traditions. Indeed, the Ten Commandments (found in slightly differing versions in Exod. 20:1-17 and Deut. 5:6-21) are so familiar that they have often come to function in an almost symbolic way: as a reflection of a supposed Judeo-Christian culture or set of values within North American society, as much as or more than they actually tend to be consulted as a concrete guide for daily conduct. That is, in practice we seldom allow them much opportunity to form our moral imaginations and behavior.

Still, the Decalogue can help clarify issues of crucial missional import: Who is God? What is God like? What does God care about? What are God's assumptions, values, and priorities? And what does a faithful covenant community look like?

The Decalogue is presented as a collection of "laws," but that term can be a bit misleading. The style of these commandments is unusual. The most common type of law is what is called *casuistic* (or case) law. Such laws address certain situations or cases, and they are written in an "if . . . then" format. For example, *if* someone is convicted of murdering another person in cold blood, *then* the murderer will be punished according to a set of established sentencing guidelines.

Note that the Ten Commandments do *not* have this casuistic "if . . . then" format. Instead, these laws represent wide-ranging commands ("You shall . . ." or "You shall not . . .") that are not limited to specific situations or cases and do not stipulate penalties for those who might be convicted. This type of legal statement is known as *apodictic* law. Unlike casuistic law, which can be expanded and updated as new situations arise, the non-situation-specific character of apodictic law does not easily lend itself to enforcement. Rather, apodictic law conveys fundamental and lasting principles. The Ten Commandments, therefore, provide a window into God's vision and purposes—and the divine will for God's people. The Decalogue declares, for example, that a faithful and obedient Israelite people will neither murder nor steal. There is no circumstantial information provided. The laws simply command that those things not be done.

But what would happen if a member of the Israelite community *did* kill someone? A wide range of circumstances could be involved. What would constitute murder, exactly? Does every killing involve murder? What about intent? Would it matter whether or not the killing was premeditated, or whether someone was killed in a moment of anger? What if someone were to kill another person accidentally? Should all of these potential situations be punished in exactly the same way? Casuistic law seeks to provide clarity in at least some of these circumstances.

Again, by contrast, apodictic law tends to reflect fundamental values and principles, regardless of the situation. Whereas casuistic law can stand on its own, apodictic law needs to be supplemented by casuistic in the course of concrete, communal life. As apodictic law, the Decalogue offers broad, summarizing statements that indicate, as it were, the central convictions of the community and, in this case, of its God, and it illuminates what a healthy covenantal relationship between God and people should look like.

The Decalogue (Exodus 20:1-17; Deuteronomy 5:6-21)

Exodus 20:1 describes the Decalogue as coming straight from God: "Then God spoke all these words." There can be no more authoritative message for the Israelites than what is about to come (cf. Deut. 5:1-5). The commandments begin in Exodus 20:2 with a reminder of God's liberation of the oppressed people: "I am the LORD your God, who brought you out of the land of Egypt, out of the house of slavery." God's self-description here is crucial for the commandments to follow. The conduct that Yahweh will expect from the people is predicated on prior divine action on their behalf. They have been rescued miraculously, and against all odds. Their freedom has nothing to do with their own efforts. They owe everything to God. How shall this people respond? They are to live together, as a community, as those who serve Yahweh, the "I Am" who met Moses at the burning bush, the one who acted decisively on their behalf. In effect, their conduct together should testify to the character and actions of their God, who demonstrated compassion toward them and who delivered them from slavery. They are thus to live together in such a way that they never inflict on others the kind of injustice, oppression, and slavery that they themselves experienced. The consistent use of the second-person singular pronoun ("you") as the subject of each item in the Decalogue suggests that the Israelites will be held individually responsible for maintaining the community's faithfulness to the covenant.

"No Gods before Me"

Exodus 20:3 commands that "you shall have no other gods before me." Note that monotheism (the belief in the existence of only one God) is *not* presupposed in verse 3. The commandment does presuppose a divine-human relationship, but the question is not *whether* there may be other gods; rather, the text is concerned with loyalty. The question is about w*hich* god the Israelites honor, serve, and obey: above all others, they are to serve Yahweh. The God of the Exodus, who now has a relationship with the Israelites, demands a privileged status in the hearts and minds of this people.

"You Shall Not Make for Yourself an Idol"

How, concretely, do the Israelites demonstrate that no other gods hold pride of place in their lives, individually and corporately, particularly when God is unseen? That is the burden of verses 4-6. The Israelites were familiar with other gods: deities were ever-present in the Ancient Near East, associated with particular places and phenomena (e.g., weather events). Archaeological evidence and the narratives in the Deuteronomic history (Joshua through 2 Kings) suggest that multiple deities were worshiped in various stages of Israel's history. Most of these gods were made present to their worshipers in some tangible form, via a physical image or idol, even if they were understood to exist beyond such specific, local manifestations.

The human tendency is to search for something tangible to make up for what seems to be absent. God is intangible, and thus humans seek to make God present in concrete ways. Images and idols, given that they are visible, can ultimately threaten to take the place of Yahweh. At one level, the concern in this command is to avoid substituting for God what is not God. The physical statues and images common in the ancient world are not, of course, the primary idols we need to avoid today. The commandment against idolatry is worded broadly and, by implication, should be understood to prohibit the worship of anything that could be exchanged for God. If idols are things valued as only God is to be valued, the forms of potential idolatry are nearly endless. Indeed, almost anything, physical or otherwise, can in one way or another become an idol. Objects, wealth, ideologies—even things that otherwise might be considered healthy and positive—can become idols when inappropriately valued. To whom or what are we most committed? That is, in whom or in what do we really place our trust? What are our most basic and nonnegotiable assumptions about the world and the way it works?

Luke 4:14-30 and 6:17-26 (see chap. 3 above) imply that God's people in the contemporary world should resist and constantly be on guard against economic, political, and social idols. Note that we do not create idols and exchange them for God unless they first represent something that we value. Those things we prioritize—material or otherwise, intentionally or unintentionally—are thus most at risk of becoming our idols. Today, potential objects of devotion could include, among other things, material items (e.g., property, possessions, wealth), values and priorities (e.g., profit, efficiency, growth, security, success, freedom, autonomy, individualism, self-sufficiency, self-interest, technological progress, success), and a whole range of social, political, and economic ideologies. Even our religious and theological beliefs, perspectives, and practices can become idols. Perhaps the most troublesome and insidious idols are those that we do not consciously recognize as elements that we have begun to honor and serve, whatever they may be.

The prohibition against making imagery to represent God effectively condemns any attempt to fashion God according to our imaginations, as a deity representing what we want God to be rather than who God is. This seems to be a constant temptation. Remember the reaction of those in the Nazareth synagogue in Luke 4 after Jesus reminded them how God had acted during the difficult days of Elijah and Elisha. Jesus suggested that their vision of God was too small, too parochial; then, according to Luke, they became enraged—to the point of attempting to kill God's anointed one. Part of the tendency toward idolatry is a temptation to understand God entirely—or, at least, largely—on our terms. Given that Jesus's statements flew in the face of their assumptions about God, the Nazarenes assumed that they were justified in treating him as they did. Likewise, Christians today often assume that God supports their assumptions, proclivities, values, and priorities. We assume that God sees and evaluates the world as we do. In short, we are tempted to create the God we want. But this commandment forbids any attempt to do so.

Exodus 20:5 articulates why idolatry must be avoided: "[F]or I the LORD your God am a jealous God, punishing children for the iniquity of parents, to the third and fourth generation of those who reject me, but showing steadfast love to the thousandth generation of those who love me and keep my commandments." This description of a "jealous God" meting out ongoing punishments—and blessings—is troubling to our modern ears. Does God vindictively execute punishment on the innocent because of a divine grudge? No matter how we interpret God's punishment "to the third and fourth generation," the language certainly reflects the reality that harmful choices tend to have implications that go far beyond the immediate persons involved.

By way of illustration, we know that perpetrators and their immediate victims are rarely the only ones affected by emotional or sexual abuse. Entire systems—social, emotional, and otherwise—develop within families, for example, to deal with the effects of abuse, often across generations. It can take years for wounds to heal, even for those uninvolved in the original abuse. Is there, perhaps, an analogy here with regard to idolatry?

The negative effects of idolatry can also last for generations, and they are understood in the biblical text as direct, ongoing punishments. Rampant consumerism in contemporary society may be a good example. Greed and acquisitiveness have become pervasive, and the fallout can and will be felt in myriad ways for generations. Our economic behavior—individually and within the larger and increasingly globalized society—has the tendency to breed various forms of social alienation, self-loathing, and insatiability, among other things. At one level, cries of indignation against clothing corporations, for example, that perpetuate the idea that only thin people are beautiful tend to focus mostly on the symptoms of a sociocultural and economic problem, rather than getting at the deeper roots of the problem itself, a problem that has become bigger and more multigenerational than anyone would have been able to predict. When we participate in idolatry—for example, when we metaphorically "worship" at the altar of the modern market—we set in motion consequences that may be as far-reaching ("to the third and fourth generation") as they are unrecognized and unheeded. By contrast, the effects of loyalty to God continue to bear fruit, also for years and years (v. 6).

"A Jealous God"

But how can God be "jealous" (v. 5)? Some of my students find that idea confusing and even repellant: Isn't Yahweh supposed to be—well, *God*—and thus beyond such seemingly petty emotional entanglements? A jealous God sounds reactive, vindictive, and unattractive. Indeed, God often seems to be "having a bad day" in many places in the Old Testament. Why is God portrayed so unappealingly?

76

With regard to jealousy, perhaps the marital analogy can again be helpful. If we think about times when we might feel jealous, especially within a committed relationship, the imagery of jealousy may actually become more intelligible. I ask my students to imagine what would happen if I were to find my wife amorously involved with someone else. What would I feel? Sadness? Anger? Jealousy? Surely, no one would fault me for feeling such emotions. We know what disloyalty and rejection feel like, and that it is natural to have strong negative feelings. Indeed, my students recognize that it would be strange if I did *not* feel angry or jealous if I were to find my wife cheating on me. Not to feel anything would suggest that our relationship was, to a significant degree, already over.

Feelings of anger or jealousy point to some level of emotional investment in the relationship. If I am angry or jealous, it is because I have something to lose. If I feel no emotion, I have nothing invested in the relationship. Anger and jealousy can sometimes be positive indicators of commitment. In biblical imagery, divine anger and jealousy do not imply pettiness or immaturity. Rather, the God of the Bible gets angry and jealous precisely because God is deeply invested in the covenantal relationship with the Israelite community. God is committed and has something to lose. The relationship matters to God, and, like a jilted lover, God is moved to strong emotion in the face of infidelity. Such feelings do not point to divine weakness, but rather to strength. Again, a relationship devoid of emotion is not much of a relationship.

Jealousy, in this case, points to love and devotion. God is fiercely loyal to the Israelites, and God expects fierce loyalty from them in return. In short, the Bible's "jealous God" imagery functions as a robust, though jarring, way to illustrate that Yahweh's loving, committed relationship with the people really matters—particularly to God.

"You Shall Not Make Wrongful Use of the Name of the LORD *Your God"*

The next "word" in the Decalogue (v. 7) refers to the wrongful use of the LORD's name. When I was young, I assumed that this commandment intended to prohibit foul language in reference to God. And, of course, the implication is that God's people should refer to God only with the deepest reverence and respect. Still, this commandment's context in ancient Israel probably referred primarily to using the LORD's name inappropriately or falsely in the context of worship, economic activity, and legal proceedings.

People in the Ancient Near East would often seal a business transaction, for example, by swearing an oath to a god. This commandment suggests, at the very least, that one must never use Yahweh's name as a way to camouflage economic dishonesty or other inappropriate behavior. The divine name is not to be associated with any form of deceit or injustice. The punishment for those who break this command is severe: "The LORD will not acquit anyone who misuses his name" (v. 7).

"Remember the Sabbath Day, and Keep It Holy"

Holiness refers to something being set apart for a special purpose, and the Sabbath day is to be set apart, devoted to God. No work is to be done by anyone, including slaves, animals, and resident aliens (v. 10). All are commanded to rest—which means, of course, that those under authority must be allowed to rest. There is a distinctively democratic quality to the Sabbath command. Everyone enjoys a day to rest and recuperate.

Within the two versions of the Decalogue, the Sabbath commandments form transitional bridges between commands that are oriented primarily toward God and those oriented primarily toward other human beings. The commandments prior to the Sabbath "word" are focused on how God is to be honored and treated; subsequent commandments concentrate on human relationships in the covenant community. The Sabbath commandments incorporate both concerns: while certainly oriented toward God, they also focus explicitly, in light of who God is and what God has done, on human needs within the larger covenant community. Although the two forms of the Decalogue (Exod. 20:1-17 and Deut. 5:6-21) are in most details very similar, these two passages offer intriguingly different rationales for the Sabbath day.

In Exodus, Sabbath observance is rooted in the first creation account in Genesis (1:1-2:4a). Creation itself comes into being through God's work, yet God does not work unceasingly without rest, any more than humans or animals should. God works and ceases from work. Creation is effectively commanded to do the same. Both work and Sabbath rest are patterned on the divine template established in creation. And creation is sustained through an ongoing cycle of work and rest.

What if we were to take the radical Sabbath vision of Exodus 20:8-11 seriously today in terms of how we think about our lives and our communities? Don't we function best when we experience a balance between work and rest? What would it look like for North American Christians to commit themselves to a sustainable balance between work and rest, one rooted in creation itself, according to Exodus? What would it take for us to view even the poorest and most marginalized as being entitled to both work and rest, as an integral function of the created order?

To rest regularly has often been a countercultural behavior. Ancient Near Eastern societies did not necessarily view rest as part of the human life cycle. The vast majority of humanity was expected to work every day— without a break. In the Roman Empire, Jews were considered odd, even burdensome to the wider society, given that they would not participate in a seven-day workweek. While the Sabbath commandment represents a covenantal obligation for God's people, it was also a gift. Of course, some saw it as an obstacle to productivity (see, e.g., Amos 8:4-6), but many, especially those burdened with heavy labor, surely experienced it as a blessing, as a time to recover and recuperate.

North American Christians are not especially known for living creatively sustainable, Sabbath-formed lives. We have ample evidence today of what happens when work begins to take over our lives, when we do not observe a rhythmic cycle of work and rest. We become unbalanced, our efforts become unsustainable, and the powerless inevitably suffer. The surprise, even for many Christians, is that a sustainable balance between work and rest is linked, in Exodus 20:8-11, to the very architecture of the cosmos as created by God.

The other version of the Sabbath commandment, in Deuteronomy 5:12-15, offers a different, though complementary, rationale for observing a regular day in which no work is to be done, even by slaves, resident aliens, or animals. Sabbath observance is rooted not in creation (as in Exod. 20:11) but in the Exodus experience: "Remember that you were a slave in the land of Egypt, and the LORD your God brought you out from there with a mighty hand and an outstretched arm; therefore the LORD your God commanded you to keep the sabbath day." God's people are enjoined to commemorate Yahweh's liberating action on behalf of the oppressed slaves in Egypt by including all members of the community, human and animal alike, in a day of rest.

Deuteronomy portrays Moses as addressing a new generation of God's people, those who did not personally experience the divine rescue from Egyptian slavery. Still, Moses speaks to them as if they were, indeed, part of the original escape: "*[You]* were a slave in the land of Egypt, and the LORD *your* God brought *you* out from there" (v. 15). As far as Moses is concerned, this is their story, and they are to conduct themselves in light of that story, providing for the rest demanded by their divine liberator. The Israelite people had experienced forced labor in Egypt themselves, so subsequent generations were to avoid reenacting the worst features of that ubiquitous ancient institution. God had provided rest and relief for the Hebrew slaves, and the Israelites were expected to do likewise for the vulnerable in their midst. Regular opportunities for rest were to be provided for everyone, even for the marginalized. Sabbath observance represented a weekly memorial to the justice that God can—and, in Egypt, did—provide.

The Sabbath commandment in Exodus, linked to creation, may be more familiar to many contemporary readers than the version in Deuteronomy. Many North American Christians have little personal experience as victims of social injustice, making it no less difficult to relate to Moses's affirmation that "you were a slave in the land of Egypt" (Deut. 5:15) than it would have been for the generation of Israelites who were not involved in the original Exodus.

Surely, as Christians, we are to understand the Exodus, along with its challenging and transformative implications, as our own story, always relevant in any context. What would it mean for us to think more consciously about observing the Sabbath as a testament to the just actions of God on behalf of those who suffered in Egypt, to recognize ourselves as those who, as part of the faith community, have been incorporated into their suffering and struggle, in order to embody justice for others in the broader community? What if we were to link Sabbath observance more explicitly to justice and liberation, as in Deuteronomy? What would it mean for the Sabbath to be consciously and intentionally celebrated as a day of justice, as a holy moment instituted by the God who sees and responds to the plight of the marginalized and oppressed?

"Honor Your Father and Mother"

Showing respect for elders in ancient Israel was a social norm, but this commandment had specific economic implications. To "honor your father and mother" seems to have meant that adult children were expected to provide for their parents' needs once age or infirmity made it difficult for them to care for themselves. In other words, the commandment required that senior members of the community not be forgotten or shunned once they had passed their most productive years—regardless of any economic burden that might pose for younger generations.

Within the framework of the Israelite covenant, therefore, productivity and economic clout are inadequate indices for determining who merits care in society. Even aged parents, who may have nothing to contribute financially to the larger family, are to be honored—in concrete economic terms.

In the Israelite familial structure presupposed by the Decalogue, it would have been quite normal for extended families to live and work together in close proximity. Today, by contrast, nuclear family households are common, at least in North American communities. Again, the commandment to honor parents points to the need within ancient Israel to make explicit provision for those who could no longer provide for themselves; the family structure, as an extended kinship unit, would have offered a ready framework and mechanism for such care. But we should not assume that the Israelites found it easy to comply with this expectation simply as a matter of course.

The financial implications of this command were real in ancient Israel, and they remain challenging today. Our economic system has a tendency to neglect the aged, to leave the aged behind, especially those whose economic clout has waned. To the extent that people participate productively and consumptively in the economic system, they have, at least theoretically, a functional voice within the larger market mechanism (e.g., in terms of purchasing power). Those who lack economic resources, however, can be rendered nearly voiceless and invisible. Given these realities, how might we understand the commandment to "honor your father and mother" today?

Clearly, the terms of the Decalogue specifically put obligations on members of the covenant community. Christians in North America today, however, live in a religiously pluralistic society that is not framed or shaped by a divine covenant. We might assume, then, that the command to "honor your father and mother," even with its proper economic force, may be irrelevant for us, at least with respect to elders beyond our own families, and those within the larger Christian community. But we should understand this "word" today in light of the fact that God loves and values all people, including dependent elderly persons. From that perspective, every elderly person should be honored concretely, by all of us, whether or not we share blood relations or religious affiliations. Every aging member of society—including those who cannot participate fully in the activities of the community, economically and otherwise—should be valued and esteemed, in concrete ways. To honor one's own biological parents while abandoning other elders would seem to be a rather shallow reading of the commandment.

Scholars often note that this commandment is the only one in the Decalogue that includes a future promise: obedience will result in a long life "in the land that the LORD your God is giving you" (v. 12). Presumably, human life would improve—in both duration and quality—as each generation intentionally honored and cared for the others. Sadly, our contemporary culture seems to have a short attention span, forgetting one generation after another as we gravitate toward novelty and youth.

This commandment is framed positively: members of the community are told what they are to do instead of what they are not to do. But the text also implicitly forbids what is due to parents to be withheld or taken from them. Treating parents with honor and respect is not understood to be something special, as some kind of charitable gift for which parents should be especially grateful. Rather, the commandment assumes that honor and respect—again, understood primarily in terms of adequate care late in life—are things that are due to parents as a matter of course. These are things that parents have a right to expect, and that their children have a duty to provide. To fail to honor parents is akin to taking something away from them that is already theirs. This dynamic links this commandment, thematically, with those that follow.

"You Shall Not Murder"

Each of the remaining commands, which can be treated relatively briefly for our purposes, effectively prohibits taking something that belongs to someone else. Economic considerations are presupposed, even if they are not explicitly highlighted. In the case of murder (v. 13), for example, one steals the life of another. Life, in all its forms, is to be protected, valued, and cherished. No one may take the life of another. It is worth noting that in both ancient and contemporary contexts, taking a human life has far more than emotional effects for loved ones. Serious economic losses are also involved. In this sense, unjustly taking a life is understood within the Decalogue to be a form of stealing. Murder steals the victim's life and thus robs from those who survive the victim—including spouses, children, and co-workers.

"You Shall Not Commit Adultery"

With regard to adultery (v. 14), no one may have sexual relations with another man's wife or fiancée. As often noted, this commandment seeks to protect marital and family cohesion, which were at the heart of communal health and vitality. The intimacy of the marital relationship is to be guarded, and any violation of that intimacy amounts to stealing what effectively belongs to someone else. Given the complex financial arrangements that were often involved in ancient Israelite marriages, as interfamilial economic negotiations often began long before any emotional attachments had developed between two potential spouses, adultery would have entailed economic fallout as well as relational pain. Perhaps it is easier in our contemporary environment to hide adultery and its wider effects than would have been the case in ancient Israel, and certainly the social sanctions that pertain to adultery are less severe today. Nevertheless, there is little doubt that the results of adultery can be devastating to marriages, families, and communities—relationally and economically.

"You Shall Not Steal"

Some commentators suggest that the original sense of this specific commandment against stealing (v. 15) had to do with kidnapping—for example, stealing a slave who belonged to another—but the commandment should probably not be understood so narrowly.[1] In any event, stealing breaks down the trust that holds a community together, even as it diminishes the resources of the victims. If a healthy covenant community is to be established and maintained, stealing is forbidden.

"You Shall Not Bear False Witness against Your Neighbor"

To "bear false witness" (v. 16) is, in effect, to steal the truth from others. Jewish law required at least two witnesses to convict someone of a crime. And there is an economic connection here as well: bearing false witness can and often does occur when money issues are at stake. Ancient legal

---

1. Carol Meyers, *Exodus,* New Cambridge Bible Commentary (New York: Cambridge University Press, 2005), 176.

cases, for example, often involved people's financial situations—robberies, property disputes, and so on—and those with something to gain economically had a significant motive for shading the truth. Some things never change.

"You Shall Not Covet"

Finally, the Decalogue prohibits covetousness (Exod. 20:17; cf. Deut. 5:21). Covenantal members were not to allow the desire to take something belonging to another to fester. This commandment harks back to several of the previous commandments by emphasizing that God does not merely forbid particular behaviors within the community, such as murder or theft; instead, God is also concerned about the motives that might lead one to commit murder or adultery, to steal, or to bear false witness. Inasmuch as the commandment concerning covetousness effectively prohibits an internal matter known only to each individual and to God, it reminds readers that God is the final authority with regard to all of these "words." The same God who liberated the community from slavery in Egypt is the one who demands certain behaviors and, indeed, appropriate motives. It is not enough merely to avoid committing murder or adultery or theft; God is concerned about the inordinate—that is, disordered—desires that give rise to murder, adultery, and theft in the first place.

The economic implications of covetousness should be fairly obvious, and the importance of the commandment in this regard is underscored through the specificity and range of the items that are not to be coveted (houses, wives, fields, slaves, oxen, donkeys, "or anything that belongs to your neighbor"). Covetousness, despite its primarily internal character, is placed on the same level of importance as the other commandments, implying that it can do as much to break down relationships within a community, and with God, as anything else. Needless to say, our contemporary economic values are often at odds with this final command. Not only are there few, if any, public sanctions against covetousness today, it has effectively become, in the form of self-interest and in the absence of obvious divine judgment, one of the primary drivers of our economy.

The "words" of the Decalogue, individually and together, assume that life, and the provisions and resources necessary for life, are to be protected. Those who are weak and marginalized (e.g., slaves and elderly parents) are to be cared for—not merely emotionally, but also in terms of their concrete needs for physical rest and economic sustenance. The health and integrity of the community must be upheld, and the basic framework for doing so requires that human life not be taken by others, that marital relationships be faithful, that personal property be respected, and that the truth be articulated. To ensure that this framework holds, the Decalogue ends by paying attention to covetousness, which is both common to human experience and the most destructive agent in the breakdown of the covenantal relationship. The commandments effectively begin and end with the awareness that the health of the community is rooted in healthy relationships with God.

Ultimately, these commandments demand from the community of faith far more than lip service or rote memory. These commandments demand and seek to form lives that reflect God's liberating love and action, lives that embody in concrete ways the kind of community that such liberating love creates and sustains. If we reduce the Decalogue to a series of rules, we truncate its significance, since these "ten words" function to illuminate the kind of witness God's people are to have in the world. They seek to form—and, in effect, to transform—not only behavior but also the moral imagination and reasoning on which faithful behavior would be based. Understood within its larger covenantal framework, the Decalogue thus serves a missional function for the communities that not only read the commandments but are, in effect, read by and ultimately held accountable by God, from whom these "words" are understood to have come.

FOR FURTHER REFLECTION

▶ Do we participate in idolatry today? In what ways?

▶ Readers often find biblical imagery (particularly in the Hebrew Bible, the Old Testament) of God as angry and "jealous" to be odd and even off-putting. In this chapter I have suggested that the portrayal of God as a "jealous God" in the context of a covenant would have been understood positively. Do you view God's anger and jealousy differently after reading this chapter?

▶ Biblical laws were understood to be part of a larger covenantal relationship between God and God's people, and obedience to those laws was conceived in positive terms, as the means by which the Israelites could "choose" to live and experience "life" most fully. Reflect on what you have just read about the Ten Commandments. What were some of the ancient economic dynamics embedded within those laws? Has your understanding of them changed after reading this chapter—and, if so, in what ways?

▶ What do the Ten Commandments contribute to our understanding of God and what God cares about? How might the Ten Commandments affect our understanding of God's mission in the world—and, by implication, the church's mission?

CHAPTER 6

Economic Formation in the Covenantal Legal Codes

I n addition to the Ten Commandments, there are three bodies of legal material in the Bible that were designed to form and guide the Israelite people: the "Book of the Covenant" (Exod. 20:22–23:33); the "Holiness Code" (Lev. 17–26); and the "Deuteronomic Code" (Deut. 12–26). We need not concern ourselves with the complex details and vigorous scholarly debates regarding the sociohistorical contexts of these codes. Suffice it to say that the biblical evidence is clear that each of these Israelite legal collections developed over time—in some cases, hundreds of years—in different historical, religious, and political situations.

Our exploration of these legal traditions does not ultimately rest on any particular historical or sociological reconstruction of ancient Israel. In general, scholars have tended to date the various covenantal legal materials on the basis of textual clues in the Bible itself; one example of such information would be the extent to which a legal corpus seems to presuppose a primarily decentralized, rural context, or whether it seems to reflect a more centralized, urban environment.[1] The "Book of the Covenant" in Exodus (20:22–23:33) appears to presuppose the former (though some of the data may reflect historical retrojection by biblical writers). The other codes, by contrast, seem generally to reflect later urban environments. In general, going along with the majority of scholarship, we will assume that the materials in Exodus tend to be older than those in Deuteronomy and Leviticus. Leviticus represents some of the most recent material in the Pen-

---

1. The work of Douglas A. Knight, *Law, Power, and Justice in Ancient Israel* (Louisville: Westminster John Knox, 2011), is reflected in this and the following paragraph.

87

tateuch; Deuteronomy is a somewhat older (if not roughly contemporary) document.

Only a tiny minority of the Israelite population would have been able to read and write, and those with access to the education requisite for literacy would have come almost exclusively from the upper strata of society; these legal traditions will undoubtedly reflect the perspectives—theological, political, socioeconomic, and so forth—of those who wrote and collected them. Few Israelites would have been familiar with the full extent of these legal collections, especially given a largely rural, decentralized population, low levels of literacy, and the fact that most of the codes seem to have been committed to writing and compiled over the course of many years. The majority of the population, especially the rural poor, probably had relatively little personal contact with any written law codes. Indeed, rural experience with law would have been predominantly limited to oral traditions rooted in customs and social norms. Those who lived in urban centers—near institutions such as the temple and the throne—may have had more opportunities than those in rural areas to become acquainted with written law codes.

The legal statements in Exodus, Leviticus, and Deuteronomy are not designed merely—or, in some cases, at all—for practical, everyday adjudication in the law courts. Indeed, some of these laws are functionally unenforceable. Such law codes function primarily as exhortations to faithful and healthy living in the covenant community, whether or not they envision specific, concrete situations that may need adjudication and, potentially, the meting out of consequences for those who would break them. In addition to guiding and regulating behavior in a practical legal sense, then, these law codes provide their communities with clear indications of who God is, what God cares about, and what it would look like to live together in faithful, covenantal relationship—both with God and with others. In this sense, the legal traditions in Torah are fundamentally missional in nature, seeking to form their reading communities for appropriate covenantal and moral reasoning—and for faithful conduct in the world.

General Socioeconomic Realities in Ancient Israel

The world in which most ancient Israelites lived was a challenging one.[2] Economies were not, by and large, oriented to markets or growth. Urban power centers, whose needs were supplied by surrounding rural communities, fostered what were effectively command economies that dictated rural production practices and priorities. The vast majority of the rural population spent the majority of their time seeking to produce and procure adequate resources—especially food, but also shelter and clothing—for themselves, their families, and, in some cases, for urban consumption. For most, securing sufficient calories for basic health was a full-time occupation. Human lives were short, maternal and infant mortality rates were high, and most people would seldom, if ever, travel more than several miles from their homes in their lifetimes.

Land figured prominently, even centrally, in this context. Land was the basic form of economic capital, and the primary means by which the population made a living. Most people engaged in small-scale, subsistence agriculture, perhaps with limited resources in terms of livestock. Those who had productive land would have tended to do well, or at least to subsist; those who had relatively unproductive land (due to poor-quality soil, sparse rainfall, or other factors) tended to struggle. All of those who depended, even indirectly, on the productivity of the rural, agricultural sector experienced difficulty during times of drought (which were not uncommon) and following poor harvests (e.g., as a result of diseases or pestilence). Those who had inadequate capital resources in terms of land—and especially those without access to land of their own—were particularly vulnerable in ancient Israelite society.

Perhaps not surprisingly, ancient Mediterranean cultures were characterized by a notion of "limited good," such that people tended to assume that life reflected something of a zero-sum game. Resources were limited and finite, and there were only so many goods—material or otherwise—to go around. For example, additional money could not be created (e.g., through investment). If one person had a larger slice of the financial pie, others naturally had less. There was assumed to be a direct connection between those who possessed or controlled more resources and those with

---

2. On this and the following paragraph, see, e.g., Knight, *Law, Power, and Justice;* see also Samuel L. Adams, *Social and Economic Life in Second Temple Judea* (Louisville: Westminster John Knox, 2014).

access to fewer. When one person had more than necessary, he or she was effectively hoarding the excess at the expense of the others.

Biblically speaking, land was much more than a capital resource; it had deep theological significance. God is understood throughout the covenantal legal tradition as the ultimate owner of all land. The Israelites possessed the gift of the long-awaited Promised Land in trust. The Israelites were understood to be tenants and sojourners on God's land, serving as stewards on what was ultimately a divine possession. Such perspectives would color the way appropriate economic conduct is understood in the covenantal legal codes.

Israelite Laws Protecting Widows, Orphans, and Resident Aliens

Several texts in Exodus, Leviticus, and Deuteronomy demand that poor people, those at "bottom" of ancient Israel's socioeconomic ladder—widows, orphans, and resident aliens—be treated with compassion and justice. Such people lacked traditional resources and kinship networks to assist in mitigating economic difficulties, and thus they found themselves especially vulnerable to extreme poverty and exploitation. Exodus and Deuteronomy give particular attention to widows, orphans, and resident aliens, and Leviticus refers to the situation of resident aliens on numerous occasions.

Having lost their husbands, widows were vulnerable in numerous ways. In many cases, they were in danger of losing their housing and land, given that, in most cases, only men owned property. Women had few, if any, property rights, and thus they often found themselves at grave economic risk when their husbands died. Ruthless creditors, tax officials, and even neighbors undoubtedly found it tempting to take advantage of the limited economic power women had.

Although most women worked extremely hard in and around the family's household, engaged in daily activities such as childrearing, agriculture, and cooking, they had relatively limited opportunity for independent activity outside the home. Similarly, certain covenantal laws highlight the situation of orphans, who, in an Israelite context, had lost either a father or both parents. As with widows, the absence of a male breadwinner in the family placed orphans in danger of poverty and potential exploitation.

A third group, the "resident aliens," or "strangers" (Hebrew: *gerim*), resided in areas where they were outsiders. These were foreigners, non-Israelites, those "sojourning" in Israelite regions—temporarily or permanently—or Israelites living away from their ancestral areas.[3] Some resident aliens may have had ample economic resources despite being separated from their normal familial and cultural networks, but the presence of biblical laws designed to protect resident aliens indicates clearly that many suffered difficulties. The potential challenges facing such outsiders could be daunting: ethnocentrism and exclusion, inadequate access to land and employment, lack of local kinship networks and other resources. As with widows and orphans, resident aliens regularly found themselves in precarious economic situations—dependent on those outside of their traditional networks of support for economic and social survival. In fact, the circumstances facing numerous resident aliens in ancient Israel would have paralleled the experience of many economic refugees in our world today—including undocumented workers and immigrants in the United States, who represent a rather close analogy to the biblical *gerim*.

We now turn to covenantal texts in Torah that refer to widows, orphans, and aliens, beginning with Exodus 22:21-24, a passage brimming with violent imagery. Biblical references to widows, orphans, and resident aliens—especially, perhaps, when they are grouped together as they are here—function as synonyms for the materially poor in Israel. They represent the most vulnerable and exploitable persons in society. This passage prohibits any form of abuse or oppression against any of these individuals, using three largely interchangeable Hebrew verbs (here translated as "wrong," "oppress," and "abuse"). In view of what we have already noted about socioeconomic realities facing widows, orphans, and resident aliens, there can be no doubt that abuse and oppression in this context includes treatment that would create or exacerbate economic difficulties for the poor and marginalized. Any form of taking advantage of the vulnerable is forbidden.

To be sure, the presence of such biblical laws does not imply that the Israelites found it any easier to obey God than people do today; laws exist when compliance cannot be taken for granted. Undoubtedly, the powerful in Israel found it no less tempting to exploit the vulnerable than the rich and powerful do today. The passage offers two negative motivations in order to inspire obedience. First, the Israelites are told to avoid mistreating resident aliens because "you were aliens in the land of Egypt." In other words, the text reminds the Israelites of their own—or at least their ances-

---

3. See, e.g., Christina Van Houten, *Alien in Israelite Law: A Study of the Changing Legal Status of Strangers in Ancient Israel.* JSOTSS 107 (Sheffield, UK: JSOT Press, 1991).

tors'—status as oppressed foreigners without rights or economic stability. Even those who were never in Egypt are described as having participated in Israel's visceral experience of injustice: "*You* were aliens."

Readers of this text are to see themselves existentially and morally implicated by the memory of oppression in Egypt. In effect, the passage reminds them that, in one way or another, they have been in the position of the resident alien. That would also be true of Christians today, who read the Exodus as a story into which they have been incorporated through faith.

A similar biblical passage makes the same point even more explicitly: "You shall not oppress a resident alien; you know the heart of an alien, for you were aliens in the land of Egypt" (Exod. 23:9). Again, readers are addressed directly: "*You* know how it feels to be a vulnerable outsider. That is *your* experience." Deuteronomy 10:19 goes further: "You shall also love the stranger ('the alien'), for you were strangers in the land of Egypt." And Leviticus 19:33-34 demands that aliens be treated as insiders, as citizens to be loved. Remarkably, the demand to "love the alien as yourself" is a striking echo of Leviticus 19:18 ("You shall love your neighbor as yourself"). All distinctions between insiders and outsiders are effectively obliterated by this demand.

To love others as oneself requires a commitment to seek the best for others. Deciding to do no harm to them is inadequate. Polite avoidance is insufficient. Conscious, proactive goodwill is necessary. To "love the alien as yourself"—now, effectively "*your* neighbor"—means that a vulnerable foreigner's needs, economic and otherwise, are to be seen and addressed as if they were one's own needs. Readers of these texts are to treat resident aliens with tangible and proactive love, reasoning from the personal experience of oppression in the Exodus story.

Let us return to Exodus 22:21-24, in which a second motive clause is linked specifically to the abuse of widows and orphans; meanwhile, the memory of the Exodus remains front and center. If the Israelites ("you") mistreat widows or orphans, God will hear and "heed their cry." When God's people were enslaved in Egypt, their cry was heard and heeded (see Exod. 3:7-10). In this new context, in which formerly oppressed Israelites can now act as oppressors, God promises to remain attentive to those who experience abuse.

Punishment for disobedience will be ruthless. Those who oppress widows and orphans will meet the same fate as did the Egyptians: God's "wrath will burn" and God will personally attack and "kill" them (i.e., "you"), presumably by means of military conquest ("with the sword").

Given Israel's repeated experience of subjugation at the hands of powerful, militaristic empires, this was apparently not an idle threat. The end result would be a complete reversal of fortunes: the oppressors' "wives shall become widows" and the "children orphans." The viciousness of the divine response to oppression should leave no doubt as to God's concern for society's most vulnerable.

Many of us recoil in horror at such violent rhetoric. How could any God be so unhinged and vindictive? While such reactions are certainly understandable, this kind of hyperbolic rhetoric probably functions not so much as a literal prediction of divine behavior as an indication of how economically important just relationships are within the biblical vision of a healthy Israelite society. Everyone is responsible for treating the weak and marginalized justly. As part of a covenant renewal ritual, community members affirmed the statement "Cursed be anyone who deprives the alien, the orphan, and the widow of justice," with a collective and vocal "Amen" (Deut. 27:19). It is incumbent on the entire community to foster justice as they participate actively in God's purposes.

Deuteronomy 24 provides two specific examples of exploitation to be avoided in Israel. The first passage (24:14-15) illustrates how, by withholding pay, employers could economically abuse day laborers, effectively cheating workers of earnings necessary for daily survival. The text requires that "wages" be paid by the end of the workday, presumably so that workers would at least have minimal funds with which to purchase food for immediate consumption (see also Lev. 19:13). Failure to comply could result in a "cry to the LORD against" the powerful (not unlike the Exodus story), who would be guilty before God.

The second text in Deuteronomy 24 (verses 17-18), in prohibiting the abuse of widows, orphans, and resident aliens, echoes the kinds of motive clauses we have already seen: Yahweh orders compliance in view of the Israelite experience of oppression and deliverance. Memories of slavery in Egypt, from which the people were "redeemed," should inspire just conduct with regard to society's poorest and most vulnerable. To demand a "widow's garment" as a "pledge" on a loan serves as a specific example of exploitation. A widow poor enough to need a loan must be helped; she must not be subjected to humiliation and physical exposure to the elements. God has already redeemed the people; they are not to turn around and economically enslave one another.

Deuteronomy 25:5-10 also demonstrates a noteworthy level of concern for the well-being of widows, at least from our cultural perspective.

In the event that a man died without a son as an heir, the brother of the deceased man was expected to marry the widow and sire a child with her. That child would be raised up to carry on the name of the dead brother. Complying with this legal practice would obviously have imposed additional responsibilities and significant economic burdens on a dead man's brother, who would be required to provide long-term financial support not only for the child but also for the widow. The account of Judah and his daughter-in-law, Tamar (Gen. 38:1-30), provides an especially striking illustration of this phenomenon; despite numerous, rather shocking plot revelations (including, among other things, prostitution and incest),[4] Judah ultimately declares that he is more in the wrong than Tamar is, apparently because he withheld economic and social support from her (by rejecting her and banishing her to her ancestral home, as well as by refusing to provide her with a marriage to his third son). Deuteronomy 25:5-10 and Genesis 38:1-30 thus underscore the extent to which Israelite custom and law was oriented to the protection of the economically vulnerable.

Additional texts are worthy of note in this discussion, despite the fact that they do not explicitly refer to widows, orphans, or resident aliens. Leviticus 19:35-37 prohibits cheating, particularly in economic contexts in which the poorest members of the community would be most vulnerable. Those without resources or power would be most vulnerable to exploitation in everyday business transactions; therefore, merchants, traders, and buyers were not to misrepresent their marketplace interactions. Measurements had to be honest and accurate. Merchants were prohibited from selling less than a pound of flour for the price of a pound. (See also Leviticus 19:13, which prohibits fraud and stealing, crimes also relevant in this regard.) As is often the case, the character and actions of God, who liberated the Israelites during the Exodus, serve as motivation for compliance.

Legal environments could be challenging for the poor as well (see, e.g., Exod. 23:1-3, 6-8). The poor do not tend to have friends in high places. In ancient Israel, where judges were drawn from the local community, often from among its more powerful members, litigants with resources and status—or prior relationships with judges—could normally expect to fare

---

4. It is unlikely, despite what some moralists apparently assumed, that Onan was put to death for masturbating or for enacting a form of birth control per se. The passage suggests that he is considered guilty because he did not want to be saddled with the burden—economic and otherwise—of supporting both Tamar and a son who would not be considered his (38:9-10).

better in disputes than those without wealth or influence. Bribery and false testimony could be used to exploit the vulnerable. These legal statements sought to ensure that justice was appropriately blind—so that no one was allowed to receive partial treatment. The same emphasis is evident in Deuteronomy 16:18-20. The Israelites were to seek "justice, and only justice" for all (see also Lev. 19:15). These kinds of laws would have been especially welcome among the poor and marginalized in Israel.

Ultimately, God's character was to guide Israelite behavior: In Deuteronomy 10:17-18, God is described as one who does not play favorites or accept bribes, "who executes justice for the orphan and the widow, and who loves the strangers, providing them food and clothing." God's people are to "love the stranger" as well (v. 19), putting aside their stubborn refusal to remain faithful to divine commands (vv. 12-16). So how do these laws concerning widows, orphans, and resident aliens serve to form and even transform the Israelites' economic reasoning for faithful participation in God's purposes? I will highlight two primary points here.

First, biblical laws concerning the treatment of widows, orphans, and resident aliens indicate that God cares deeply about the most vulnerable members of the covenant community. Covenantal faithfulness thus requires that God's people treat such people justly as well; if not, God will hold the responsible parties to account—personally. God will not remain neutral in unjust situations. God will act decisively on the side of the weak and vulnerable—and will come to their rescue. This does not mean that God loves the poor more than the rich; but it does mean that, for God and for God's people, to remain neutral in the face of injustice is to side with the oppressor.

To contextualize our discussion a bit, we might say that these legal texts concerning the treatment of widows, orphans, and aliens illustrate that, from a divine perspective, economically depressed and marginalized lives matter. This does not deny the fact that all lives matter. God loves everyone, and all lives *do* matter. Nevertheless, those who suffer economically at the hands of individuals and systems of power must, from God's perspective, be acknowledged, valued, vindicated, supported, and restored. Justice, according to these biblical laws, begins at the bottom of a society (a point we will return to later in the chapter).

To affirm, as it were, that lives on the financial margins do matter is not to imply that all members of the community who are not poor foster economic oppression; instead, it acknowledges that community members who are not poor inevitably benefit from systems and structures that allow some to amass increasing wealth and resources, often at the expense of others, whether directly or indirectly.

Second, these laws make it abundantly clear that God's people are to reason economically in light of their experience of divine deliverance from oppression in Egypt. The Israelite slaves were once the poor and marginalized whose lives mattered to God. They are now repeatedly reminded of their story—a personal one ("*you* were a slave in Egypt" [Deut. 24:18]) that must inform and transform their behavior toward those who are currently poor and marginalized. The legal motivation for treating widows, orphans, and resident aliens justly is rooted in the believers' prior redemption. Inasmuch as the redemption story is personal for everyone, all are responsible for fostering justice for those who now find themselves suffering at the bottom of society.

Contemporary North Americans tend to reason rather differently, of course. We root our economic choices and our attitudes toward the poor in stories we find more palatable than the Exodus narrative, such as the mythology of the American Dream or the saving power of self-interest. Our narratives tend to valorize the powerful, the popular, and the well fed. Our narratives do not encourage justice for the weak; instead, they teach us to look out primarily for Number One. The liberation and redemption at the heart of the Exodus story thus remain deeply relevant for those today who are willing to have their economic reasoning transformed in line with God's concerns and purposes.

Gleaning Laws: Food for the Poor

Today it is relatively easy, as it undoubtedly was for the Israelites, to ignore the plight of hungry poor people. But according to a few covenantal texts, God is deeply concerned for the hungry, and God's people should be as well. As always, the covenant people were called to maintain healthy, just relationships with God and one another, which ultimately meant that God's people are to meet the basic needs of the poor in tangible, concrete ways. They are the hands and feet of divine care.

Deuteronomy 24:19-22 provides an example of law codes concerning what could be gleaned at harvest time: specifically, landowners were not to harvest the produce from their fields or orchards completely. What they left in the fields was to be intentionally left for the poor—such as the widows, orphans, and resident aliens. (For an example, see Ruth, especially chap. 2; in that same context, see also the related laws in Deuteronomy concerning the triennial tithe [14:28–29] and pilgrimage feasts [16:11, 14]; these passages contain further instructions about the provision of food for Israel's poor.)

The Israelite experience of poverty and oppression in Egypt provides the philosophical underpinning for the text from Deuteronomy. Indeed, leaving the gleanings of the field for the poor is linked to Israelite flourishing in the Promised Land. Similar passages in Leviticus (19:9–10 and 23:22) explicitly and bluntly indicate that the motivation for the law itself—and for obedience to it—is rooted in the character of Yahweh, the same God who rescued the Israelites in the Exodus.

These gleaning laws are remarkable provisions. They remind us that property rights were not absolute in the Bible, and that owners were not allowed to do whatever they wanted with what they possessed. To be sure, private property is a biblical notion: one of the Ten Commandments prohibits stealing, for example, and the gleaning laws presuppose that some own private land on which they grow food. Nevertheless, biblical gleaning laws illustrate that landowners do not completely own or control everything they grow. Ownership is limited, as are the ways in which owners may use what they own. All land belongs to God, and humans are understood to be tenants of the divine property. Landholders are essentially indebted to God, even as God looks out for the landless poor. In effect, the final gleanings belong to God, and thus to the poor, because they are entitled to harvest them by divine decree.

We might ask whether gleaning laws represent a form of charity—that is, providing a needed dressing for a wound, or whether this kind of legal provision is better understood as a matter of justice, in which inequities and poverty are ameliorated by permanently adjusting societal structures. Charity is absolutely necessary. Hungry people need to be fed right away, on a daily basis. Still, while it is obviously necessary to meet immediate needs, the fundamental causes of poverty and suffering go unaddressed. The powerful remain powerful, and the poor remain poor.

Justice means that the status quo has been permanently changed, that the power dynamics between the rich and poor have been fundamentally altered. Biblical gleaning laws did not create that kind of structural change. Even so, since gleaning laws gave poor people the right to keep what they harvested, we must recognize that landowners were *not giving* something to the poor when they complied with a biblical gleaning ordinance. Gleanings were not handouts. The right of people to work for their own food and sustenance was protected. Gleaning laws presupposed that there was an inherent dignity in working for one's food. And the opportunity for such work was not a privilege, but a right. Gleaning laws thus seem to fall somewhere between what we might think of as a distinction between justice, on the one hand, and charity, on the other. While they did not entirely alter the dynamics of power, neither did those laws rely on the goodwill of the landowner (as would be the case in charitable giving).

Given that biblical gleaning laws do not articulate specific sanctions or penalties for those who break them, they are not like most laws with which we are familiar. Rather, they function as a form of exhortation, describing the character of the society and the relationships that God expects in Israel. Biblical gleaning laws point to a relational God who attends to those at the bottom of society—the widow, orphan, alien, and other poor people—and who expects human relations to be worked out compassionately and mercifully within the covenantal community. Jesus reiterates something quite similar in Luke 4 and 6 (see chap. 3 above).

We sometimes justify economic inequities by resorting to categories of merit and worthiness, assuming that those with resources are hardworking, skillful, and entitled to what they possess. Less successful people are often blamed for their plight, regardless of the circumstances. Ultimately, though, such categories are functionally irrelevant for biblical gleaning laws: the burden of responsibility falls upon those with ample resources.

I often ask my students to try to propose modern analogies for gleaning laws. It's not easy to do. But despite radical differences between ancient and contemporary socioeconomic realities, we are not absolved of the need to reflect on what such laws suggest about God's character and concerns—and about the church's identity and mission today. At first glance, biblical gleaning laws may seem analogous to modern taxation, inasmuch as both systems legally require contributions for the poor. But there is a fundamental difference between the two. Modern taxation is almost entirely impersonal. We do not know with any specificity whom our taxes will end up helping; resource disbursement is automated, impersonal, and anonymous. By contrast, gleaning laws presume that landowners may personally see and directly encounter the poor who harvest in their fields (see, e.g., the book of Ruth).

To allow hungry people to rummage through our household gardens would be a closer analogy, though this would still lack the legal requirement of biblical gleaning laws. Part of the socioeconomic force of these legal provisions is that they require the "haves" regularly to experience, in a direct and uncomfortable way, the concrete effects of radical poverty upon the "have-nots." Imagine watching widows struggling to get by, perhaps with children in tow, gleaning tomatoes in your garden. Gleaning laws make it impossible not to see the pain of poverty and its marginalizing effects.

What would it mean for contemporary Christian communities to reason about and to respond to the poor and marginalized as God does, as illustrated in these gleaning laws, rather than as our individualistic, market-driven, pick-yourself-up-by-your-own-bootstraps society generally encourages us to do? How might our conduct change if we were to recognize the common humanity all of us share? What would it look like for the entire community to have the opportunity to live in dignity and in wholeness?

Recall the Ancient Near Eastern concept of "limited good": resources of all kinds—such as food, money, power, honor, and so on—were understood to exist in a finite supply. Surplus and scarcity were directly and causally connected. Unequal distribution was the result of someone maintaining excess at the expense of others. Indeed, some early Christian church leaders held that those who possessed more than they needed were guilty of stealing from those who did not have enough. In short, many ancients recognized a direct correlation between those who were poor and those who were rich. By contrast, many Americans assume that differing levels of economic well-being exist naturally and in relative isolation from one another.

Today we recognize, of course, that many economic resources are not limited goods. Nevertheless, overconsumption has led to a contemporary situation in which many resources have been dangerously depleted, and global distribution of many resources is wildly inequitable. Perhaps the situations in which the rich and the poor find themselves are more interrelated than many of us would want to admit.

Let us be clear: The Israelites did not find it any easier to care about others than we do today. In general, laws are unnecessary if people already live appropriately without them. But in the absence of adequate conduct, laws develop. The presence of biblical laws about gleaning thus suggests that the people did not care for the poor appropriately when gleaning laws were not in effect. Like the Israelites, the Christian community has been called to bear witness to the character and purposes of God, often in ways that do not come naturally. Biblical gleaning laws remind us that the *missio Dei* must inform—and transform—how we reason about and respond to the poor.

Laws concerning Collateral and Loans

In this section I wish to consider laws that pertain to loans and collateral, such as Exodus 22:25-27; Deuteronomy 23:19-20; 24:6, 10-13; and Leviticus 25:35-38. The earliest of these texts is probably Exodus 22:25-27.

If we remember that land was the primary form of capital in ancient Israel, and that agricultural production was primarily of a subsistence variety, we can better grasp the context of this text. The assumption here is that poor people do not seek loans for capital investment or for other moneymaking ventures, but rather to stave off complete destitution. To add interest to loans made to a needy people would be to exploit their misfortune, adding insult to injury.

If subsistence farmers' fields yielded poor crops, growers would lack adequate food to supply their families' needs as well as seed for the subsequent year's planting. In such situations, extended kinship connections could often provide temporary support. But if such resources were insufficient, it might prove necessary to seek out a loan in order to purchase food and seed. If adverse conditions continued, relatively self-sufficient families could find themselves trapped in massive and debilitating debt. In extreme cases, poor people might have to sell off not only their land and homes, but even their children—and sometimes even themselves, as hired laborers—in order to pay off debts. Ruthless lenders could make things especially bad by offering loans with usurious rates of interest, leaving the poor bound in chains of debt that could last for generations.

Indeed, incarceration and slavery were real threats for the desperately poor. Contemporary readers may be horrified, and rightly so, to discover that slavery was practiced and tolerated in Israel. This is one of the clear examples of the ways in which Israel's perspectives and practices reflected their ancient context, and in ways that we now recognize as deeply problematic. Slavery was an endemic and well-known feature of ancient societies in that part of the world. Indeed, in some areas the majority of the population was enslaved.

We cannot gloss over the presence of slavery in the Bible, nor should we. Nevertheless, there were differences between the chattel slavery system known in the antebellum United States and the phenomenon of most Ancient Near Eastern slavery. In the biblical world, slavery was not built and justified predominantly on notions of racial inferiority, as it was in the United States. In the ancient Mediterranean world, slavery was normally linked to warfare or poverty. Prisoners of war were often enslaved, as were those who became slaves as a result of economic hardship. While those realities do not excuse the practice, it is true that a few slaves—an extreme minority, to be sure—could actually attain relatively high levels of stature, enjoying significant autonomy, for example, as managers of large estates. The point is that slavery, while still fundamentally involving the control of one individual by another, was rarely identical to what we imagine based on slavery in the United States.

While we can lament the fact that God's people practiced and tolerated slavery, it is worth noting that biblical laws did place limits on the institution, particularly in terms of its financial dynamics, so as to mitigate some of its worst effects. Biblical texts describe how those in slavery—often as a result of financial destitution—were to be treated, reflecting the fact that crippling debt was a potential danger for many in that part of the world during biblical times.

Exodus 21:2 prohibits a member of the covenantal community (i.e., a Hebrew) from serving as a slave (presumably as a result of financial ruin) for more than six years; in the seventh, the slave is to be set free. Deuteronomy 15:12 concurs, and verse 13 adds that, once the financial debt has been paid off, after six years of work, the slave was to be freed and provided with sufficient provisions for the freed person to succeed economically. Again, despite the presence of debt slavery, the poor in Israel were not to be treated ruthlessly, and the expectation was that they would be released from bondage with dignity; moreover, according to biblical law, slavery was term-limited.

It is interesting to note that Leviticus 25:39-40, which likely reflects a later corpus of legal material, actually goes further than the texts we have just considered. It prohibits treating Israelites as debt slaves; it requires that members of the covenant community be treated as laborers, whether "hired" or indentured. They had to be released in the year of Jubilee, a special debt-forgiveness celebration that we will consider later in this chapter.

To be sure, taking advantage of the poor who needed loans could be a prosperous venture. Interest rates on loans in the ancient world were often exorbitant, which meant that creditors could effectively control debtors for years, as peasants could find themselves buried under insurmountable debt from interest, not to mention the original loan amount. Exodus 22:25 prohibits charging interest to fellow members of the covenantal community, another measure that would avoid exploitation of poor Israelites. There is a noteworthy difference, however, between that verse and a related text in Deuteronomy 23:19-20. In both cases, it is unlawful to charge interest on loans to Israelites. Deuteronomy, though, explicitly *permits* interest to be charged on non-Israelites. Readers may legitimately ask why the Deuteronomic code considers it okay to charge interest to foreigners. If it is unjust to take advantage of one's own people, how can it be legitimate to turn around and do the same thing to others?

From a biblical perspective, the legal distinctions here are related to the Israelites' special calling within the context of their covenant with God. Internally, the community of God's people was to manifest healthy and holistic relationships; righteousness was inherently covenantal and thus communal. To pile debilitating interest on one's fellow covenant members would not keep relationships healthy and whole. By contrast, Deuteronomy probably envisions the outsiders, on whom interest could be charged, as being foreign traders and merchants—evidently not members of the covenant community—who were engaged in business dealings; far from fighting off financial destitution, those traders were seeking economic gain among the Israelites. As outsiders to the covenant, they were considered to be in a different category. It was apparently considered legitimate for God's people to participate in business relationships with them, including the charging of interest on what were most likely commercial loans. Thus, ultimately, the primary distinction between insiders and outsiders had to do with the fact that loans *within* Israel were to mirror and manifest the kinds of relationships that were expected by God within the terms of the covenant. Charging interest on the poor within Israel would not do so.

In addition to restricting interest on loans to Israelites, the covenant codes also regulated how collateral (or advanced security for loans) was to be handled. A strikingly specific example is found in Exodus 22:26–27. In ancient Israel, people typically wore two long garments—an inner garment and an outer cloak. For the poorest people, the cloak may well have served double duty as a blanket for sleeping. Therefore, this code (see also Deut. 24:12–13, 17) prohibits the exploitation of a destitute (and perhaps homeless) person by requiring a piece of clothing as pledge on a potential loan. If someone is so poor that he has only the "shirt on his back" with which to secure even a (presumably) miniscule loan, a creditor had to return the garment before sundown. The needs of the poor person superseded the profit motive of the person collecting the pledge. The specificity of the situation envisioned here suggests that the prohibited behavior was common enough to necessitate a legal injunction. As we have noted before, the presence of a law does not suggest that compliance was normal, but rather the opposite: laws seek to inspire conduct that would not necessarily occur otherwise.

Exodus 22:26-27 closes with a pointed statement that God is attentive to the cries of the oppressed. If God is "compassionate" and "will listen" to a poor neighbor's "cries," the implication is that God's people must also be compassionate and attentive to the needs of their poor neighbors.

Deuteronomy 24:6 contains another specific prohibition regarding collateral. The tools with which one turns coarse grains into flour, such as a mortar and pestle, are not to be taken as collateral on a loan. The reasoning is as simple as it is profound. If the poor lose the ability to grind grain, they will not have food to eat. To keep someone from eating is to take a person's very life as collateral on a loan. Again, the prerogatives and strategies of the lender take a back seat to the needs of the poor borrower.

Deuteronomy 24:10-11 adds a further consideration. Why should a creditor not be allowed into a debtor's house in order to collect a pledge on a loan? Most likely, the law reflects an awareness of what it feels like to be a debtor. Needing to take out a loan is bad enough, but to have one's entire family witness the indignity of a creditor barging into the house to demand a pledge would be even worse. To enter the house of a debtor is to shame him or her in front of loved ones, to add insult to injury. This law indicates that God cares about the fundamental human dignity of every person, including those who are destitute.

Most of these lending laws include some form of a motive clause explaining why obedience is important within the context of the Israelite covenant. For example, see the statement in Leviticus 25:38. This verse reminds the Israelite community that God had liberated them from slavery under Pharaoh and gave them the land that had been promised to Abraham centuries earlier. As we have seen, personal (or at least ancestral) experience of oppression often forms the backdrop and rationale for obedience to God's commands. Those divinely rescued from slavery should never inflict similar kinds of oppression on others. To do so would amount to a denial of the liberating experience of the Exodus that was to define and guide the Israelites as a people.

Even centuries after the Exodus, Leviticus 25:38 addresses the covenant community as if its contemporary members participated in the original liberation: "I am the LORD *your* God, who brought *you* out of the land of Egypt, to give *you* the land of Canaan, to be *your* God." The text invokes the Exodus as a living memory, as an identity-forming story, the personal and communal narrative that is to guide and inspire the moral sensibilities and the missional identity of each successive generation of Israel.

Deuteronomy 23:20 offers a different motivation for prohibiting interest on loans to fellow Israelites: ". . . so that the LORD your God may bless you in all your undertakings in the land that you are about to enter and possess." Well-being in the Promised Land is explicitly linked to obedience and just behavior toward the poor. The same expectations and blessings surely apply to those Israelites who were to occupy the land in subsequent generations.

These legal statutes may seem naïve and irrelevant in the context of our very different socioeconomic realities today. Loans and credit are now ubiquitous, and interest is one of the drivers of our economy. The availability of credit has certainly aided economic development. Should Christians even concern themselves with such seemingly outdated biblical laws? Although these legal codes may seem out of touch with contemporary economic orthodoxy and conduct, we should not dismiss them too readily. "Predatory lending" is not only an ancient problem. We have ready examples of what happens today when creditors take advantage of the poor by way of interest on credit and loans, whether this is transacted via credit-default swaps on Wall Street or via payday loan businesses in poor neighborhoods. These biblical laws illuminate God's character and concerns. For God, the needs and dignity of the poor and the health of the community at large must supersede individual economic prerogatives and the profit motive.

Again, the narrative of divine liberation from Egypt was supposed to inform and transform how the Israelites—now as potential oppressors—were to conduct themselves. Christians today, having been grafted into the Israelite family, also claim the Exodus as our story. Does the compassion and liberation of God revealed in the Exodus inform and shape our economic reasoning and behavior? It is worth noting that in Luke 6:35, Jesus instructs his followers to "love your enemies, do good, and lend, expecting nothing in return," which goes well beyond biblical laws prohibiting interest on loans. To "love . . . enemies" and to "do good" obviously rules out exploitation in any form. Indeed, to lend without expecting anything in return comes close to giving a gift. Jesus's understanding of life within the new covenant community, the kingdom of God, is thus quite unconventional—even radical, reflecting what just relationships look like from God's perspective.

It is worth noting that the charging of any interest on loans was, for about the first 1,500 years of the Christian church, considered a heinous sin known as *usury*. Indeed, Christian leaders and writers universally condemned charging interest on loans. It is thus remarkable how different things are today, when charging interest is part of the engine that drives our economy. Living in a different economic context does not excuse Jesus's contemporary followers from bearing faithful and authentic witness to the character and mission of God in the world. Biblical prohibitions against charging interest on loans suggest, at the very least, that our lending and credit practices must not exploit the poor. That divine concern is always relevant, no matter what the current economic system may be. God makes the poor a priority, something that is demonstrably not the case in our own economic context, often not even in the church. To the extent that God's economic reasoning differs significantly from our own, to the extent that we are "conformed to this world," a conceptual revolution will be necessary. That is why the apostle Paul calls us to allow the Spirit of God to transform us by renewing our minds, so that we may be able to discern God's merciful and often surprising will.

The Sabbatical Year and Debt Remission

We begin with Leviticus 25:1-7, which portrays Moses on Mount Sinai receiving final instructions from the LORD as the Israelites stand poised to enter the Promised Land. God tells Moses to inform the people that during every seventh year, the land is to be given a "sabbath" rest (v. 2). All work on the land is to cease. The idea was that the land, like human life, would be best sustained through a rhythm of work and rest. Today, we know that leaving land fallow aids in the replenishment of soil nutrients. Even though nothing would be tilled or planted during a sabbatical year, whatever the land produced could be eaten (vv. 6-7). I will return to the subsequent material (Lev. 25:8-17) later in the chapter; but at this point, let us jump ahead briefly to note verses 18-22.

Leviticus 25:18-22 responds to an obvious objection that the Israelites might raise: "But wait! What will we eat during the seventh year?" (v. 20). God promises to provide extra food every sixth year, a bumper crop that will amount to three years' worth of bounty (v. 21). Therefore, during the seventh year the people will eat one-third of the sixth year's crop; and they would do likewise every eighth year (when the farmers again plant seeds, to be harvested in the ninth year of each cycle [v. 22]).

We can understand Leviticus 25:18-22 as a text that is designed to form not only the concrete behavior of God's people, but also—and no less importantly—their economic reasoning. That is, this passage requires both that the Israelites act obediently with respect to agricultural cycles *and* that they trust God to provide sufficiently. The covenant community cannot rely on its own resourcefulness or investment skills during sabbatical years; the people must trust in God's faithfulness. In effect, by calling for radical and sustained obedience in the face of tangible sabbatical-year scarcity, this passage emphasizes that the Israelites must reason economically on the basis of a divine promise as opposed to human ingenuity or willpower.

Consider a similar story in Exodus 16, where God promises to provide manna on a daily basis for the recently escaped Hebrew slaves to eat in the wilderness. The people were instructed to collect only the amount of manna that they actually needed for each day's sustenance. But on the sixth day of the week—reminiscent of the sixth year's harvest in Leviticus 25:21-22—they were to gather enough manna for two days, in anticipation of the coming sabbath, when no manna would appear. According to the account in Exodus, those who took more manna than they needed on a given day, hoarding it for the future, found that it turned to worms. Both Exodus 16 and Leviticus 25:18-22 seek to form the Israelites into a people who will rely on God, not themselves, for their economic security.

Contemporary readers contemplating the church's mission in the world today will do well to reflect on analogous ways that we may be tempted to gather too much manna—or not to trust that God will provide enough over the long haul (as in Lev. 25:18-22). Given our society's commitments to self-reliance, independence, and economic security, perhaps we *claim* to trust in God far more readily than we actually do.

We now turn to Deuteronomy 15:1-3, which describes a remission of debts to be held every seventh year, similar to the sabbath for the land in Leviticus. Once again, from the perspective of our contemporary economic environment, this is a remarkable law. Who would make a loan if the debt would soon be erased? Every seventh year, all debts were to be forgiven, except those owed by foreigners. As in Deuteronomy 23:20, the reference to "foreigners" probably refers primarily to traders and merchants engaged in profit-oriented business transactions; the law really reflects a covenantal commitment to those within the Israelite community who might be suffering or anticipating potential economic ruin.

It was not unheard of for kings of empires in the Ancient Near East to announce a cancellation of debts, especially to commemorate the beginning of a new king's rule. Doing so would have had the sociopolitical benefit of consolidating loyalty among the masses while at the same time undermining the economic standing of a ruler's potential rivals—that is, debt relief as a calculated form of political manipulation. But rarely, if ever, were such remissions of debt held regularly in a repeated cyclical fashion.[5]

Note that the text describes debt forgiveness every seventh year as "the LORD's remission" (v. 2). The requirement to forgive debts was not to be understood merely as a human law, whether promulgated by Moses or subsequent Israelite kings. Rather, remission of debts was described as a regular event sponsored by Yahweh. It is striking that repayment of outstanding debts to lenders would seem to be less important to God than that the poor not remain indebted.

That brings us to a stunning statement in Deuteronomy 15:4-6. The claim in verse 4—that "there will be no one in need among you"—has inspired extensive discussion over the centuries, particularly in light of the fact that what follows (in verses 7-11) explicitly presumes that poverty *will* persist. Whereas 15:4 envisions "no one in need," verse 11 assumes that "there will never cease to be some in need on the earth." How are we to understand this seeming contradiction? Verses 4-5 point to a specific context within which no Israelites will be in need. This will happen only if the people faithfully observe the terms of the covenant. In other words, *if* the Israelites obey all of God's commands, including the economically oriented ones, then there will be no needy people. This is tantamount to suggesting that covenant faithfulness is the key to poverty elimination; by implication, a faithful community will have no need to pardon any debts.

Verses 7-11, by contrast, indicate that the remission of debts demanded in Deuteronomy 15:1-3 will be needed every seven years precisely *because* there will be needy people—presumably because the Israelites will not have obeyed all of God's covenantal commands, including the economically oriented ones. So the initial affirmation that "there will be no one in need among you" (v. 4) is predicated on the idea that the Israelites are obedient and treat one another as God would treat them (v. 5). Given the overwhelming likelihood that they will *not* actually live that way (given both their own history and typical human behavior), some of them will inevitably fall into difficulty. Every seventh year, therefore, God's people are instructed to forgive all debts that have accumulated.

The obvious objection that could be, and surely was, raised against

5. See Knight, *Law, Power, and Justice in Ancient Israel*, 18-22.

the notion of debt remission is that it would not make much sense for those with resources to loan money as the year of debt forgiveness approached. The passage addresses such concerns directly and forcefully: *If* anyone is found to be in need in the community, which would mean that the people have not fully kept the terms of the covenant, then the Israelites are to be generous and not "hard-hearted or tight-fisted . . . willingly lending enough to meet the need, whatever it may be" (vv. 7-8). In other words, God expects need to prompt generosity.

The caveat in verse 9 is crucial: "Be careful that you do not entertain a mean thought, thinking, 'The seventh year, the year of remission, is near,' and therefore view your needy neighbor with hostility and give nothing; your neighbor might cry to the LORD against you, and you would incur guilt." Even though it appeared economically irrational to require the wealthier members of Israelite society to subvert their own economic interests in order to loan money, especially when there was little likelihood of repayment, biblical law expected that they do so. According to verse 9, to withhold aid from a needy person would be "mean"; to act thus would result in guilt before God. In short, those in a position to lend and to forgive debts were to be generous, and they could anticipate divine blessing for such behavior (v. 10). Clearly, God does not assess economic self-interest in the same ways that humans typically do.

Verse 11 merits serious consideration: "Since there will never cease to be some in need on the earth, I therefore command you, 'Open your hand to the poor and needy neighbor in your land.'" The Bible makes it abundantly clear that the Israelite community often failed to uphold and obey the terms of the covenant. Ultimately, at least in part because of that disobedience, poverty would never be completely eradicated (v. 11). Note that God explicitly commands that his people act generously *since* poverty would persist. The proper response to economic marginalization involves compassion and generosity. We must recognize that this verse does not hold the poor responsible for the situation in which they find themselves; rather, those with adequate resources are required to be generous. Resignation and complacency in the face of widespread and chronic poverty are inadequate responses to the suffering of the poor. The burden of responsibility rests squarely on the "haves," not the "have-nots."

Verses 4 and 11 are not, in fact, as contradictory as interpreters have sometimes assumed. Verse 4, which imagines "no one in need among you," presupposes complete fidelity to the terms of the covenant. Still the statement is absolutely conditional: no one will be poor *if* you are obedient.

Verse 11 recognizes that the people in Israel (and elsewhere: "there will never cease to be some in need on the earth") will not, in fact, be completely faithful. As a result, there will always be poor people. The key in both verses is faithful generosity.

In this context, we should note that one of the most egregious misconceptions among many Christians today is the notion that Jesus was not particularly concerned about poverty. John 12:8 is often cited to that effect: "You always have the poor among you, but you do not always have me" (see also Matt. 26:11; Mark 14:7). Many have understood Jesus to be saying, in effect: "There will always be poor people around. So, don't worry about them." But this is a profoundly misguided interpretation. Let us consider John 12:1–8.

Judas is not pleased when Mary pours costly perfume over Jesus, anointing him and using her hair to wipe his feet. He asks, "Why was this perfume not sold for three hundred denarii and the money given to the poor?" Under the circumstances, Judas's question seems to be a legitimate one. The cost of the perfume (300 denarii) is nearly equal to a year's wages for a first-century day laborer. Why would Mary spend so much money on such an ephemeral moment, when it could have been used more effectively to help the poor? Wouldn't that have been a more worthy cause?

As the narrator, though, John parenthetically provides some key information about Judas Iscariot: "He said this not because he cared about the poor, but because he was a thief; he kept the common purse and used to steal what was put into it" (v. 6). John knows that Judas, rather than having a real heart for the economically marginalized, is actually a thief who, as the holder of the disciples' purse, has been stealing from Jesus and the other disciples and is now feigning a concern for poor people, which reveals the hardness of his heart. In verse 8, Jesus says, "You always have the poor with you, but you do not always have me." Again, on its own this verse might imply that Jesus is not particularly concerned about the poor either. But what many have missed is that, in verse 8, Jesus is actually *quoting* Deuteronomy 15:11.

Indeed, Jesus's statement probably presupposes all of Deuteronomy 15:1–11: that disobedience to the full terms of the covenant, including its legal provisions related to economic justice, actually contributes to the presence of poverty. It is precisely in that context, in which there are always poor people, that Deuteronomy 15:11 requires generosity. The words "since" and "therefore" in 15:11 are important in this regard: "*Since* there will never cease to be some in need on the earth, I *therefore* command you,

'Open your hand to the poor and needy neighbor in your land.'" The assumption is that "you" (the Israelites) have not been completely faithful to the covenant. "Since" that is the case, "therefore" you must be generous—concretely and in an ongoing, continuous way.

Given John's characterization of Judas (in v. 6), Jesus is effectively saying: "Judas, I know that you're not really concerned about the poor or you would have been acting generously toward them on a daily basis (but you haven't been doing so)." It is true that Jesus's presence with Judas and his other followers was destined to be temporary, and thus honoring him as Mary did—in effect, preparing Jesus for his burial—was appropriate. But in this biblical scene Jesus is not devaluing the poor or diminishing the need to care for them. Rather, he is calling Judas out for his lack of concrete and ongoing concern for the poor. Jesus is in effect saying: "Mary is doing something special for me in this moment, but you have not shown the kind of generosity toward the poor that is expected as part of the covenant." Jesus is not driving a wedge between himself and the poor. On the contrary, he is pointing out that Judas's typical behavior illuminates his opposition to Jesus's mission, an opposition that cannot be papered over with a few words of concern about wastefulness and the poor.

As I have suggested, Jesus highlights (in John 12:8) the perpetual presence of the poor—citing Deuteronomy 15:11—to demonstrate that Judas and the rest of the covenant community have not been faithful to the covenant. In effect, Jesus underscores the negative consequences of covenantal disobedience: When God's laws are not observed faithfully (see 15:5), "you always have the poor among you" (Deut. 15:11 *and* John 12:8).

What might Deuteronomy 15:1-11 have to contribute to contemporary Christian communities seeking to be faithful to divine purposes? At the very least, the divine commitment to keep people from being swallowed up by debt or poverty should influence how Christians reason and behave, including how we use our economic resources, how we think about and interact with poor people, and how we vote. For those guided by Deuteronomy 15:1-11, thinking and acting on the basis of radical and consistent generosity will be the rule, not the exception, despite any potentially negative economic effects that such liberality might be assumed to engender. Indeed, this passage further suggests that our contemporary faith in the salutary effects of pursuing narrowly personal self-interest is often profoundly at odds with divine economic reasoning. The interests of the poor must always trump the interests of those who are not poor. In fact, the notion of self-interest itself should be rethought. Deuteronomy 15:1-11 assumes that any benefit that one might "lose" through generosity—specifically, in this case, through debt forgiveness—will be outweighed by the benefit that will come through divine blessing. In light of this passage, therefore, radical generosity can actually be understood as self-interested behavior, individually and communally. Choosing obedience benefits everyone since it fosters life (see, again, Deut. 30:19).

Christians need to be a people who forgive others' debts, both real and metaphorical, even as our own indebtedness has been cancelled through God's mercy. Given the lavishness of divine generosity that we have received, we can certainly afford to be less calculating in terms of how we treat others in need.

To what extent are we guilty of having harbored "mean thoughts" (Deut. 15:9) toward poor people? The American Dream is supposedly within everyone's reach: hard work and dedication can lead anyone to financial security; the corollary is that a poor person must not have demonstrated adequate drive or commitment and thus is to blame for his or her plight. Deuteronomy 15:1-11, by contrast, assumes that poverty is largely the result of people with resources disobeying the terms of their covenantal relationship with God. The passage functions as an indictment against those who fail to act generously in the face of need. Divine judgment comes upon the haves for not tending to the needs of the have nots, a direct reversal of contemporary economic assumptions about the poor and their responsibility for being so. In these ways and more, Deuteronomy 15:1-11 should encourage Christians to reflect thoughtfully about whether their reasoning and their behavior toward the poor reflect contemporary economic orthodoxies more than God's own values and purposes.

The Jubilee

Let us return to Leviticus 25, beginning with verses 8-12, which follow the instructions (in verses 1-7) to leave the ground fallow every seven years. Every seventh cycle of seven years, on the fiftieth year, the Israelites were to sound a trumpet on the Day of Atonement, the day of national repentance before God. On that holiest of days, the *only* occasion during every year when the high priest would enter the most sacred space ("the holy of holies") in the temple to offer sacrifices for the sins of the people as an entire community, the Israelites were to celebrate the "Jubilee" as a nation. Every fiftieth year was to be sanctified, and during that year Israel was to "proclaim liberty throughout the land to all its inhabitants" (v. 10). During that Jubilee year, all Israelites were to return to their ancestral properties, and they were to observe a sabbath for the land as they did during every other seventh-year cycle.

In effect, the Jubilee represents the greatest of sabbaths. Notice the repetitive and ascending pattern of sevens in the passage: there was to be a sabbath day (rest from work) observed every seventh day; a sabbath year (oriented to agricultural land and indebtedness) every seventh year; and a Jubilee (a sabbath oriented to the land, indebtedness, and ancestral property) every seventh seven-year cycle (or fifty years). Seven is a number that often connotes completeness and perfection in biblical symbolism. Beyond this symbolic pattern, highlighting the importance of the Jubilee from a biblical perspective, what makes the Jubilee so noteworthy?

Let us consider Leviticus 25:13-29. This passage rehearses a number of instructions for the Jubilee year: prohibitions against cheating in the process of selling land; clarification regarding the relative prices that should be paid, depending on the number of harvests remaining until the next Jubilee; further explanation regarding how the Israelites will be able to feed themselves during the land's sabbath (cf. verses 1-7); and stipulations pertaining to the rights, responsibilities, and restrictions governing redemption of the land. These verses represent one of the Bible's most revolutionary visions.

The most striking aspect of the passage is the divine command that all rural ancestral land is to be returned to its original owner during the Jubilee year (Lev. 25:13, 31). This radical redistribution law is predicated on the following Israelite narrative: After wandering in the wilderness for years, God's people under Joshua's leadership (following the death of Moses) came into the Promised Land. Eventually, that land was divided among the various Israelite tribes. Tribal land was further subdivided by kinship clans, and then apportioned even further among families (see Joshua 13-21). Thus, the Promised Land was distributed among the Israelites so that each family had its own portion of the land that had been promised to Abraham by God—centuries earlier.

Scholars recognize that the biblical portrait of an original, largely egalitarian, distribution of land is an idealized schematization of Israelite origins in the land of Canaan. Nevertheless, the imagery provides the crucial conceptual framework within which the Jubilee year commandment functions. Leviticus 25:13 informs the Israelites that in the Jubilee year, "every one of you" is to "return . . . to your property." The assumption is that between Jubilee years (that is, during the intervening forty-nine years), there would inevitably have been some changes in landholdings through buying and selling, and, as a result, various forms of migration throughout the land. Between Jubilee celebrations, economic hardship would have forced some members of the community to sell their land or otherwise lose control of it. Terrible debt, as a consequence of drought, crop failure, or other issues, would have caused more than a few Israelites to lose their ancestral land.

There are at least two keys to understanding the Jubilee provisions, and both are articulated in Leviticus 25:23: "The land shall not be sold in perpetuity, for the land is mine; with me you are but aliens and tenants." First, all of the Israelites' land ultimately belonged to God; second, ancestral lands were not to be sold permanently. The Israelites held their plots of land in trust, by means of a free loan from God, the divine landlord. Ancestral lands had a certain destiny: they were to remain in the hands of the specific families who had been hired, as it were, to be God's tenants living on those plots. Jubilee redistribution ensured that the poorest of God's tenants would not remain poor forever and that any exchange of land (due to debt, bankruptcy, land speculation, exploitation, or whatever) would be temporary. The land would return to its original owner every fiftieth year.

It is worth noting that the Jubilee law in Leviticus 25 applied to rural land, the lifeblood of a subsistence economy. It does not apply "to a dwelling house in a walled city" (vv. 29-30). Still, the law provided opportunities for the "redemption" of both rural land (the cost of which would be prorated relative to the number of crop years left until the Jubilee [vv. 25-28]) and, within a year of the original purchase, of urban houses (vv. 29-30). Those who had lost their rural land through economic hardship were to be "rescued," so to speak, by their closest kin—people who, in biblical law, had first right of redemption for property sold (or defaulted on) by their relatives. A kinship "redeemer" could purchase the land that would otherwise be sold to nonfamily members in order to keep it within the family. In other words, land would stay in the hands of its ancestral families either by means of Jubilee redistribution or through familial rights of redemption.

The Jubilee year was designed to ensure that no Israelite family would remain poor and landless forever. Life expectancies in the ancient world were short; those who lived much beyond the age of forty would have been elders. Rates of infant and maternal mortality, in particular, were extremely high, and disease was a significant killer. So, a significant redistribution of wealth (in the form of land) every fiftieth year during the Jubilee would have kept poor families from being relegated to grinding poverty for more than one or, at most, two generations. Given that land was the primary form of effective economic capital—and subsistence agriculture was, for many, the most basic form of work—any loss of ancestral land would have been utterly devastating. If a family had lost land through the accumulation of crippling debt, perhaps due to the loss of a parental or spousal breadwinner, or as a result of unfortunate agricultural conditions, at least they would know that they (or one of their near descendants) would eventually recover the familial land in the Jubilee year.

The Jubilee commands assume that the Israelites *did not* care for one another as advocated by many of the legal provisions in Exodus, Leviticus, and Deuteronomy that we have examined. Prohibitions against cheating (Lev. 25:13–17) would be unnecessary unless such conduct was already a problem. Covenantal relationships were breaking down. Many poor people had lost their land—perhaps commonly as a result of usurious interest rates on loans. In the Jubilee, God calls a game-changing time-out: traditional behavior had to cease on this ultimate sabbath, and the negative effects of such conduct had to be reversed. The Jubilee thus functions as a divine reset button for society, resulting in a massive redistribution of land in such a way that God's purposes will again be reflected tangibly among the Israelites.

After sketching this picture of the Jubilee, however, we have to acknowledge that no clear evidence exists, biblical or otherwise, that the Jubilee was *ever* celebrated in Israel. As was true of many of God's directives, God's people were disobedient in this regard. Again, the notion that there was a single, original landowning family for every spot in ancient Israel is idealized and schematic. In truth, it would have been no less impossible to enact a Jubilee in ancient Israel than it would be in the United States today. Given the lack of historical and literary evidence for the *practice* of Jubilee, readers today may be tempted to ignore Leviticus 25. Why spend time reflecting on the Jubilee, and any economic implications it might have for Christians today, when it was clearly not important even for the Israelites to observe?

We must not ignore the Jubilee, however, for at least two reasons. First, even though the Israelites apparently *never* obeyed God's law regarding the Jubilee, neither did they excise it from their scriptures. The biblical law codes—including the Jubilee law in Leviticus—were not finalized until late in Israel's history. The writers and editors who preserved the biblical manuscripts knew how the course of Israel's history had played out in the several centuries since Moses's time; they knew that the poor in Israel had been repeatedly marginalized and oppressed; the writers knew that, rather than celebrating a Jubilee every fifty years, which would have clearly set Israel apart from other nations as one committed to God's justice, the poor in Israel were regularly exploited; they knew that Israel was thus disobedient to the terms of their covenant with God.

The fact that the Jubilee year provisions were included and *remained* in Israel's Scripture, despite the lack of historical evidence for the practice, is significant. Leviticus 25 does not merely detail an ancient practice; rather, in light of the fact that there is no record of its enactment, we might say that this text functions as something akin to an economic parable. In short, the Jubilee communicates something crucial about God. It provides a vision of what God intends.

The biblical writers and editors found in the Jubilee law a means by which to illustrate divine values and priorities, whether or not the Jubilee ever occurred. The text envisions a God concerned enough about the poor to require cyclical and massive redistribution of wealth, and calls the Israelites to imitate God's radical and unremitting concern for the poor. Deep and enduring economic inequities in Israel demonstrate, however, that God's people have failed to live into the divine vision for them as a community. In effect, the presence of the Jubilee law within the biblical canon functions as an enduring acknowledgment and reminder that while God thoroughly cares for the poor, Israel does not.

A second reason that we should take the Jubilee seriously has to do with the first text we considered as we began our study: Luke 4:14-30. Recall the last line that Jesus read from the book of Isaiah in the synagogue in Nazareth: "He has sent me . . . to proclaim the year of the Lord's favor" (4:18-19). The wording of this quote, particularly in Greek, suggests very strongly to most scholars that Jesus has in mind the year of Jubilee. As he reads the words of Isaiah and claims that "today this scripture has been fulfilled in your hearing" (v. 21), Jesus is announcing good news to those who have suffered in various concrete and often economic ways. Again, the last line refers to the Jubilee. In Nazareth, then, Jesus is proclaiming a new, first-time-ever celebration of the Jubilee, one that he is inaugurating!

The economic implications of the Jubilee imagery would have resonated with the rural poor in Nazareth during Jesus's time. Indeed, at least some—perhaps most—of those listening to Jesus that day would have had at least some experience with heavy indebtedness, loss of land, or employment as tenant farmers (or even as irregular day laborers) on someone else's land. They would have heard Jesus's allusion to the Jubilee year as a revolutionary announcement of hope.

If Jesus were to come today and read the lines from Isaiah cited in Luke 4:18-19, how would we hear his words? Would we hear Jesus's announcement of a Jubilee as good news from God, or would his words threaten our understanding of economic rights and property ownership? How might the biblical Jubilee law help to inform and ultimately transform the economic reasoning of those who seek to participate faithfully within the larger *missio Dei*? In our contemporary economic environment, redistribution of wealth is often viewed with suspicion. Many Americans, Christians and non-Christians alike, believe—almost as an article of faith—that even legal forms of redistribution are fundamentally unjust, especially to those who have wealth. For example, some view taxation, a common mechanism for redistribution, as government-sponsored robbery to the extent that compliance is effectively coerced.

It is noteworthy that the Jubilee law, by contrast, unequivocally advocates wealth redistribution as a *matter of justice* for the poor. This is an issue that merits ongoing reflection in the Christian community. We need not try to enact, in our contemporary world, a literal Jubilee as it is envisioned in Leviticus 25. Of course, it would be impossible to trace back to the original ownership of all landholdings. None of us today would be entitled to any of the land we currently hold. Note that God does not command that all humans carry out the Jubilee; rather, God commands that the Jubilee be carried out by the Israelites with whom God is in covenant relationship. The question today is not about literal compliance with the Jubilee law; instead, we must consider how Leviticus 25 might help to form and even transform our contemporary economic reasoning, just as it served as an enduring, if unrealized, vision of justice for the Israelites. What would it look like for Christians—Jesus's followers, the community called to embody a new covenant—to live, as it were, according to a "Jubilee economy"?

The historic Liberty Bell of the United States, it is interesting to note, contains a quotation from Leviticus 25:10: "Proclaim liberty throughout all the land unto all inhabitants thereof." In the context of the Jubilee law, "liberty" pertains to debt forgiveness and the recovery of land tenure; it refers to the redistribution of Israelite wealth. It is unlikely that the Liberty Bell's designers intended to invoke those particular connotations of liberty. Indeed, the quotation on the Liberty Bell is rather ironic today, given that contemporary conceptions of liberty in the United States often have more to do with libertarian self-determination and private property rights than with freeing poor people from the economic burdens that entrap them.

Concluding Reflections: Justice from the Bottom Up

Whatever we make of these legal traditions today, we must not assume that they are irrelevant. The good news that Jesus proclaims in passages such as Luke 4:14-30 and 6:17-26 is *not* entirely new and unprecedented. His words in Luke 4:18-21 make it clear that he is at least to some extent harking back to the way God had acted in Israel's past, indicating that God has always looked out for the poor, marginalized, and oppressed. The covenantal laws we have considered in this chapter were intended to form the economic reasoning and behavior of the Israelite people; they were certainly part of Jesus's transformational vision, and we must take them seriously if we are to understand Jesus's concerns.

Bible readers often marvel at the seeming disparity between the characterization of God in the Hebrew Bible, on the one hand, and in the New Testament, on the other. That is, many see the God of the Old Testament as an angry, terrifying, violent, arbitrary, unpredictable, and punitive deity; many see the God of the New Testament, by contrast, as merciful, forgiving, loving, gentle, and steadfast. That view is an oversimplification: while there are indeed differences in the portrayals, there is actually a remarkable level of continuity across the two Testaments concerning what God is like and what God cares about.

In the Torah, God is always concerned for the poor and oppressed. The divine character and will as clearly revealed in the Exodus and Israel's covenantal legal tradition reflects the same passion. Jesus's teachings in the Gospels are not opposed to this material: they are in radical agreement with both the letter and spirit of what we find in the Torah.

It will not do for Christians to dismiss Old Testament legal texts as irrelevant just because in Christ we live under grace rather than under the law, an objection I have heard raised frequently with respect to the kinds of economically oriented laws we have been exploring in this chapter. It is true that the specific demands of Torah do not remain concretely in effect, whether they be kosher food laws, specific holiness pronouncements, or even certain highly contextualized economic ordinances. That fact, however, does not negate the relevance of such laws today.

In various ways, the laws in Torah point to the divine character and will, illuminating God's presuppositions, assumptions, values, purposes, and priorities; in that sense, they remain invaluable and authoritative for Christian readers today. That is, even if the covenantal legal codes such as those concerned with gleaning or the year of Jubilee are not binding on the Christian community in every detail and nuance, the biblical writers wanted to communicate to their readers who God is and what God considers important. The laws sought to form the reading community for its life and mission in the world. So even if the specifics of various laws make little or no sense in our very different contextual situation, what they seek to communicate about God remains in force. Again, there is remarkable continuity in terms of how God is portrayed across the Old and New Testaments.

At the most basic level, Israel's law codes suggest, for example, that God is ready and willing to take sides in contexts in which people are being oppressed. God seems to be remarkably less concerned with individual rights, profitmaking, and economic efficiency than with the well-being of the poor. Indeed, for God, justice is not adequately reckoned from the top of community (from the vantage point of the rich and comfortable), but rather from the bottom, where we find those without resources, power or voice: the widows, orphans, and resident aliens. The Israelite legal codes seem to suggest that God is especially interested in what is happening to those most easily forgotten and trampled on, even if they are not the ones who drive the economy (whether ancient or contemporary). Economic choices are to be rooted in human need and in the character of Yahweh, who rescued and formed the covenant people, not in self-interest or any other form of economic reasoning, no matter how productive they may be in the short term.

In short, biblical justice is reckoned from the bottom up. In our economic decision-making, we must consider how the poor are faring. Such consideration is, to a significant degree, the divine metric for a just society. If today's Christian community were to come to terms with the implications of that realization alone, the transformation in our economic reasoning would be stunning. In short, when we begin to think economically from the bottom up, we will begin to think increasingly as the God of the Bible does, and we will begin to participate more faithfully in the divine mission into which we have been called and caught up.

As a final thought, we should not forget that one of the New Testament's primary words for salvation is "redemption." Christians believe that we have been redeemed through Christ. The explicitly economic imagery of passages such as Leviticus 25 forms the conceptual backdrop for such terminology. We would do well to ponder the economic connotations of this key New Testament metaphor. If "redemption" was integrally linked to poverty and radical need in the covenantal legal tradition, how is it that many Christians today can celebrate their own spiritual redemption in Christ even as they functionally oppose potential forms of economic redemption for others in need?

FOR FURTHER REFLECTION

▶ Reflect on the various laws discussed in this chapter. Were there any that surprised you?

▶ Many of the covenantal laws discussed in this chapter encourage obedience by appealing to God's character ("I am the LORD") or the Israelite experience in the Exodus (e.g., "you were aliens"). How might these laws contribute to our understanding of God and what God values? Might Christians today need to identify more closely with the Exodus story? Discuss the implications of your answer.

▶ Who are the widows, orphans, and resident aliens in our contemporary context?

▶ How might our reasoning and behavior toward the poor and marginalized today need to be transformed, given what we have read about how the covenantal community is to treat the poor and marginalized (e.g., widows, orphans, and resident aliens)?

▶ What might be some contemporary analogies for the laws regarding gleaning or loans or the Jubilee, for example?

▶ How might these laws challenge us today to reason and behave differently, with regard, for example, to poverty, indebtedness, and other forms of economic marginalization?

▶ How might our reasoning and behavior change if we were to evaluate the quality and extent of economic justice in our society from the bottom up, by emphasizing first and foremost how the poor and marginalized are faring?

▶ Do you think about God's mission—and the mission of the church—differently after reflecting on these laws?

CHAPTER 7

Prophetic Formation for Economic Reasoning

I n this chapter we consider what a few biblical prophets had to say about matters of economic justice. Figures such as Amos, Isaiah, and Jeremiah are known for critiquing Israelite unfaithfulness to God, defending the powerless, and speaking truth to power. There is a wealth of material from the prophets concerning economic justice in the Bible, much of it well known and amply surveyed by others. Our discussion will be brief and illustrative, focusing on some short passages in three of the classic eighth-century BCE prophets—Amos, Isaiah, and Micah. Beyond our treatment of these three, I encourage readers to continue exploring how other biblical prophets indicted God's people, often with devastatingly powerful rhetoric, when the latter were treating the poor and marginalized unjustly.

Despite what many contemporary readers assume, biblical prophecy was not primarily about foretelling the future. Prophets were, first and foremost, spokespersons for God, whether or not their messages had anything to do with the future. The biblical books bearing their names suggest that Amos, Isaiah, and Micah talked *a lot* about economic and social justice, often announcing judgment on current injustice.

Amos, Isaiah, and Micah spoke into a grave geopolitical situation in eighth-century Israel. Assyria, a powerful, militaristic empire, was threatening at the nation's doorstep, and these prophets warned the people, in various ways and contexts, to wake up and change their behavior. Otherwise, the Assyrians would carry out God's judgment on their conduct. First, some context: By this time the once unified nation of "Israel" (from 1020 to 922 BCE, under Saul, David, and Solomon) had actually split into two separate entities. In 922 BCE, Jeroboam, one of Solomon's military leaders, revolted against Solomon's son Rehoboam. Jeroboam ended up consolidating the northern part of the land and becoming king of what became known as the nation of Israel. The southern part of the original nation, ruled initially by Rehoboam, was now called Judah. The two nations were never unified again, and the Bible goes on to detail a long series of kings ruling each country, following Jeroboam and Rehoboam, respectively.

As two separate nations, Israel and Judah existed next to each other, often as political rivals, and eventually were caught up in a much larger geopolitical conflict between the superpowers of Egypt (to the southwest) and Assyria (to the northeast). As the Egyptians and Assyrians waged repeated struggles for supremacy, the tiny nations of Israel and Judah—geographically located directly between the two imperial powers on major trade and military routes—often bore the brunt of the larger empires' animosities. They would sometimes try to enter into strategic alliances with one of those larger empires, but the expansionist designs of Egypt and Assyria (and, during a later period, the Babylonian Empire) made them ongoing threats to the security of Israel and Judah. Eventually, in 722 BCE, the Assyrians succeeded in completely wiping Israel off the map. Only Judah remained, though it would be eventually destroyed by the Babylonians in 586 BCE.

Amos

Amos was from the small town of Tekoa, located near Jerusalem, within the southern nation of Judah, when his prophetic career began. Around 760 BCE, God sent Amos north to Israel to tell the people that their societal injustice would bring harsh punishment in the form of an Assyrian invasion if they did not change their ways.

The northern economy was booming in the middle of the eighth century BCE, and things were going well in Israel—at least for the wealthy. In today's terms, the Israelite stock market was in great shape, major building projects were underway, and the GDP was at an all-time high. Into this context, Amos, a foreigner from the south, arrived to rain on Israel's parade. Amos was very critical of the way the Israelite elites were living, especially in an economic sense. But he faced a difficult task: political, religious, and economic elites in Israel were not particularly interested in listening to a naysayer, even one claiming to speak for God.

Let's first look at Amos 3:1-2, where the prophet slams Israel for mistreating the poor and for forgetting its fundamental identity. Speaking judgment in the name of Yahweh, Amos rooted his critique of Israel in the story of the Exodus from Egypt. Even though God had liberated the Israelites from Egyptian slavery, social elites in Amos's day were effectively reenacting Pharaoh's injustices. Israel's God had been revealed as a liberator, but God's people had become oppressors. Given that covenant faithfulness required good relationships with both God and with one another, Israel was actively violating its covenant with God. Moreover, *since* they were God's special, chosen people, uniquely known by God, they were "therefore" responsible for their behavior and would be punished. In other words, being the chosen people did not give them a free pass, but instead, a special responsibility to act appropriately.

What were the Israelites doing that made Amos so upset? Take a look at the shocking description in Amos 2:6-8. The phrase "for three transgressions of Israel, and for four" is a Hebrew idiom that highlights the extreme unfaithfulness of God's people, as if Amos were saying, "How sinful have you been? Let me count the ways!" Their guilt is not restricted to individual behavior. Indeed, Amos addresses "Israel" and its national, societal sinfulness. According to Amos, the people "sell the righteous for silver, and the needy for a pair of sandals" (v. 6), implying that they are buying human beings, probably for labor or sexual exploitation, and they value the poor no more than they would a pair of cheap footwear—an apparent reference to debt slavery, a form of exploitation that Amos rejects, even if it may have been technically legal.

Amos's language is visceral: People "trample the head of the poor into the dust of the earth and push the afflicted out of the way" (v. 7). In other words, the Israelites are brutalizing the most vulnerable, including, we can assume, the widows, orphans, and resident aliens. Israel has completely forgotten what kind of people they are to be according to the covenantal codes in Exodus, Leviticus, and Deuteronomy; by implication they have effectively forgotten who God is and what God cares about.

Notice the multiple levels of sin Amos describes: "Father and son go in to the same girl" (using the same prostitute, perhaps together), "so that my holy name is profaned" (instead of being glorified and honored by covenantally faithful behavior). Moreover, "they lay themselves down beside every altar" (participating in idolatrous worship not devoted to Yahweh, perhaps in a sexual context) "on garments taken in pledge" (on clothing taking from the poor as pledges for loans) and "in the house of their God" (even when ostensibly worshiping Yahweh) "they drink wine bought with fines they imposed" (getting drunk with wine they purchased through taxation and other fees levied on the poor). In short, Amos describes a pattern of idolatrous, sex-addled exploitation. What images might Amos use to describe our contemporary context?

The material in Amos 5:10–13 is similarly harsh and challenging. According to the prophet, the people hated to be scolded for the injustices in their society. To "hate the one who reproves in the gate" was to resent communal elders who sat at the town gate and ruled on local disputes, many of which would have been economic in nature. They detested people who spoke "the truth" about injustice. The economic conduct of powerful Israelites was reprehensible to the prophet: The powerful "trample[d] on the poor," imposing burdensome taxes (on grain, for example) on them. Elites used the proceeds of their unjust economic conduct to build lavish homes ("of hewn stone"). But according to Amos, those homes and the vineyards of the very rich would end up vacant (following an Assyrian invasion).

Amos reminds the Israelites that he—and ultimately, *God*—is aware of the extent and gravity of the sins of those "who afflict the righteous, who take a bribe, and push aside the needy in the gate" (v. 12). The litany of crimes against the weak and marginalized closely echoes the behaviors prohibited by the various covenantal laws we explored in the preceding chapter. Amos's assertion that "it is an evil time" during which "the prudent will keep silent" (v. 13) is not an attempt to encourage passivity or quietism in the face of injustice, as if evil were best handled by people sticking their heads in the sand. Instead, Amos advises thoughtful, faithful people not to participate in any form of social rhetoric implying that "all is well" when it is not. To respond appropriately to "evil," the Israelites would have to change their ways, as Amos demands in 5:14–15.

Amos implores the people of Israel to "seek good and not evil," for their own survival and in order that Yahweh may be present in their midst, as they claim. The search for "good" will enable them "to live"; they must actively pursue "good" by moving in a direction opposite to the one they are currently heading in. The last clause of verse 14 is especially striking: according to Amos, at least some of the (elite) Israelites assume incorrectly that God is with them. But God will actually be with them only when they "seek good and not evil." In other words, though people may *say* that God is with them, such statements amount to nothing more than human rhetoric and have no bearing on God's actual whereabouts. What might Amos's reaction be to some of our contemporary rhetoric? We often invoke God's blessing for ourselves (e.g., "God Bless America"), even as we participate actively in an economic system that is, like the one in eighth-century Israel, tough on the poor.

Amos continues in verse 15, exhorting the Israelites to "hate evil and love good, and establish justice in the gate." Most of us are taught not to hate anyone or anything. But here, Amos is explicitly calling for hatred because it is an appropriate response to the evil of economic injustice. In light of what Amos says, we should ask ourselves whether contemporary North American Christians express adequate hatred for economic injustice. In what ways and to what extent might Christians be colluding too readily with the kinds of evil that Amos has in mind? Is our own context really that different from the one in Israel?

Amos 5:18-20 also provides some striking images, as Amos declares a "woe" upon those who "desire the day of the LORD!" "Woes" are statements of prophetic judgment—the opposite of blessings—and the prophet's language drips with sarcasm: "Why are you waiting for the day when God will vindicate you against your enemies? The day of Yahweh will be a day of judgment against *you* because of *your* injustice. You will be shocked to find God acting against you, not for you!" God's anticipated intervention will be something dramatically different from what the Israelites expect. It is worth considering what resonance Amos's message might have today. Are we opposing God through our economic conduct and, if so, might we find ourselves surprised by God's reaction? As we eagerly anticipate God's judgment on our enemies, will we be shocked to find God opposing us as a consequence of our injustice toward the poor and marginalized?

Finally, let's consider Amos 5:21-24, where Amos condemns shallow and insincere religious practices in Israel that fail to foster a just society. God is sick of Israel's worship: "I hate, I despise your festivals, and I take no delight in your solemn assemblies." Nor will God "accept" or even "look upon" their sacrifices. It is true, of course, that God expected worship involving sacrifice. So, this is not a blanket rejection of the divinely instituted sacrificial system per se. God is not opposed to sacrifices and worship, but God "hates" that Israel is going through the religious motions of required ritual practice while its everyday economic behavior fails to reflect the God they claim to worship. God utterly rejects Israel's hypocritical music and rituals: in a community of rank injustice, worship songs are nothing but noise. Amos demands that the Israelites truly enact what God desires: "But let justice roll down like waters, and righteousness like an everflowing stream" (v. 24).

There was scant rainfall in Israel during most of the year; water was often scarce, and drought was common. When meager rains eventually fell on the parched landscape, it could be difficult for the water to penetrate into the ground. Fast-running rainwater would create vigorous, temporary rivers that carved large gullies and crevices (called *wadis*) into the ground. Amos probably has these *wadis* in mind when he indicates (v. 24) that justice must be a powerful force in Israel, like the waters that rush down the parched gullies. But unlike the *wadis*, which are dry and deserted most of the year, Amos does not merely want occasional just behavior in Israel; rather, he wants righteous conduct to flow all the time—like an "everflowing stream." In other words, justice and righteousness are not to be merely seasonal, when, for example, the people are ostensibly worshiping God or having some kind of religious "festival." Rather, justice and righteousness must *always* flow, like a river that never stops moving. It is striking that it was in this sense that Martin Luther King Jr., seeking racial and economic justice that would be constant and enduring, famously quoted verse 24.

I conclude our brief treatment of Amos with two final observations. First, Amos repeatedly describes how livid God gets in the face of economic injustice. Whatever we may want to say about capitalism or any other economic system, Christians should take Amos's message seriously: If the poor are being mistreated, God is angry. Might God actually be angry with us and, if so, what might we need to do about it? Second, Amos reminds his audience what it looks like to remain faithful to God in a covenantal relationship, making it clear that authentic worship and religion must be paired with just economic behavior. Our economic conduct, and how it affects the poor and marginalized, is and will always be a matter of Christian faithfulness, theologically speaking. Have we effectively divorced our orthodox religious claims from our economic practices? To what extent might God be tired of our worship, of our religious rituals, given the ways the poor and marginalized are affected by our economic priorities and choices? Such questions point to the heart of the gospel, both for Amos and, as we shall see elsewhere in the Bible, for Jesus as well.

Isaiah 1

The first section of the book of Isaiah (chapters 1-39) reflects the work of a prophet who was active in the southern nation of Judah for some forty years, beginning in 742 BCE (making him a younger contemporary of Amos). Subsequent portions of the book apparently come from later periods: Isaiah 40–55 is rooted in the exilic period of the sixth century, and chapters 56–66 reflect a time following the exile.

I will focus on the first chapter of Isaiah, so the historical and literary complexities of the overall document need not detain us. In brief, the first chapter reflects the situation in eighth-century Judah, when foreign threats from the regions of Syria and Ephraim—and later, from Assyria—had become real and increasingly palpable. The people of Judah watched nervously as the Assyrian menace hovered over Israelites in the north, before its military force eventually destroyed them (722 BCE). Politically, Judah's leaders struggled for years to figure out how to avoid a similar fate; a few of those Judean kings sought to establish alliances with neighboring powers, but Judah ultimately succumbed to the Babylonians (586 BCE). The elite members of Judah's society were then exiled to Babylon.

Isaiah addressed the volatile environment prior to the final Assyrian and Babylonian conquests: the elites in Judah were experiencing economic growth and burgeoning prosperity even as foreign nations threatened. Unlike Amos, Isaiah was an insider: he may have been a priest who had access to those in power. Following a brief historical note in Isaiah 1:1, situating the prophet's career during the reigns of Judah's mid- to late-eighth-century kings—Uzziah, Jotham, Ahaz, and Hezekiah—Isaiah declares God's judgment, in the form of a public announcement or legal summons (v. 2): "Hear, O heavens, and listen, O earth; for the LORD has spoken" (v. 2). Speaking God's words, he alludes to Israel's covenant with Yahweh, claiming that the people have turned on God.

Verse 3 contains fascinating imagery concerning what has happened in the relationship between God and the people. Even brute beasts such as oxen can recognize their owners; and donkeys, known for their stubbornness, understand when they are at home benefiting from their owners' care. Israel, however, is clueless. In other words, God's people in Judah do not even recognize the most basic facets of their relationship with God: they are put to shame by the most intellectually limited and stubborn of pack animals! Verses 4–9 go on to describe, in vivid word pictures, the plight of God's rebellious people. There is, Isaiah says, a consuming sickness in this rebellious community.

In verse 10, Isaiah brutally equates Judah with the proverbially evil cities of Sodom and Gomorrah (see Genesis 18–19): "Hear the word of the LORD, you rulers of Sodom! Listen to the teaching of our God, you people of Gomorrah!" The prophet could not be more insulting; and, given what was done to those cities, God could not have been more offended by Judah's conduct.

In verses 11-15, Isaiah sounds like Amos (e.g., 5:21-24) as he lambasts the community's worship practices. Isaiah asks, rhetorically, "Why are you bringing these animal sacrifices to me? Enough already! Your rituals do nothing for me!" In fact, according to Isaiah, God denies requesting these sacrifices, instructing the worshipers to stay out of the temple: "Trample my courts no more." Judah's offerings have become futile, and incense has become "an abomination to" God (v. 13) because of widespread unjust conduct ("your hands are full of blood," v. 15). Yahweh is not interested in worship mixed with sinfulness; festivals and assemblies are now nothing but a burden (vv. 13-14). Yahweh promises that Judah's prayers will fall on deaf ears, and God will hide from them because they have bloody hands (v. 15).

Verses 16-17 succinctly describe what Judah must do to rectify the situation. God's people must repent and turn from their evil ways (v. 16). They will need to "learn to do good," which, at the very least, means to "seek justice, rescue the oppressed, defend the orphan" and "plead for the widow" (v. 17). In short, Judah must begin to act as God does, responding compassionately and intentionally to the needs of those at the bottom of society.

These poor and marginalized members of the community have relatively little, if anything, of economic value to contribute: they are vulnerable, dependent, and, from a modern market perspective, relatively unproductive. Intermittent handouts will not suffice in this context: occasional acts of charity, while they are crucial, will never replace the need for enduring social change. The scope of societal injustice will require more personal investment and long-term solidarity from those able to help. The people of Judah must go beyond sporadic acts of charity, and in order to do good and seek justice, they must act as Yahweh did in the Exodus: look out for the interests of the weakest and most defenseless and do so as an ongoing pattern.

The people are out of practice with justice; they need a radical reorientation in their thinking, accompanied by drastically different conduct. To "seek justice" in a covenantal context is to foster a holistic community of interdependent relationships in which all, including the most vulnerable, flourish consistently. "Rescuing the oppressed" (v. 17) suggests that God's people must be willing to be inconvenienced, to show up in those places where oppression is occurring, and even to participate in unmasking and opposing forms and sources of oppression. For Isaiah—and in the Bible more broadly—victims of oppression are not at fault for their suffering, nor is the burden of proof of change theirs to bear. In our contemporary culture we often assume that the poor and marginalized are at least partly to blame for their difficulties. But to "defend the orphan" and to "plead for the widow" imply active engagement in the situations of suffering people, a willingness to join orphans or widows in their struggle against injustice, adopting and engaging in that struggle as our own.

Isaiah's words raise a critical question for the Christian community today: Are we willing to reason and behave as God demands? Remember, Isaiah is not merely offering good advice. Instead, he suggests that the people can only recover their "understanding" of who God is and what God cares about (v. 3) by making significant changes in their reasoning and conduct. Currently, the people are "utterly estranged" from God (v. 4), even if they are unaware of that fact. Their injustice has left them completely in the dark about God. Is there any sense in which the same thing might be true of us today?

As Isaiah continues to prophesy in verses 18-23, he invokes the imagery of a courtroom or a debate, as the biblical prophets often do. Here God is indicting Judah for its transgressions. It is remarkable, though, that Isaiah immediately indicates that the people's guilt will be forgiven: "Though your sins are like scarlet, they shall be like snow; though they are red like crimson, they shall become like wool" (v. 18b). But a radical change of behavior, even a conversion, will be necessary. And the outcome of the people's situation is contingent on their response: Obedience, as in Deuteronomy, will lead to a good life in the Promised Land; disobedience will result in violent destruction (vv. 19-20). Again, we know what ultimately happened: the Babylonians came in and slaughtered Judah in 586 BCE.

In verse 21, Isaiah ruthlessly denounces the elites of Judah. The once "faithful" Jerusalem "has become a whore!" Formerly "full of justice and righteousness," the holy city is now populated by "murderers"! At least two aspects of this description are noteworthy. First, the horrible epithet "whore" appears here as a correlate of the marital metaphor some biblical prophets use in describing God's covenant with the people of Israel. For Isaiah, the economic and political conduct of God's people is akin to prostitution: they are, in effect, "whoring around," giving themselves to any and every suitor. They are anything but faithful to Yahweh, their husband. This is a disturbing image, but one that contemporary Christians would probably do well to ponder. Do we understand the economic injustice in which we participate—directly or indirectly—in terms of radical unfaithfulness to God? To draw on Isaiah's imagery, could our typical economic reasoning and conduct reflect a form of marital infidelity against God?

Second, Isaiah describes Jerusalem as a city of murderers. His language is at least partly metaphorical and hyperbolic, which is to say that his imagery is not to be restricted to murder in a literal sense. The entire city is now characterized by economic injustice. From Isaiah's perspective, then, the Jerusalem elites, in particular, are accessories to murder, whether literally or figuratively. The poor and vulnerable are being destroyed, crushed by the economic conduct of the powerful in Jerusalem. For Isaiah, this is tantamount to murder, and all who participate in the system and profit from the status quo have a hand in such crimes. Could that also be more true of us than we would like to admit?

In verses 22-23, Isaiah asserts that God's people have become impure, as when "silver" becomes "dross" or when "wine is mixed with water." The powerful are "rebels" and the "companions of thieves." Bribes are now universally considered objects of desire. And, unlike God's covenantal behavior toward orphans and widows, the people fail to take up the cause of the oppressed, refraining from getting involved. How might we be failing to "defend the orphan" and to take up "the widow's cause" today?

Eventually, in verses 24-26, Isaiah's tirade comes to a climax, as he announces how God will respond to the situation in Judah. Yahweh will not hold back, promising to wage war on his "enemies," who have fostered injustice (v. 24). God promises to "turn . . . against" the people in order to purify them (v. 25). Leaders will be replaced so that the people will be guided appropriately, and eventually Jerusalem will again "be called the city of righteousness, the faithful city" (v. 26). But Jerusalem, the current capital of Judah, effectively serves as the headquarters of economic injustice, guided by elites who have turned from the terms of the covenant. Restoration will be painful—even excruciating—but God is determined to bring about necessary change. Notice that God's people have utterly failed to uphold their end of the covenantal relationship and that God now will, in effect, take the lead—through punishment—to wake them up and bring them back to relational faithfulness.

Isaiah closes out the chapter in verses 27-31, ultimately affirming that a remarkable turnaround is coming. Justice will "redeem" Zion, the holy city of Jerusalem, and righteousness will redeem the city's residents who "repent." Destruction is not inevitable; indeed, justice, repentance, and righteousness can turn the tide (v. 27). But destruction will come to those who refuse to change (v. 28). Isaiah's message could hardly be more direct: Change—or else!

As I have noted, North Americans are often more comfortable thinking about poverty as something that is rooted in the conduct of the poor themselves rather than in wider social and economic structures. We speak in terms of the American Dream, assuming that anyone can make it in the United States. Those who fail to do so, given the mythology of the American Dream, are, in effect, blameworthy because they have not achieved "success." According to Isaiah, God's perspective is quite different. Isaiah suggests that God is not impressed by our societal perspectives that portray the poor as benighted, as undeserving—as moral failures. God seems to think that economic injustice and oppression are things for which the comfortable and powerful bear responsibility—and, indeed, merit punishment. What difference might it make if we were to take Isaiah's message from God seriously and concretely today? What would happen if we were to think as God does, according to Isaiah: that is, focusing less on how poor people are responsible for their situations and more on the responsibility of the powerful toward the weak and marginalized? There might even be other areas in which such a reorientation in our reasoning could have significant effects—such as, for example, how we might think about racial injustice, environmental issues, and so forth.

Isaiah's message probably took many of the elite in Judah by surprise. As we often do today, many would have assumed that the way things were going economically simply reflected the way the system worked. Notice that it is Isaiah, speaking for God, who identifies the system as unjust. Those committing injustices, by contrast, did not think anything was wrong. For most people in Judah, the economic system may have seemed largely unavoidable—simply a fact of life. That is certainly true in our complex, globalized world today. We often shrug our shoulders, feeling that while poverty is unfortunate, it simply comes with the territory, as it were. Many in ancient Jerusalem would have agreed, but Isaiah does not. Mistreatment of the poor is not merely an unfortunate circumstance; poverty is something that a society, through the behavior of individuals and groups, effectively perpetrates on its weakest members. In general, poverty reflects injustice. And injustice is not merely unfortunate. Injustice is evil. It must be rooted out of a society via repentance, through righteousness and justice. Or else, as Isaiah indicates, God will have the final say. How might we need to "be transformed by the renewing of our minds" so as to begin to understand God's perspective as articulated by Isaiah—and to respond faithfully?

Micah 6

Micah was a prophet in Judah toward the end of the eighth century BCE, during some of the time that the prophet Isaiah was active. Micah was likely in Judah in 722 BCE, when the Assyrians wiped out the northern country of Israel, and he probably experienced the Assyrian invasion of Judah in 701. Micah's comments were thus made within the context of war and political instability, and he raised themes similar to those we have encountered in Amos and Isaiah. I focus here on Micah 6.

In Micah 6:1-2, using a striking image, the prophet announces that God is filing a lawsuit against them. God is calling the people to task and taking them to court. God demands that the people face the charges that will be brought. (The reference to "Israel" in v. 2 may be intended to represent all of the people, given that the divided nations of Israel and Judah had once been a single entity.)

In Micah 6:3-5, God, speaking through Micah, turns directly to the people of Judah, demanding a response. Yahweh wants to understand why the people have turned away from their covenantal relationship: "O my people, what have I done to you? In what have I wearied you? Answer me!" God is clearly exasperated, and these rhetorical questions indicate that the culpability for the breakdown in divine-human relations rests with the people, not God. Yahweh immediately reminds the people what has been done for them, beginning with the Exodus (v. 4), suggesting that the entire story of God's deliverance from Egypt—and perhaps the entire covenantal relationship between God and people established in the wake of that liberation—is being brought to the table, so to speak. The LORD is angry because the people are not responding appropriately to their own rescue and to God's ongoing relationship with them.

Verse 5 reflects events that are described in Numbers, beginning in chapter 22. Balaam was a prophet who was hired by Balak, king of Moab, to curse God's people. The prophet, though, found himself unable to curse God's people because the only word he was given by God to speak was a blessing. Furthermore, the phrase "from Shittim to Gilgal" recalls events that took place in the final stages of the wilderness wandering (after the escape from Egypt and the Exodus), as the people were entering the Promised Land. Although the implications of these references are not drawn out extensively, it seems that God, through Micah, makes the point in the final phrase of verse 5: ". . . that you may know the saving acts of the LORD." In other words, "God has been with you, Israel, through thick and thin, rescuing and guiding you throughout your entire history as a people. How can you have turned against Yahweh so completely?"

In verses 6-7, the context seems to have changed a bit. Now a voice ("I"), presumably the prophet Micah as a representative member of God's people, asks several questions about what the Lord requires. Micah asks four questions in rapid succession. First he asks, "With what shall I come before the LORD, and bow myself before God on high?" This question sets up three others, about offering and sacrifice, to which the anticipated answer in each case is "no." The topic throughout this portion of the passage involves sacrifice, though the hyperbole ("thousands of rams," "ten thousands of rivers of oil," and "my firstborn for my transgression")—as well as the answer that Micah will provide in verse 8—suggest that at issue here is not merely sacrifice, but, more broadly, what God has always expected from the covenant people. In fact, these hyperbolic rhetorical questions are intended sarcastically: that is, Micah is not primarily concerned about how, or how much, to sacrifice to God. The real question is, "What does the LORD require of you?"

In verse 8, Micah succinctly answers the rhetorical questions he has just posed—in the form of a question: "He has told you, O mortal, what is good; and what does the LORD require of you but to do justice, and to love kindness, and to walk humbly with your God?" Micah insists that there is no great mystery here: as God's people, they already know what God wants!

In covenantal terms, relationships are to be just and whole, and people must foster such relationships actively. The Hebrew term here for justice is *mishpat*, which reflects active commitment to whole and harmonious relationships, economically and otherwise. The people are to "love kindness" as well. The term translated as "kindness" here is *hesed*, which is often translated "loving-kindness," "mercy," or "steadfast love." God is described in the Bible as one who exhibits *hesed*, a term that emphasizes loyalty and ongoing commitment in relationship.

And the people are to "walk humbly with [their] God." This last phrase is especially interesting. Notice that the requirement to "walk humbly with God" does not emphasize the content of what they believe. For many today, Christian belief is understood primarily in philosophical or intellectual terms, as something like a set of propositional statements to which believers give their assent. In effect, *what* is believed sometimes becomes more or less distinct from *how* that belief translates into behavior. The Israelites did not understand their beliefs in such philosophical terms. Everyone in the ancient world believed in a divine realm—in some form or fashion. The question of believing the right things, intellectually, would have struck the Israelites as an odd abstraction, and one that would have made relatively little sense to them. There was a God, Yahweh, with whom they had a covenantal relationship. The important thing was not so much whether or not they believed in God—though, of course, they did believe—but how they lived out the implications of their belief in their conduct.

For Micah, the most important thing for Yahweh—"what the LORD requires"—is not that the people intellectually believe in certain propositional affirmations about God, but that they live (literally, "walk") humbly with their God. Walking was a basic Hebrew idiom for life, one that focused on conduct and behavior. How one "walks"—how one "journeys through life" in relationship with God, we might say—is crucial. Notice that Micah emphasizes the relationship that the people already have with God, by referring intentionally to "your God." The people should already know how to please Yahweh; they should already know what the LORD requires. They have been in relationship with God for generations, and such things should be clear.

Micah 6:8 coheres well with what we have been exploring in this book. We would do well to read Luke 4:14-21 alongside this passage. What would it look like, concretely—that is, economically and otherwise—for us to live into the implications of what Micah 6:8 says? Whatever Micah is doing in this text, he is not interested in pious platitudes. He is indicating that Yahweh expects tangibly enacted faithfulness. We need to reflect carefully and continually on what "doing justice, loving kindness, and walking humbly with our God" would look like in our context today.

The second section of the larger passage (verses 9-16) points to some potential implications of what verse 8 might mean for us. First, in verses 9-10, Yahweh cries out "to the city," highlighting things that God cannot abide. The reference here to "the city" is significant. Whether the reference is to Jerusalem specifically, or to another city (such as Samaria, in view of the reference to the Israelite [northern] kings Omri and Ahab in v. 16), urban areas were, of course, where most of the elites resided and the locations from which they exerted their power, economically and otherwise. Cities were often understood as places where various forms of injustice flourished. Today, we might think of the colloquial contrast that is sometimes made between "Wall Street" (and its urban elites) and "Main Street" (where non-elites tend to live).

Next, in verses 10-11, Yahweh asks two rhetorical questions and provides a summary critique, demonstrating how far the behavior of the people has been from what is expected as part of their covenantal relationship with God. As with the rhetorical questions in verses 6-7, the implied answer to these two questions is obviously No. God is unable to overlook what "the wicked" accumulate through their wickedness, nor the measurements used, for example, in the marketplace, that are smaller than they are supposed to be. Such cheating in measurement is forbidden in the Torah (see Lev. 19:35-37) and elsewhere (e.g., Amos 8:5).

Notice how closely the two clauses in verse 10 relate to each other: One of the ways in which "wicked" people in the city end up with treasures in their homes is by cheating others in marketplace measurements (see v. 11). It is significant that God reminds the people that such cheating is "accursed." Verse 12 is phrased as a declaration (rather than as a question, as in verses 10-11): "Your wealthy are full of violence; your inhabitants speak lies, with tongues of deceit in their mouths." Yahweh directly accuses those in the city of various transgressions, crimes that will ultimately lead to their own destruction. The "wealthy are full of violence." This assessment presumably includes physical violence, though it probably also incorporates the idea that economic injustice is a form of violence against the oppressed. In connection with that, the people fail to speak the truth, apparently as a means to continue taking advantage of others, whether in the marketplace or elsewhere. In what ways do similar practices occur in our economic behavior today? Even though most of us are not involved in measuring salt or spices in the marketplace, there are analogous modern forms of cheating that people still get away with, even in ways that may be technically legal.

Finally, in verses 13-16, Yahweh articulates the consequences that will befall the people as a result of their wicked and unjust conduct. It is only a matter of time before the people reap what they have sown: "I have begun to strike you down." Indeed, the punishment will be severe: they will be made "desolate because of [their] sins." Verse 14 is especially noteworthy: "You shall eat [something for which wealthy elites in the city were certainly known, even as the rural poor may have often struggled for daily subsistence] but not be satisfied, and there shall be a gnawing hunger within you." Isn't this an apt description of our experience of hyperconsumerism? We are never satisfied. We have more than enough, but we cannot get enough. The ancient Israelite city dwellers, according to Micah, would experience the same thing as a result of the injustice they had been perpetrating. Saving for later would not help, because everything saved would be forfeited in war.

Verse 15 continues the theme: The wealthy, presumably those who owned vineyards and fields of olives, would continue to plant and harvest. But the fruits of their labors would end up in other hands. Why? The reason, as Micah explains in verse 16, is that the wealthy have acted according to the ways of Omri and Ahab, wicked kings of Israel who had been—or soon would be—destroyed by the Assyrians (in 722 BCE). Theologically, this explanation clearly links verses 9–16 to verses 1–8. Rather than do what the LORD requires (verses 1–8), the people described in verses 9–16 "kept the statutes of Omri" and "the works of the house of Ahab." They obeyed the contemporary economic expectations and dogmas of those who did not stay faithful to Yahweh. The result would be catastrophic: "Therefore I will make you a desolation, and your inhabitants an object of hissing; so you shall bear the scorn of my people" (v. 16). According to Micah, the full truth of injustice and its consequences would eventually come out. The wealthy elites who had so cruelly mistreated the rest of God's people would come to destruction (at the hands of foreign powers, if not before), and those members of God's community whom they had crushed would shame them.

Micah 6:1–16 is a tough passage. Among many things worthy of reflection, we should consider the "gnawing hunger" that Micah promises in verse 14. How do we experience that phenomenon, and what might that have to say about our own conduct, in light of Micah 6:1–16? Ultimately, the heart of the passage is Micah 6:8:

> He has told you, O mortal, what is good;
> and what does the LORD require of you
> but to do justice, and to love kindness,
> and to walk humbly with your God?

Many Bible readers are familiar with this verse. In the context of Micah 6:1–16, it is a statement of both hope and judgment. Fundamental in any discussion of Micah 6:8 is the covenantal and relational quality of God's expectations. In other words, the verse is not simply about an abstract principle or "requirement"; it is not a slogan or disembodied rule. Rather, it is about our relationships with God and with one another. One cannot, for example, live out the implications of Micah 6:8 from the perspective of contemporary libertarian individualism. This passage requires more than merely avoiding harm. It calls for positive regard, for the active pursuit of justice—in relationships, in community, in economics, and otherwise.

There are, of course, many other prophetic texts on matters of economic justice and discipleship that we could explore. References to "the poor" and "justice" abound (see, e.g., Jer. 9:23-24; Ezek. 18; Zech. 7:8-14). In that regard, material related to economic justice in the biblical prophets is abundant, and the few short passages we have examined here represent merely the tip of the prophetic iceberg—at most, a starting point. Readers will do well to explore widely in the prophetic literature, as the prophets' frequent attention to matters of economic justice reminds us how central such concerns are within the *missio Dei*—and thus how important they are also for the church's missional identity and faithfulness.

FOR FURTHER REFLECTION

▶ How do Amos, Isaiah 1, and Micah 6 describe economic and social justice?

▶ What do the prophetic passages discussed in this chapter contribute to your understanding of God and what God considers important?

▶ Reflect on Micah 6:8: "What does the LORD require of you but to do justice, and to love kindness, and to walk humbly with your God?" What would it look like, today, to live out the implications of this verse in tangible, concrete ways—individually and as a community of faith?

CHAPTER 8

Creation and Its Discontents

In chapter 4 we discussed the important role that stories play in our lives. In particular, we noted that the Exodus functioned as the foundational Israelite story, highlighting for each successive generation incorporated into that narrative a sense of communal identity and purpose—mission— within the world. For Christians, that story is also our story, one that is to inform, form, and transform how we understand God, ourselves, and our mission within God's larger purposes. But sadly, rival stories often compete for our attention and allegiance, often shaping our perspectives, practices, and policies more than the account of divine liberation that we find in the Exodus narrative. The stories that we choose to tell and retell really matter.

In this chapter we will explore biblical narratives in Genesis 1–3 that describe not only the creation of the world but also the choices and alienation that characterize our lives as human beings. These stories intend to shape our theological and moral imaginations, and thus our awareness of and participation in the divine mission into which we have been called.

Literary Genre and Genesis 1–3

Some readers may find it troubling to think of the accounts in Genesis 1–3 as "stories," inasmuch as we sometimes distinguish "stories" from "facts." We recognize that stories can be fictional—that is, entirely invented in the minds of their authors. Other stories may be rooted in facts, even if they are not entirely factual. If the Bible is to be understood as communicating "truth," aren't facts crucial? Don't we lose something important—like "truth"—if we call the biblical accounts of creation "stories"? That is, don't

Bible narratives communicate truth in a way unlike other stories that we tell? If we refer to the creation accounts as stories, don't we imply that the Bible is factually questionable—and therefore untrue? These concerns bring us to the question of genre in the Bible.

The Bible is a large and diverse collection of books. It communicates its truth by means of different types, or *genres*, of literature that its various authors used to get their message across, including epic sagas about famous figures, law codes, historical and prophetic literature, poems, songs, Gospel narratives, letters, and apocalyptic narratives and imagery. Interpreting those rather different genres appropriately requires sensitivity to the ways in which they each seek to communicate to readers.

We recognize that the kinds of information we expect to find in a newspaper differ from section to section. We know that we would not read a comic strip or the sports page with the same expectations we might have when we read the front-page news—or, for that matter, an internet meme, an academic journal article, or a classroom textbook. We do not approach a poem in the same way we would a sermon, or even a comment by a friend. The point is that we pay close attention to matters of genre all the time, even if we may not always be conscious of doing so.

Many Christians, however, do not pay adequate attention to biblical genres, and they end up interpreting the Bible as if everything in it represents the same kind of literature—often as something like a God-ordained collection of factual truths or laws governing human behavior. The assumption is that, because the Bible is God's word, everything in it by definition communicates truth. And what could be more truthful than a collection of facts from Almighty God? While a commitment to the truth of the Bible is certainly well intentioned, that kind of approach to truth and biblical genre is profoundly problematic. Although it does seem appropriate, in general, to view what is factual as true, it is worth asking ourselves what happens when we imagine truth to be *limited* to what is factual. We recognize that something may be true even if we cannot marshal—or have not yet marshaled—adequate facts to prove it. Christians claim that God exists even though they cannot prove it factually. Indeed, truth is not always reducible to demonstrable facts, and truth often transcends mere facts. This is also true with regard to the Bible.

Genesis 1–3 serves as an apt demonstration of this distinction between facts and truth. This section of the Bible reflects a particular type of literary genre known throughout the world, one that often explores matters of human origin, group identity and purpose, and the relationship between humanity and the natural world. Literary and biblical scholars regularly refer to the genre of these stories as *myth*. While some readers will, no doubt, hear the word "myth" as a synonym for "false" or "untrue," that is not how scholars use the term. Rather, myth, technically understood, refers to stories that communicate truths beyond what is demonstrably factual. Across human societies and cultures, accounts describing the creation of the world abound. These so-called creation myths often describe, among other things, actions of divine beings. Since it is impossible to verify the activity of God or the gods, such stories are categorized in literary terms within the genre of myth. Therefore— and this is the crucial point—referring to something in the Bible as a myth is not the same as declaring it to be false; instead, the genre includes stories that relate unverifiable details even as they communicate significant truths. Hence truth is a crucial component of myth. In the process, myths often explain and reinforce the communal identity and purpose of those who share and value them.

In chapter 4, I discussed the so-called American Dream, a story that has been and continues to be influential for citizens of the United States. While the American Dream does not explicitly incorporate divine actors, for example, it nevertheless seems to function as a kind of myth within the wider culture. The evidence that *anyone* can succeed through hard work is dubious. Factually speaking, many experience little of the dream despite having relentless personal initiative, hard work, and persistence. And many who do realize the dream begin their pursuit of it with clear advantages that they have not necessarily merited. The truth is that not all who are "losers" in the race are culpable, and none of those who are "winners" do it entirely under their own power. Nevertheless, the story of the American Dream provides a sense of communal identity and purpose for those influenced by it.

So, is the myth of the American Dream true or false? Perhaps it is, in some ways, both. The key point is that while this myth may not be entirely true in terms of factual evidence, whatever truth it does communicate is significant and profoundly formative for many people in the United States. As we have already noted, the story forms our sense of who we are, how we should live, whom we should admire, and whose conduct we should question. The story shapes our economic priorities, our legal structures, and our behavior—individually and socially—and to a remarkable degree, we believe in it and act in accordance with it. Truth in this story is not reducible to facts and data; rather, the story's truth provides a vision for our identity and purpose as a people. We value and repeat the story, from generation to generation—even when its details are not explicitly borne out factually—revealing that it is one of our most cherished and influential myths. Myths can be relatively particular and parochial, like the American Dream, or they can be universal in their scope and claims. Among the latter variety, myths of origin—such as those that describe how everything began—are especially common.

It is important to recognize that the creation narratives in Genesis (yes, there are two of them) clearly belong within the genre of myth. The stories do not purport to provide scientific or historical data regarding the origin of the cosmos, at least not in the sense in which we traditionally think of science and history in the twenty-first century; rather, the stories in Genesis 1–3 describe the origins of the world in order to form and shape God's people for their life in it.

The biblical creation narratives are not factual, even though they are deeply true. Some readers may find that statement shocking, but we need to acknowledge that the writers themselves chose to communicate via the ancient genre of mythic narrative and not via some other means. Emphasizing theological meaning and significance over demonstrable evidence, the biblical storytellers were not as concerned as we tend to be with historical "facts." And, in the end, we must read the Bible as it presents itself, not as we assume it to be or want it to be.

The two creation stories in Genesis 1–3 (see Gen. 1:1–2:4a and Gen. 2:4b–3:24) are clearly distinct from each other. The first has an orderly, declarative, and repetitive style, while the second consists of a comparatively meandering plot and includes fascinating conversations among the lead characters. The two stories consistently refer to the name of God in different ways: "God" in the first and "LORD God" in the second. Perhaps most notably, the sequence of creation differs radically in the two accounts: in the first one, humans (both male and female, Gen. 1:26–27) are created last, after everything else in creation has been brought into existence; in the second, God specifically creates a human being before the existence of vegetation or animals of any kind (2:4b–8, 18–20). And then, only after the Garden of Eden has been planted with vegetation and populated with animals does a second human being appear (2:21–23).

Those differences alone make it rather difficult to claim that both stories communicate the same facts: Was the human race created first or last? In the face of such differences, which story is true? If truth were reducible to a question of fact, we would be forced to question both of the accounts. But when we understand them as myths, both stories convey significant truths; moreover, the ancient editors of the Bible left no indication that they were at all concerned about simply placing the two contrasting accounts side by side, allowing each of them to communicate to readers the truths they could reveal.

The two creation stories in Genesis 1–3 did not arise in a historical vacuum, dropping wholly formed from heaven, as it were. Each story is a product of, and a message to, its time. Most scholars understand the first creation story (Gen. 1:1–2:4a) as a response to a well-known Babylonian account of the origin of the world, the Enuma Elish, which would likely have become familiar to the Jews exiled to Babylon in the sixth century BCE. The second story (Gen. 2:4b–3:24) seems to be older than the first, likely reflecting a rather different political and religious environment—probably a few hundred years earlier, during the monarchical period in Israel.

Stories of Creation: The Biblical and the Babylonian

Certain details in both Genesis 1 and a Babylonian creation myth, the Enuma Elish, suggest that the first biblical account of creation may well represent an intentional and polemical *response* to the Babylonian story. According to the Enuma Elish, the world came into existence as the result of a violent war among the gods. In an effort to defeat Tiamat, the goddess of the deep and chaotic salt waters, and her divine allies, the gods who opposed her created another god, Marduk, a fearsome warrior. Endowed with incredible power, Marduk defeated Tiamat and her divine comrades, ultimately splitting her in two with his bow and arrow. Having brought a measure of order to a formerly chaotic situation, Marduk—now acknowledged (by prior agreement among the gods) as the king of all divinities—uses half of Tiamat's dead body to form the earth, and places the other half in the heavens to create the sky. As the sun, the highest god, Marduk fashions the rest of the divine bodies (e.g., moon and stars). And human beings—created from the blood of Qingu, the god responsible for inciting Tiamat's original rebellion—are purposely designed to provide a perpetual labor force for the gods, who desire rest for themselves. Ultimately, humans are formed to do the work the gods do not want to do, and the great city of Babylon is established as a terrestrial resting place for the gods.

Clearly, the Enuma Elish is not rooted primarily in empirical, scientific facts. It is a classic example of what biblical scholars call a *myth*: the story provided foundational and valued truths for the Babylonians, who told and retold it. For example, the Enuma Elish explained to the Babylonian people how the world came to be, helped them understand who they were as a people within that world, and informed them about and formed them for their purpose—their mission—in the world.

A story of this type would have wielded great social force, articulating a communal vision such that all people would know their roles and responsibilities and how they were designed to fit within the larger society. The Enuma Elish established clear social hierarchies (from the gods, at the top, to common laborers, at the bottom); it validated the warlike character and reputation of the Babylonian Empire (locating its militaristic imperialism in the primordial actions of the gods); and it authorized the exploitation of the Babylonian labor force by the imperial regime in support of its divine overlords. To the extent that the Enuma Elish reinforced submission to the will of the gods—and, by implication, to those who wielded power on earth in their stead—the Babylonian rulers would have had a vested interest in keeping the story alive and popular.

By proffering a particular *theological* view of reality in the form of a creation myth, the Enuma Elish helped to shape a relatively stable society and a willing and compliant workforce. The myth encouraged the masses to accept their lot in life, as laborers whose fundamental purpose, authorized and intended by the gods, was to contribute effectively to the larger imperial Babylonian machine. As those created expressly for the purpose of doing the work that the gods wanted to avoid, the people of the Babylonian labor force would have understood and accepted their work responsibilities as a divine inheritance. Individual humans may have had a modicum of functional value as workers, but there was relatively little room for individuality and freedom of choice within the worldview engendered by the creation myth.

If the Enuma Elish helped to foster a certain stability *within* Babylonian society, it undoubtedly inspired a competitive and warlike perspective concerning other human communities. The militaristic imperialism that characterized Babylonian foreign policy was understood to be rooted in the very nature of the cosmos: the world owed its very creation to the chaos and competition characteristic of the divine realm. Thus, chaos and disorder were viewed as normal and to be expected as the default categories for human existence. In this context, human worth and individual prerogative would have been subsumed under the needs of the society. Human beings would have been valued particularly for their ability to contribute productively to the empire and its communal war machine. In summary, the Babylonian myth formed and fostered a competitive and imperialistic society in which the populace accepted militaristic violence, unceasing labor, and an entrenched authoritarian hierarchy as natural and unavoidable factors of life.

Genesis 1 offers a strong counterpoint to the Enuma Elish. Instead of creation by means of chaos and war, this story suggests—in terms of both style and content—that God brings order out of the watery chaos (compare the actions of Tiamat, the Babylonian goddess of the chaotic salt waters), thoughtfully and purposefully speaking the world into existence. In contrast to the Babylonian account, not only is the divinely created order intentional, it is repeatedly affirmed as "good." Everything is the way it is supposed to be, the way God intends. The sun, moon, and stars are divine creations, but they are not themselves divine, as they are in the Enuma Elish. God is truly other, transcendent over *all* of creation—even the celestial bodies in the sky. Genesis 1 asserts, among other things, that God is purposeful, unrivaled in power, and endlessly creative. Only God is divine. But the story does not stop with the nature and power of God. The first story of creation has much to say about the function and value of human beings.

Humans, both male and female, are created in the divine image and given a mission as representatives of God on earth (verses 26-28). Their vocational calling involves labor, to be sure, but notice how it differs here from what is described in the Enuma Elish. In Genesis 1, human work is understood as an *extension* of divine work, not (as in the Babylonian perspective) as a *replacement* for a lack of divine willingness to labor. That is, human beings in Genesis are understood to work within and for the larger creative purposes of God, whereas in the Enuma Elish they serve as substitutes for the work that the gods want to avoid. Human labor is thus elevated in Genesis to a divinely ordained calling. It is valuable, worthwhile, purposive, missional. Humans are doing God's work—and not instead of God, but *with* God. Human work is thus integrally linked to the creation itself. Indeed, human beings participate through work in God's ongoing creative activity.

Human beings are created in the very image of God, an affirmation that points to their value within this non-Babylonian, biblical worldview. In order to illustrate this point, I often ask my students to reflect on the value, in economic terms, of the God envisioned in Genesis 1. That is, given what the story affirms about God—a divinity powerful enough to create everything simply by verbally calling it into existence—how much would God be worth? The question is a bit crude, perhaps, but it is still one worth asking. Could we ever put a price tag on that kind of power, on that kind of God? No, of course not. Such a God would clearly be beyond price; indeed, the God of Genesis 1 is literally priceless. The story then describes humans as being created in the divine image. What truth is this biblical creation myth trying to affirm here? Whatever else we might say, it is clear that if humans reflect the very image of a God beyond price, they are rather valuable. In other words, if God's value is inestimable, those created in God's image and sent as ambassadors to care for creation in God's stead must have inestimable value as well. Moreover, note that God's "worth," if we may put the matter so crassly, is not merely based on God's functionality or on God's ability to create per se. God has inherent value, in addition to being the source of all that is and can be. Similarly, we can say that human value is not primarily functional, as if it is simply tied to what they can or cannot do. Rather, human beings have inherent value as those who reflect God, those who are in the image of God.

But how different are our contemporary calculations of human worth from those of the Babylonians? Today's economic orthodoxy encourages us to view everything, including human beings, in competitive, market-oriented, functionalist terms. That is, everything can be valued on the basis of its market utility. When humans are productive (or when they consume) in ways that markets can recognize and calculate, they are understood to be worth more than those who "fail" to produce or consume as effectively. The young, the elderly, the disabled, and the marginalized are readily devalued in this functionalist framework. Some of these views of humans echo, in our context, the Babylonian mythos. Genesis 1 suggests a different vision: human beings have inherent worth, whether they are functionally valuable to others—and in market contexts—or not.

Particularly in the Roman Catholic tradition, the affirmation that humans are created in the image of God, the *imago Dei,* leads to the assertion of human dignity: that all human beings have fundamental and inherent dignity, regardless of their specific characteristics, situations, or behaviors. Human life is understood to be sacred, something that we must treat with utmost seriousness, care, and compassion. In the Catholic tradition, of course, this commitment to life serves as the basis for opposing abortion. And, while the abortion issue may receive most of the attention, it is important to recognize that the Catholic emphasis on human dignity affirms the value of all human lives, at all stages of life and in all contexts. In other words, a commitment to life, properly understood, seeks to foster life in a comprehensive sense, not merely at conception and birth, but also as life continues. Thus, thoroughgoing concern for human dignity also necessitates attention to what happens *during* life: beyond opposition to abortion, for example, workers' rights (e.g., livable wages, safety, unionization), and many other economic, racial, and social-justice matters (e.g., health care, military- and prison-industrial complexes, and the death penalty) become matters of "life."

The first creation story declares that complete abundance is provided for humans and animals alike (verses 29-31). Nothing necessary is lacking: there are no deficits, no deficiencies, and scarcity is a nonreality. Everything in creation is ordered, abundant, purposeful, and good. Humans are to serve as God's representatives in attending to creation, a point that completely obliterates any tendency to claim biblical authorization for environmental exploitation and destruction. And, apparently satisfied with a job well done, on the seventh day, God ceased from the process of divine creativity and enjoyed a day of rest (Gen. 2:2-3). What a contrast with the violent and chaotic Babylonian vision of creation!

If we read the first story of creation looking for facts, for scientific verifiability, we will find ourselves struggling to reconcile this story with contemporary scientific knowledge. To read Genesis 1 as if it is designed to provide empirical truths about the nature of the cosmos, however, is to impose our own foreign expectations on it. The story is properly understood on its own terms: it is an ancient creation myth. We need not assume, for example, that it precludes the possibility of an expanding universe or that it contradicts our observations about evolutionary processes. While Genesis 1 offers an explanation for the origin of the world, it makes no claim to provide verifiable scientific evidence about those origins. The story, as a myth, was written not to provide scientific facts so much as to supply a picture of fundamental truths that its author wanted to convey.

The first creation story also subverts the Babylonian concept that the world has always been characterized by cutthroat competition, militarism, violence, and chaos. Rather, it asserts that creation was, from the beginning, intentional, orderly, endlessly abundant, and good. In other words, the story declares that the Babylonian vision of reality is not the only paradigm or framework within which the Israelites—or contemporary readers, for that matter—can understand the world around them. Even if Genesis 1 does not claim to provide empirically based scientific claims about the world, it does intend to provide a more truthful vision of reality than does the Babylonian Enuma Elish. Readers are invited to embrace the mythic vision of Genesis 1, invited to their lives on the basis of abundance, order, human dignity, and the goodness of the created order rather than presupposing that violence, disorder, and domination are the only options for human existence and conduct.

The Second Biblical Creation Story

For its part, the second creation story in Genesis (2:4b–3:24) provides a different, albeit theologically complementary, depiction of creation. In this case, the LORD God forms from the dust of the ground (Hebrew: *adamah*) a human being, an *Adam* (Hebrew: *adam*)—better, an "earthling," "groundling," or "dirtling"—into whom God breathes life (v. 7). Literally, the *adam* is brought forth from the *adamah* and given life. This imagery suggests the deep connections between human beings and their environment, illustrating in a tangible way how linked human life and death are to the earth (see Gen. 3:19). This creature is placed in a garden of complete and utter abundance (2:8–9) and given the task of caring for it (v. 15). Again, readers must recognize that neither of these biblical creation stories provides support for a transactional, functional view of the environment that might permit its short-term, market-driven exploitation. Adam is told not to eat from only one tree in the entire garden (vv. 16–17), underscoring the lavishness of divine provision for him.

The LORD God then recognizes that it is not healthy for the human to be alone, and so proceeds to create every animal and bird "out of the ground" in order to find a partner for the human being. It is worth noting that, unlike the first biblical creation story, in which God appears completely competent and intentional throughout the process of creation, this second account implies that God is, in effect, learning by doing, as God produces prototypes that might serve as partners for Adam. The original creature names each of the new ones, but no suitable match is found (vv. 18–20) until the LORD God forms a woman, Eve (see 3:20), from a rib of Adam (now identified explicitly as a man, 2:21–23). Although the authorial context of this story could scarcely be more patriarchal in character, the imagery here is primarily of interdependence and closeness. The emphasis is not on the order of human creation, as though the man, created first, is more important, or that the woman—created from a piece of relatively unnecessary anatomy—is unimportant. Rather, the sense is that Eve is of crucial importance in the created order: she provides the one thing that was not provided in abundance for Adam at the beginning: full human relationship and partnership. She is the last of God's creations—the pinnacle of the created order! And she and Adam are literally related at a bosom level. Eve is created from Adam's innards, so they could not be more integrally related and closely connected. The chapter closes with an etiology that explains and roots the phenomenon of marriage within the context of the created order itself, affirming an original state of human innocence and openness, which is reflected in their nakedness without shame (vv. 24–25).

Genesis 2 symbolically emphasizes the interdependent nature of humanity, a stark contrast to the overwhelming tendency in contemporary North American economic thinking to conceive of human experience primarily in terms of an isolationist, self-interested individualism. Adam is not complete without another human being: according to Genesis 2, human beings are intrinsically relational; we need each other even though our contemporary environment regularly encourages us to think of our relationships as optional, transactional exchanges subject to calculations of utility. In view of the story, rugged individualism may be ideologically attractive, but it does not square well with human nature.

Genesis 3 goes on to relate a conversation between the woman and a serpent, the most "crafty" animal created by the LORD God. (Despite common misperceptions, we should note that this reptile with legs is never described within this story itself as the embodiment of evil [i.e., Satan; cf. Rom. 16:20; Rev. 20:2].) The serpent challenges the prohibition against eating from the one tree by asking a question (v. 1) that is designed to get the woman focused on what she lacks: "Did God say, 'You shall not eat from any tree in the garden'?" Notice that the serpent's question does not merely confirm the original command from the LORD; he also sows a seed of discontent by asking whether *everything* is off limits. The serpent's question symbolizes the human tendency to reason from the vantage point of scarcity, from consciousness of what we do not or cannot have. (It is worth noting that scarcity provides the fundamental rationale and philosophical point of departure for mainstream capitalist economic reasoning and theory today, as any introductory macroeconomics textbook readily demonstrates.) Sometimes, a narrow restriction (e.g., to avoid this one thing) can feel as though all of our freedom has been denied (e.g., you cannot have the fruit from any of the trees). The one thing we are prohibited from having can quickly become the one thing we really want. Even though Eve knows that God did not say that they were prohibited from eating of every tree, the serpent's question effectively suggests that she should ask why God would prohibit eating the fruit from *any* of the trees in the first place. The question encourages the woman to doubt God's goodness, authority, wisdom, and trustworthiness. If we are honest with ourselves, that probably sounds familiar.

Eve assures the serpent that only the tree in the middle of the garden is forbidden (vv. 2-3), seemingly extending the original command ("nor shall you touch it") in order to ensure compliance. The serpent tells her that disobedience will not bring death, and that God is actually keeping her from becoming godlike, having an awareness of the difference between good and evil (vv. 4-5). The woman ponders this matter carefully, recognizing that choosing to eat the forbidden fruit promises to bring three undeniably good things: sustenance, beauty, and wisdom. She eats—and so does Adam, who, we should clearly note, has apparently been with her the whole time! (We should not miss the fact that the imagery in the story suggests that, while Eve thoughtfully reflects on the potential reasons for and benefits of eating the forbidden fruit, it appears that Adam mindlessly chomps down without paying much attention to the implications of his choice [v. 6].)[1] For the first time, they see reality for what it is: they have lost their innocence, and they are now aware that they are naked in front of each other and the rest of creation. Instead of remaining unhindered and open before the world, they immediately cover themselves (v. 7).

Adam and Eve decide to make their own *choices*; however, they use their freedom not to live into the full abundance of the garden but rather to reject God's instructions. Notice that within the world of this story, humans (not God) create scarcity by fixating on the one thing they do not have or exercise control over. Amid complete abundance, with every need met, they focus on what they lack. Moreover, they choose to become like God themselves and, as a result, they discover that wisdom involves the loss of innocence.

The rest of Genesis 3 offers a fascinating and haunting illustration of the destructive power of self-oriented human choices. Adam and Eve hide themselves from God, recognizing their nakedness (vv. 8-10). When confronted, Adam plays the blame game, engaging in one of the most common of human activities. Audaciously, in the same breath he has the temerity to blame his actions not only on Eve but also on God. Eve, for her part, blames

---

1. See Phyllis Trible, "Eve and Adam: Genesis 2-3 Reread," in *Biblical Studies Alternatively: An Introductory Reader*, ed. Suzanne Scholz (Upper Saddle River, NJ: Prentice Hall, 2003), 98; originally published in *Andover Newton Quarterly* 13 (1973): 74-83.

the serpent (vv. 11–13). How much like us these primordial humans are! How often do we accept full responsibility for our actions, without trying to deflect our failures onto others? Notice how quickly relationships that were once whole and healthy have become stilted and broken. Humans hide themselves from one another, and from God.

In verses 14–19, a series of curses are announced as the unfolding results of Adam and Eve's disobedient choice to eat the forbidden fruit. The serpent loses its legs and is doomed to crawl on its belly in the dirt from that day forward. Snakes and human beings become enemies, primed for violence against each other. Childbearing becomes painful, and male domination over women rears its head. Agricultural production becomes a matter of hard work; in contrast with the natural productivity and abundance of the Garden of Eden, the ground now becomes populated with "thorns and thistles." And human beings become mortal.

In the language of the text, these curses are uttered by God. In order to catch the force of the imagery, however, we might best interpret these statements as symbolic, etiological details that help to explain observable realities in the ancient world. In other words, the emphasis here is less on God's harsh punishment per se than on the consequences of problematic human choices. When Adam and Eve choose to go their own way, they unwittingly unleash a torrent of unforeseen changes in the created order. Their decision to do things their own way actually leads to the breakdown of creation.

Etiologies explain how things came to be the way they are as we observe them. In effect, they serve to address ancient empirical curiosities, such as:

Why do snakes not have legs, and why are human beings afraid of them?

Why does it hurt to give birth?

Why do men dominate women?

Why do weeds and thorns make it difficult to grow crops?

Why do we die?

The ancients were intelligent and thoughtfully observant of their world. It is not difficult to see that almost every animal has legs. So, if snakes do not have legs, ancient "science" would have wondered about the absence of those legs. Genesis 3 explains why snakes do not have legs like other animals. Likewise, how could a good thing like childbirth be so painful and, in the ancient world, so dangerous? Again, Genesis 3 provides a reason. The Garden of Eden story also explains patriarchy and human mortality.

The key thing to note, according to the larger story, is that while these curses reflect the world as we know it (and as the ancients knew it), the broken relationships, patriarchy, and death illustrated in the narrative do not reflect God's original design or intent for the world. These curses symbolically represent the breakdown of creation inaugurated by the destructiveness of human choices to turn against God. Take patriarchy, for instance: it is worth recognizing that despite the tremendously patriarchal culture in which such stories would have been told and retold, the story proposes that male domination over women is not attributable to God. As I have noted elsewhere,

> God is not held responsible for the breakdown of the created order; ironically, it is Adam and Eve who, through their actions, effectively "create" a new, "disordered" reality. Human choices have remarkable power. What God intends (in [Gen.] 2, as well as in [Gen.] 1) is subverted, even if not completely destroyed ([Gen.] 3). Self-interested and disobedient choices lead to economic scarcity, various forms of alienation, and, ultimately, death. Genesis 3 thus serves as a brilliant and brutal illustration of the extent to which humans are responsible for the way things are—indeed, far more responsible than we would like to admit.[2]

Genesis 3 ends with a note of compassion and grace, as God makes clothes for the newly self-aware humans (which provides an etiological explanation for clothing), while simultaneously reaffirming the great distance between God's original creative intent and the situation in which humanity finds itself (i.e., the humans are now shut out of the garden altogether). Symbolically, humans find themselves alienated from God and each other.

2. Michael Barram, "'Occupying' Genesis 1–3: Missionally Located Reflections on Biblical Values and Economic Justice," *Missiology* 42 (2014): 393–94. This chapter reflects a thorough reworking and extension of issues raised in that more technical article (*Missiology* [2014]: 386–98), which readers seeking more in-depth exegetical treatment of Genesis 1–3 may consult.

Abundance, Adam and Eve, and Us

We must recognize that, as a mythic story, the account of Adam and Eve is not primarily about the *facts* of what happened to the first two human beings. For many Christians, of course, that is how these stories are supposed to be read. The common assumption is that readers are being faithful to the text if they accept the Adam and Eve story as a historical account of the beginnings of the human race. The first humans sinned and, like it or not, we cannot escape the detrimental effects of their choices. If they would not have made such poor choices, we assume, the world would not be so troubled. The problem is that such an interpretation fails to do justice to the way in which the text itself asks, on its own genre terms, to be understood. The account of Adam and Eve is framed within the genre of myth; we must remember that in order to interpret the text appropriately.

Indeed, to read Genesis 2 as a myth is, in fact, to interpret it with the full seriousness it deserves from its readers. If the story is understood as an account of the facts of early human history, the events in the garden pertain directly to Adam and Eve alone; we are connected to their remote story as their descendants, reaping the negative rewards of *their* poor choices. If, however, we take seriously the mythic character of the account, its contemporary relevance explodes. Rather than restricting the second creation story to the distant past, we begin to see clearly its symbolic and illustrative character as a myth: Adam and Eve are not merely two ancient characters whose lives, like it or not, have forever shaped and distorted our own; on the contrary, Adam and Eve *are us!* Those two figures represent every human being who has ever lived, and they reflect every reader's human experience. We are faced at every moment with choices to make. And each one of us makes the same choices to turn away from God, to serve ourselves and our priorities, to live according to scarcity rather than abundance. As a myth, Genesis 2–3 helps all readers see more clearly the situation they find themselves in; understood in terms of its appropriate genre, the story can serve its intended, diagnostic purpose in our lives. We are gravely mistaken if we imagine that we would not be subject to original sin had only Adam and Eve not made such a bad choice in the garden. The myth in Genesis 2–3 seeks to remind us that we ourselves regularly make the same kinds of choices that Adam and Eve are symbolically described as making; we each participate in our own state of "original sin" in the sense that we regularly choose to be Number One, refusing to live into the abundant relationships and provisions God makes available for us. As a myth, the story of Adam and Eve is not about *them;* rather, it is symbolically and strikingly about *us.*

The two creation stories in Genesis 1-3 assert that God provides complete abundance for inherently—and in effect, infinitely—valuable human beings. Unfortunately, those human beings—that is, *we*—choose to embrace not God's good and purposive design but rather our own vision of self-interest and autonomy. As a result, we hinder the created order, including ourselves, from flourishing, causing creation to cave in upon itself. We choose scarcity to our own detriment. We fail to recognize the real value of each human being as we objectify one another, treating each other as means to further ends. Relationships, both human and divine, are shattered. Patriarchy and death result. It is interesting to note that in Genesis 4, Cain, the third human (following Adam and Eve), kills Abel, the fourth human—denying that he bears any responsibility for his brother's well-being ("Am I my brother's keeper?"). What more powerful illustration of broken human relationships, alienation, and violence could there be? By the time of the second human generation, there is already a 25 percent worldwide murder rate!

The world in which we live today is broken in many ways. The mythic worlds portrayed in the Babylonian Enuma Elish and in Genesis 3 are remarkably sober—and in that sense rather brilliant, I would submit—accounts of what a competitive, destructive, and unjust world looks and feels like. Those accounts recognize quite well how it feels to live in this world, even today.

It would be incorrect, however, to assume that there are no other options. In fact, the creation stories in Genesis 1-2 suggest that there is a prior and more fundamental reality beyond what we see reflected in Genesis 3. There is another way to live and flourish together in the world, rooted in a biblical vision of divine abundance, human dignity, and healthy relationships (see Gen. 1-2). May God transform our moral and economic reasoning through these creation stories, challenging us not to settle for the broken world, to which we have become so accustomed. And may we thus participate with ever more authenticity and faithfulness in God's larger mission of liberation, justice, and mercy in the world.

- ▶ Are there ways in which our contemporary social and economic environment resembles the Babylonian worldview reflected in the Enuma Elish?

- ▶ As discussed in this chapter, the two creation stories in Genesis 1–3 fit within the literary genre of myth. Has your understanding of the two biblical creation stories changed as a result of reading this chapter? If so, how?

- ▶ Adam and Eve, understood in terms of myth, represent all of us. How do we replicate in our own lives their reasoning, choices, and behavior, particularly with regard to economic matters?

- ▶ How might our choices and behaviors be transformed if our economic reasoning, above all, were predicated on the inherent and inestimable value of each human as a creature made in the image of God?

- ▶ Contemporary economic reasoning is rooted in the assumption that resources are scarce. The biblical creation stories suggest that creation reflects not scarcity, but rather divine abundance. By implication, human beings and their fateful choices render a world of pain and scarcity. How might our economic and social reasoning and behavior change if we were to reason and live entirely in terms of divine abundance rather than scarcity?

- ▶ What does Genesis 1–3 contribute to our understanding of God's character, concerns, and mission? Of our mission as God's people?

CHAPTER 9

The Kingdom's Economy of Abundance

In this chapter I will reflect on Mark 10:17-31, a famous passage with parallels in both Matthew (19:16-30) and Luke (18:18-30). As we consider Mark's story, we should keep in mind the short section that immediately precedes it (10:13-16). In that scene, Jesus castigates his disciples for prohibiting small children from approaching him. In their culture, children were to be kept out of sight and out of mind, so the disciples' actions are understandable. But Jesus has other ideas (vv. 14-15). By placing the account of the children and the disciples next to the scene about the rich man and Jesus (vv. 17-31), Mark seems to suggest that the latter passage can be understood as an example of what it looks like "not" to "receive the kingdom of God as a little child."

"What Must I Do to Inherit Eternal Life?"

As our passage begins (v. 17), Jesus is leaving "on a journey" when someone runs up, kneels before him, and asks: "Good Teacher, what must I do to inherit eternal life?" The man's encounter with Jesus begins with a number of intriguing details. His concern is urgent: he is eager to catch Jesus before the teacher leaves. The man shows significant deference toward Jesus, falling to his knees in a sign of reverence and humility, and he acknowledges Jesus's status and authority as a "teacher." The adjective "good" probably refers to what he knows about Jesus's reputation and moral authority rather than being a strict assessment of Jesus's pedagogical talents and rhetorical skill as such, though by this point in Mark's narrative, Jesus has already developed an intriguing reputation along those lines as well.

The specifics of the man's question include at least a couple of assumptions: first, that there is something called "eternal life," and second, that this eternal life is attainable through activity. The man wants to know what he must "do" in order to obtain "eternal life." Although it is not immediately clear what the man means by this eternal life that he seeks, Jesus seems to understand his request in terms of heavenly treasure (v. 21), and his responses to the man seem to affirm, at least to a certain extent, the assumption that eternal life has something to do with what one does on earth. What the man *believes,* for example, does not seem to be central either for Jesus or for the questioner. But, as we shall see, how and what the man thinks are quite closely connected to what he will or will not do.

As he is often wont to do, Jesus does not simply answer the man's question, but he responds to the man's inquiry with a question of his own: "Why do you call me good?" (v. 18). That would seem to suggest that Jesus does not accept the premise on which the man based his initial question, or perhaps Jesus sees in the man's approach a mixed motive. For whatever reason, rather than accept the compliment from the man, Jesus declares, "No one is good but God alone" (v. 18). Given that the man's specific concerns involve the relationship between eternal life and conduct, Jesus may wish to remind him that such matters ultimately have to do with God rather than with any particular theological teaching about God (despite how high-quality that teaching, coming from Jesus, might be). Jesus appears to be foreshadowing the fact (which becomes clear by the end of the passage) that eternal life is fundamentally linked to endless devotion and obedience to God. Jesus will eventually remind the man that God and God's goodness are what he must keep in mind first and foremost; that is what is most necessary. By contrast, Jesus has little interest in whatever rhetorically skillful deference or self-oriented piety the man's initial greeting ("Good Teacher") may have reflected.

"You Know the Commandments"

Jesus then turns to respond directly to the man's query (v. 19). He identifies several biblical laws that he knows would be well known to the man: "You know the commandments: 'You shall not murder; you shall not commit adultery; you shall not steal; you shall not bear false witness; you shall not defraud; honor your father and mother.'" Much could be said about this list, including the fact that it does not contain all of the Ten Commandments, and the order of Jesus's list does not match exactly with either of the two versions of the Decalogue (Exod. 20; Deut. 5). In those two passages, honoring one's parents comes before the other commandments that Jesus quotes. Perhaps most notable is the fact that "Do not defraud" does not appear in the Ten Commandments at all.

Jesus emphasizes some of the latter commandments—statements that are clearly oriented toward appropriate covenantal behavior toward fellow humans. He does not mention the first two commandments, which concern themselves with the primacy of Yahweh and with idolatry, for example, or those about not misusing God's name and about Sabbath observance. If one of Jesus's concerns is to reorient the man toward God ("No one is good but God alone"), we might anticipate that he would emphasize the commandments that are especially focused on God. Jesus probably does not respond this way for at least two reasons. First, the evidence that a person puts God first, eschews idolatry, and lives a life consonant with the liberating framework of the Sabbath is seen, to a large extent, through the ways one lives with respect to the other commandments. In other words, devotion to God is concretely demonstrated through everyday human relationships. Secondly, as we have already noted, the Decalogue has significant economic overtones. Jesus highlights particular commandments that refer to how covenantal members treat one another, perhaps sensing already what the man's difficulties were ("he had many possessions" [v. 22]). These commandments seek to ensure economically and socially just relations between human beings. They are the ones that would ferret out at least some of what held the man back from his fullest possible relationship with God—and ultimately from eternal life, as this passage implies.

If Jesus is indeed highlighting these latter commandments that emphasize economically just covenantal relationships, we might wonder why he does not cite the last commandment from the Decalogue, the one against covetousness. Within the narrative and sociocultural framework of the passage, however, the absence of any "word" about coveting may be at least partly explained by Jesus's inclusion of one commandment that is not part of the Decalogue, namely, "Do not defraud." This commandment appears in Leviticus 19:13, where the full verse reads as follows: "You shall not defraud your neighbor; you shall not steal; and you shall not keep for yourself the wages of a laborer until morning." The absence of a "word" about coveting and the inclusion of "Do not defraud" tantalizingly suggest that Mark's Jesus is aware of and understands his interlocutor's situation. Indeed, since he was already rich in possessions, perhaps covetousness was not his primary problem; he already owned more than most of those around him.

Perhaps Jesus's inclusion of the prohibition against fraud is especially pointed for this particular man. As we have noted elsewhere, people assumed that there was a limited supply of wealth and material possessions available. Anthropologically, this is what was known as a "limited good" society. There was only so much to go around; whatever limited, scarce resources there may have been, the total size of the economic pie would not change. This notion was, of course, quite different from assumptions rooted in capitalism today, which recognizes that wealth can, in fact, grow. In a "limited good" culture, those who possessed more than others were, in some sense, hoarding what would have belonged to others under different circumstances. Some went so far as to suggest that the possession of excessive wealth was evidence of stealing or fraud: those who had more possessions than others did, must have taken it, or at least they must have acquired it by capitalizing, for example, on the laziness or foolishness of those who were less well off. Perhaps Jesus is suggesting that the man is not as innocent of fraud as he assumes, given his wealth, or as innocent as he believes he is with regard to the other commandments either.

"You Lack One Thing"

The man, addressing Jesus again as "Teacher," claims to "have kept all of these [commandments] since my youth" (v. 20). Jesus does not dispute this. Rather, Jesus looked "at him, loved him, and said, 'You lack one thing; go, sell what you own, and give the money to the poor, and you will have treasure in heaven; then come, follow me'" (v. 21). Jesus presses the man to do the one thing he cannot do, namely, divest himself of his possessions for the sake of "the poor." Jesus may well be illustrating that, while the man has been technically observing the aforementioned commandments, he has not really caught the depth and implications of what they are to mean in his life. Was he going through the motions of following the laws without attending to the deeper motivations that were to inspire obedience to them? Was he, in other words, obeying the letter but not the spirit of the law?

Regardless of how we understand the function of the commandments listed by Jesus, his final instructions effectively expose the true object of the man's devotion. It is striking that Jesus highlights something that

157

this wealthy man is lacking; ironically, for all of his possessions, he is still in need. Jesus, however, gives him the key to obtain what he most wants—eternal life. He invites the rich man to divest himself of what holds him back from experiencing the fullness of life. No matter how he has obtained his wealth—whether on the backs of those who lacked it or in some other way—Jesus effectively calls him to reverse the process of self-enrichment by giving his money away for the benefit of the poor.

We should note that Mark emphasizes Jesus's love for the man. Jesus is not a cold, judgmental prosecutor who articulates in withering fashion all of the ways in which this well-intentioned but self-secure man has fallen short in his quest to embody the commandments faithfully. Instead, Jesus is deeply committed to this man and his situation. Jesus wants to help him, but his way is not to force our hand. We, like the rich young man, are always left with our own decisions to make.

Upon hearing Jesus's final instructions, Mark tells us that the man "was shocked and went away grieving, for he had many possessions" (v. 22). His inability to part with his wealth undoubtedly demonstrates his failure with respect to serving "God alone" (v. 18). In the end, his possessions prove more important to him than "eternal life." The man's inability to part with his wealth effectively indicates more than any creed or confession could have about what he really believed in—whether God or something else. The man's commitment to his possessions means that he is not fully devoted to God: in the final analysis, his wealth takes precedence over God. And when that is the case, he is guilty of breaking the commandments at the beginning of the Decalogue—against the worship of gods other than Yahweh, and against the creation of idols. The man's possessions, and perhaps the security that they provided, became his God in actuality. Perhaps the same is true of those of us today who find ourselves able to identify with the man's difficult decision.

Mark's comment that the man "went away grieving" is worthy of our reflection. Are we as aware as this man was concerning what we must leave behind in order to follow Jesus wholeheartedly? What would you do if faced with the same stark challenge that Jesus gave this man? When we lose something or give something up, there is a natural grieving process that we experience—whether major or minor, conscious or unconscious. The man in this story knew exactly what he was being called to give up, what he had to lose. He would have grieved the loss of his wealth, but that was just the necessary, productive, and ultimately life-giving grief that Jesus called him to face. As it turned out, the man chose not to give up his wealth, but he ended up grieving nonetheless: he grieved the loss of an ongoing relationship with Jesus ("follow me") and the loss of eternal life.

Have we adequately grieved what we may be called to give up in order to follow Jesus faithfully? Or have we simply forgotten that following Jesus will indeed mean leaving some things behind—and grieving their loss—whatever those things may be for each person? The wealthy young man realized immediately what was at stake in following Jesus. Have we faced what we must be willing to leave behind? Maybe we have not grieved enough. Perhaps we want to have our cake and eat it too, so to speak. Jesus "loved" the man but did not give him the option of having it both ways. Perhaps Jesus is not giving *us* that option either. In that sense, maybe grief can function as a good indication of what it looks like to face the real stakes involved in following Jesus, and to choose appropriately in light of them, no matter where the "good teacher" may lead.

Camels and the Eyes of Needles

After the man exits the scene, the focus of the passage shifts significantly. In Mark 10:21, Jesus had "looked at" the inquiring man; now Mark tells us that Jesus "looked around" in the direction of his disciples. In each instance, Jesus's gaze effectively highlights the need for each character—the man in verse 21 and the disciples in verse 23 and beyond—to reflect seriously on what it means to follow the "good teacher" into the life of the kingdom. In the case of the disciples, as if to underscore what had just taken place with the rich man, Jesus addresses his disciples directly (v. 23): "How hard it will be for those who have wealth to enter the kingdom of God!" Mark tells us that "the disciples were perplexed at these words" (v. 24). Why would it be difficult?

Then, as now, material wealth was often understood—even in a "limited good" context—to reflect God's blessings on those who possessed such wealth. Think, for example, of Abraham, Solomon, and the character Job. Although excessive wealth could be understood in terms of greed and unjust acquisition, it could also point to divine favor. That is, economic inequality could be understood from within a "limited good" perspective either as an indicator of human injustice or of divine beneficence. The disciples were shocked because they were thinking along these latter lines. They assumed that wealth was a relatively clear indicator of God's favor. How could someone whom God has so obviously blessed with material well-being find it difficult to enter the kingdom of God? Why would wealth hinder one's participation in the kingdom? And what would that mean for those—like most of the disciples, not to mention the masses of the poor and marginalized following Jesus around—who were not so richly blessed?

Recognizing the confusion felt by the disciples, Jesus repeats his assertion, now addressing them in familial terms: "Children, how hard it is to enter the kingdom of God!" There should be no confusion, according to Jesus. He has now twice emphasized the difficulty involved in entering the kingdom. The disciples—and by extension, Mark's readers—must listen closely to understand Jesus's perspective as he continues to speak. The intimacy shown in Jesus's interaction with the disciples parallels the love that he had for the questioning young man. Remember that this story follows the scene in which Jesus announced that "whoever does not receive the kingdom of God as a little child will never enter it" (Mark 10:13-16). Now Jesus addresses his disciples as children, urging them to receive the kingdom appropriately, that is, as a child would.

Jesus's next statement is one of the most enigmatic and memorable statements in the entire Bible: "It is easier for a camel to go through the eye of a needle than for someone who is rich to enter the kingdom of God." If the disciples found it surprising to think of wealth as an impediment to entry into the kingdom, Jesus's clarification here is downright stunning.

In fact, throughout the history of Christianity, interpreters have often assumed that the extreme nature of Jesus's imagery cannot be intended literally. Of course, camels are massive animals; and needles are clearly very small. It is manifestly impossible for a camel to pass through the eye of a needle. Many readers have thus assumed that Jesus did not really mean what he said. One explanation that made the rounds, even among some biblical commentators, was that Jesus must have had in mind a small gate in the Jerusalem wall, a passageway with a remarkably low and narrow opening, supposedly known as "The Needle." Under normal circumstances, a large animal would not have been able to pass through such a doorway; but, if the animal were to kneel down just so, and inch through carefully with the assistance of multiple human handlers, it would presumably have been possible. Despite the attractiveness of that interpretation, there is no evidence that such a gateway ever existed. This explanation is nothing but wishful thinking and, very significantly, it is an approach to the text that completely misses Jesus's message about wealth.

Another misguided reading of the passage assumes that Jesus was describing the difficulty of threading a rope, rather than a camel, through the eye of a needle. In a small minority of biblical manuscripts, we find "rope"—a word in Greek that is spelled almost the same as the word for "camel"—in place of the majority reading ("camel"). Scholars now recognize that the original passage almost certainly read "camel" rather than "rope": the overwhelming majority of manuscripts read "camel"; and the appearance of such a difficult, counterintuitive word ("camel") in that context helps to explain why some copyists assumed the word should have been "rope." As manuscripts are copied and recopied, the more difficult reading is usually the original one: the appearance in this verse of the word "camel" would have readily inspired copyists to substitute "rope" for "camel," given the oddity and extreme character of "camel" in this context. To do the reverse—that is, to replace an original "rope" with "camel"— would make far less sense. Indeed, Jesus himself indicates that the most extreme form of the statement is what he has in mind: in verse 27 he says that what is impossible for mortals—such as, for example, having a camel walk through the eye of a needle—is possible for God. It is thus precisely the impossibility of a camel passing through the eye of a needle that Jesus intends to highlight.

Not surprisingly, the disciples "were greatly astounded" by Jesus's words, and they said to one another, "Then who can be saved?" If the wealthy are not in a privileged position with regard to God's favor, what does that mean for others—the poor, the marginalized, and the disciples themselves? None of what Jesus says makes sense, even to those who have been so closely following him.

It is worth reflecting on the disciples' reaction to Jesus's words. They are shocked—stunned! According to their teacher, if it is impossible for camels to pass through needles' eyes, then it is even more impossible for rich people to enter the kingdom of God. The implications of this are significant and far-reaching: The disciples incorrectly assumed that the rich man had an advantage with regard to God's kingdom. Not unlike us, perhaps, they tended to place the wealthy on pedestals of one kind or another. But Jesus's comment suggests that earthly "success" and human esteem are worth very little in God's economy. The rich have no special keys to the kingdom. Indeed, Jesus underscores the impossibility of entry into the kingdom—for all humans—while at the same time leaving the disciples (and all of us, whether rich or not) with reason for hope. Again, Jesus "looked at" his disciples—the third time that Mark emphasizes Jesus's gaze at a decisive moment in the narrative—"and said, 'For mortals it is impossible, but not for God; for God all things are possible'" (v. 27). Only God can make the kingdom available; apart from God, entry into the kingdom remains a distinct impossibility. Salvation is always an act of God; God can do for us what we cannot.

Clearly, though, humans are free to choose whether or not they will participate with God. The questioning young man had the choice of whether or not to act on Jesus's instructions and to follow him. He decided not to take Jesus's advice, with devastating consequences. He went away grieving, illustrating an example of the impossibility that Jesus describes to his disciples. Salvation is possible for God, but God will not force us into it. We have choice. God's grace is decisive, but it is not "cheap grace," as Dietrich Bonhoeffer reminds us. We must participate in the process, even if it is merely to turn away from what most captivates us and demands our loyalty—such as, in the case of the man in this passage, wealth—and to turn toward God, choosing to follow Jesus from that point onward. God's grace has a costly quality, as the man in this story found out. Human salvation is possible for God, but we must be willing to allow God to save us. Hard choices will likely be involved for us. According to Mark, the man walked away. How will we respond?

Peter is one of my favorite characters because he seems to verbalize whatever he is thinking. He seems to respond to Jesus's troubling and enigmatic statements as I might—impulsively, with some intensity and a bit of pique. He finds it necessary to remind Jesus that, unlike the rich man, as disciples "we have left everything and followed you" (v. 28). Note that Peter begins his statement by encouraging Jesus to "Look!" This is the fourth time that the theme of "looking" has appeared at key points in this passage. In one sense, Peter's call for Jesus to "look" is subtly ironic; Jesus is obviously the only one who can look and see fully and completely.

"We Have Left Everything and Followed You"

Peter's implied questions are: "So what does all this mean for us who have effectively renounced everything that we held dear, given that we have left behind families, and jobs, and security, and reputations? Will we have eternal life? Will we enter the kingdom of God?" Peter recognizes that most of those following Jesus are not wealthy; still, they had given up much in order to follow Jesus. What do Jesus's statements portend for them?

Jesus's detailed response, which closes the passage, is both encouraging and enigmatic: "Truly I tell you, there is no one who has left house or brothers or sisters or mother or father or children or fields, for my sake and for the sake of the good news, who will not receive a hundredfold now in this age—houses, brothers and sisters, mothers and children, and fields with persecutions—and in the age to come eternal life. But many who are first will be last, and the last will be first" (Mark 10:29-31). Jesus seems to be reassuring Peter that those willing to forsake their families and possessions in order to follow him—and to further the cause of the kingdom—will not be left without seeing their needs met. Indeed, according to Jesus, those who leave their homes, families, and livelihoods (which "fields" would imply for rural, nonwealthy listeners), can expect to "receive a hundredfold now in this age," presumably referring to what they will receive during their earthly lives. Moreover, "in the coming age" they will receive "eternal life."

The assurance about "eternal life" for those who leave behind their earthly commitments coheres well with what we have seen earlier in the passage with respect to the rich man. When the man refused to give up his "many possessions" (v. 22), he forfeited eternal life. Jesus now assures Peter that eternal life is indeed the reward for those who choose to do what the rich man did not.

"A Hundredfold Now in This Age"

But what are we to make of Jesus's statement about this-worldly needs being met with a hundredfold increase? Is this some kind of "prosperity gospel" that promises greater material riches for those who first give up their possessions? Such a reading is rather unlikely, particularly given the emphasis Jesus places on persecutions to come (v. 30). Jesus does not say that believers will experience instant (or eventual) and perpetual bliss; instead, he promises his present and would-be followers that opposition and hardship await them in this life.

Scholars correctly recognize that the reference to persecution—which does not appear in Matthew's or Luke's version of this scene—probably points to the social location of Mark's readers. There are a few indications in this Gospel—here and in chapter 13 especially—suggesting that Mark's narrative was probably written during or in the near aftermath of the Roman destruction of the Jerusalem temple (70 CE), an event within the larger Jewish War with Rome (66-73 CE), when Christians such as Mark and his intended audience (quite possibly in Rome) would have experienced significant opposition and difficulties as a consequence of their faith in Jesus as the Messiah. In other words, the reference to persecution in verse 30 may offer a small but telling glimpse into the Markan community's actual situation. Jesus's inclusion of persecution in Mark's account of the story would have encouraged readers to recognize that such difficulties were to be expected and that they should be understood as corroborating evidence that Jesus's other assurances in verse 30 could be trusted as well.

Beyond the emphasis on persecutions, Jesus promises remarkable this-worldly abundance for his followers. If this is not a promise of some sort of quid-pro-quo prosperity gospel, what does Jesus mean? Obviously, many of Jesus's followers in the first century experienced the persecutions he describes, but what about one-hundred-fold houses, family members, and fields? At first glance, this statement sounds so hyperbolic as to be insensitive to those followers of Jesus, who—then as now—do not experience such bounty. To be sure, relatively few Christians—then as now—have actually left everything behind in the process of following Jesus. Perhaps his statement in verses 29-30 is not so much hyperbolic as it is untested. But that interpretation seems unlikely, especially given the fact that some Christians (e.g., Mother Teresa) have indeed left everything behind, and they have rarely inherited anywhere near a hundred homes or mothers or fields for their troubles.

Our deeply ingrained individualism makes it difficult to grasp what Jesus has in mind here. Today we are used to thinking about ourselves as being radically autonomous individuals who make choices in ways that presuppose a fundamental independence from others. In Jesus's day, such notions would have been largely inconceivable. People understood themselves as deeply embedded within wider webs of relationships, communities, patronage, and status. No one was a radical individual. Familial and community relationships, vocational opportunities, future prospects, and social status were among those things that were, for most people, constrained largely by birth. Indeed, we miss the force of Jesus's teaching in this passage if we fail to recognize how counterintuitive and countercultural it was for his followers to sever their closest social ties—as if it were not enough to forego any forms of economic security and stability. Many readers in the largely individualistic West today would probably hear the challenge of Jesus's teaching in this passage as exclusively economic in nature—as an issue of what "possessions," for example, we might be required to relinquish in the process of following Jesus. By contrast, for Jesus's disciples and for Mark's original readers, Jesus's words would have been equally radical with regard to the familial and social realms of life (which were, of course, often linked to economic phenomena).

Kingdom Abundance

If we read Jesus's statement from an individualistic standpoint, it appears to be false. Most of his followers have not received one hundred times what they have given up. Westerners often express confusion and incredulity when reading this passage: "If I give up my possessions to the poor in following Jesus, won't doing so simply transfer the wealth from me to the poor—making others rich and thus placing them in the same precarious position vis-à-vis the kingdom that the rich man found himself in?" In other words, aren't we effectively shifting the onus of responsibility for wealth onto someone else when we forsake our possessions, putting the recipients of our former wealth in the unenviable position illustrated by the imagery of the camel and the needle's eye? Reading this passage individualistically can make Jesus's statement sound, as one of my students suggested, as if he is advocating a "hot-potato" kind of divestment, in which all those who would follow Jesus are encouraged to shift the danger of riches onto others.

When we read this text from a communal, covenantal perspective, however, Jesus's statement actually makes excellent sense. If the entire community of Jesus's followers were to relinquish—or even to give up their personal sense of—ownership and control of their houses, families, and fields (or the contemporary analogies for such things), they would be forced, in effect, to share with one another. There would then be many more of each of these things—houses, families, and fields—to go around, for everyone's use. That is, Jesus seems to be explaining, even promising, that the community of faith, if and when it truly operates as a community—having forfeited everything for his sake and for the sake of the gospel—becomes empowered to share with others in an entirely new kingdom economy. Everyone would, in effect, become mothers and brothers and sisters to one another. Houses would not be possessed in isolation from others, but in fellowship with them. Fields would be held in common—for the good of the entire community. As Jesus anticipated, a phenomenal multiplication of resources would result.

In effect, Jesus promises his disciples that those who have left everything will begin to experience a foretaste of life in the kingdom now, life in which sharing, cooperation, and the meeting of needs—both relational and material—take precedence over individual ownership and prerogative. When we relinquish control of what we consider to be our own, shifting our economic praxis from notions of self-interested reciprocity to sharing and mutuality, Jesus assures us that we will gain a remarkable overflow of all that we have given up. We will discover true abundance. Jesus is not, we must recognize, advocating pious rhetoric or touchy-feely sentimentality; on the contrary, he is encouraging a very concrete form of economic behavior, one patterned on the very different economic logic operative among those who participate in the kingdom of God.

It is worth noting that, though those who leave behind their family members and possessions "for [Jesus's] sake and for the sake of the good news" can expect, according to Jesus, to receive a hundredfold of "houses, brothers and sisters, mothers and children with persecutions" (verses 29-30), they will not, in Mark's account, receive a multitude of "fathers." Jesus specifically includes, in verse 29, leaving behind a "father," but there is no reference to fathers in the statement of what would be received in verse 30. It is unlikely that Jesus, as Mark records his words here, intends to imply that those who leave behind family members—including a father—would fail to receive potential father figures (e.g., elders, mentors). Jesus is probably highlighting the fact that, ultimately, those in the kingdom have only one true Father, namely, God—and thus there is no reference here to gaining additional fathers.

The meaning of Jesus's enigmatic statement at the end of the passage, "But many who are first will be last, and the last will be first" (v. 31), is not entirely clear in this context. Mark records a similar quote from Jesus in 9:35, when, in response to an argument among his disciples about "who was the greatest" (v. 34), he says, "Whoever wants to be first must be last of all and servant of all." In that instance, Jesus seems to indicate that the most important members of his community will be those who place others before themselves, serving others first and foremost. Perhaps the "last" and "first" statement in 10:31 is similar to the comment in 9:35, but the context of the former suggests that Jesus has in mind a contrast between, on the one hand, those who think they are "first" (perhaps in the sense of being included in the kingdom, or in terms of presently having wealth and status) and, on the other hand, those who are "last" (perhaps those who, from a human perspective, would not appear to be first in line at the gates of the kingdom, or those who are poor and marginalized). To the disciples, the rich man looked as if he would have been "first"—and he might have assumed as much himself—but his response to Jesus's challenging call left him, in effect, "last." It would appear that Jesus is emphasizing in verse 31 that the way things look from the vantage point of our typical, human perspective is not always the way things really are within the reality of God's economy.

Perhaps the most common question with regard to Mark 10:17-31 is whether or not sincere followers of Jesus must actually renounce all possessions and family. That is unlikely; some of Jesus's early followers were apparently not required to do so. Perhaps the most obvious example in the Gospels is Zacchaeus (Luke 19:1-10); and there were always at least some people among Jesus's followers with some means (e.g., Luke 8:1-3; see also 1 Cor. 1:26-31; 11:17-22). Moreover, consider Jesus's words in Mark 10:29 again: "Truly I tell you, there is no one who has left house or brothers or sisters or mother or father or children or fields, for my sake and for the sake of the good news. . . ." Notice that in English, as in the Greek, each of the items in Jesus's list of items that one may need to leave behind is separated by the word "or." That detail suggests that Jesus is not restricting the implications of his discussions with and about the rich man to narrow considerations of wealth or possessions. There are many things that can be left behind, given that many things can hinder complete devotion to God. One person may need to leave possessions, while another may perhaps need—in one way or another—to leave one or more family members. Indeed, Jesus's list in verse 29 is probably to be understood as illustrative more than all-inclusive; he is probably highlighting the fact that his followers will need to be willing to leave whatever is personally most valued and dear to them. That could potentially mean different things for different people. The rich man's possessions held him back from fully embracing Jesus and the good news of the kingdom, and thus he needed to be able to renounce them. Family connections could presumably hinder someone else's ability to be fully present for Jesus and the gospel. Others would need to be willing to leave their livelihood or means of security, their fields, and so forth.

In any event, for our purposes, we must recognize that abandoning the things that Jesus suggests his followers may need to leave behind—houses, family members, or fields—would have had significant economic implications for their lives (as doing so would also have for us today). Whatever else Jesus may be doing in this passage, he is inviting his followers to participate fully in a kingdom-oriented economy, one in which our standard economic reasoning, measures of efficiency and stability, and notions of appropriate conduct may not apply. This kingdom economy is rooted in the grace and provision of God rather than human self-interest.

What is impossible in one context is entirely possible in the other. A kingdom economy, this passage suggests, forms and requires a community, not merely individuals, whose loyalty is entirely given over to God (see, e.g., Mark 12:13-17), even so far as to renounce good things that might hinder that primary relationship.

But even as we recognize that Jesus may not be indicating that everyone must sell his or her possessions and give the money to the poor prior to following him, we should not assume that only others are called to do so. We may be able to acknowledge Jesus's warning—or, perhaps, given his love for the rich man, his lamentation—regarding those who are rich and the difficulty they will have in entering the kingdom of God. In my experience, though, most of us tend to assume that Jesus's message is less applicable to us than to others. We assume Jesus is addressing *that person's* problem, or at least someone else's problem.

Before discussing Mark 10:17-31 in classroom and congregational settings, I often ask those in the room what their first impression is upon hearing this text. I ask them to raise their hands to indicate whether the text generally seems to communicate "good" news or "bad" news. Invariably, whenever I ask that question (usually, in relatively comfortable North American contexts) no more than a few of those in the room experience this text as communicating good news. Every time, the vast majority of those in the room confess that the text portends bad news in some way. It is heard as a warning, as a threat—that is, as a message of danger. This is striking. It suggests that when we hear the story of the rich man and particularly Jesus's statements about those who are rich and their difficulties with regard to entering the kingdom of heaven (verses 23-25), we hear ourselves implicated—directly or indirectly.

Indeed, this is one of the primary passages I use when introducing students to the notion of social location, namely, that who we are (including gender, race, background, experiences, commitments, perspectives, economic status, and so on) affects how we interpret what we read and encounter in the world. Mark 10:17-31 provides a good illustration of this phenomenon. If we find ourselves troubled or distressed reading the passage—if it seems like "bad news" somehow—it probably means that we identify in some way with the rich man. And even implicitly, we probably recognize that we, too, may have something to lose if we really want to follow Jesus. Given what Jesus says here, that may be true even if we do not share the same socioeconomic status as the rich man. If we hear this passage as saying something essentially negative, we may be committed to things, whether money or otherwise, that make it difficult—perhaps even impossible—to participate fully in the kingdom and its radically counterintuitive economy. In other words, if we hear this text as bearing bad news, even implicitly, we may be richer than we would want to admit, since we must have something to lose.

By contrast, those who hear Mark 10:17-31 as essentially good news likely have relatively little to lose. Rather than identifying with the plight of the rich man, they would resonate more with the idea that the rich do not have a more privileged position with regard to entering into the kingdom of God. For the poor, that fact alone would be quite good news, especially in contrast to the ways in which wealth typically works in our traditional human economies. And, of course, note that Jesus instructed the rich man to distribute the proceeds of his former possessions *to the poor!*

Mark 10:17-31 is a radically important text for the missional vocation of the contemporary Christian community. The North American church has tended to operate from the perspective of cultural, economic, and political privilege, which has resulted, all too often, in a cozy relationship with the priorities, forces, and structures that reflect worldly power and wealth more than the kind of communal economy of generosity and abundance that Jesus seems to be advocating in this passage. What would it look like for the Christian community, individuals and congregations alike, to stop trying to explain how Mark 10:17-31 does not really apply to them, and rather to begin living as the kind of missional community whose God-given vocation involves a powerful new economic vision, one in which anything can and will be renounced, if necessary, for the sake of Jesus and the good news? Let us not, like the rich man, walk away grieving. The abundance of the kingdom awaits.

FOR FURTHER REFLECTION

▶ Although the rich man in Mark's story "had many possessions," he still, according to Jesus, lacked something. In what ways do many of us remain needy despite—or perhaps because of—ample resources?

▶ Reflect thoughtfully and discuss: Do you find more security in God or in wealth and possessions?

▶ Imagine yourself having a conversation with Jesus similar to the one he had with the rich man. What does Jesus say to you? How do you respond? If he advised you to sell all of your possessions in order to give the proceeds to the poor, and then to follow him, would you do so?

► How did you respond to Jesus's comments about the impossibility of a rich person entering the kingdom of God? What does your response reveal about your social location?

► Following Jesus will almost certainly require leaving something behind. Do you need to grieve something that you have relinquished (or that you may still need to relinquish) for the sake of fuller life in the kingdom of God?

► Jesus tells Peter that great abundance is in store for those who leave everything for his sake and for the gospel. What would it look like for us to reason in terms of God's abundance as opposed to what we might lack? What would it look like, concretely, for you and your community of faith to live fully into that promised kingdom abundance?

CHAPTER 10

Formation for Economic Reasoning in Matthew

There are numerous texts within Matthew's Gospel that we could explore as we reflect on the missional calling of the Christian community, particularly with regard to matters of money, wealth, poverty, economic justice, and so forth. Space considerations require, however, that we focus illustratively on Matthew 5:1–7:29, a passage known as the Sermon on the Mount (within which we will pay special attention to Matt. 6:19-34), and on the eschatological scene in Matthew 25:31-46.

The Sermon on the Mount: Renewing the Covenant

Traditional readings of the Sermon on the Mount (Matthew 5:1–7:29) have emphasized a wide range of concerns within the text, including theological, spiritual, doctrinal, political, and ethical matters, but interpreters have paid relatively little attention to the kinds of contextual economic factors that Matthew's earliest readers would have recognized as presupposed within the text.

Richard Horsley argues—correctly, I believe—that the Sermon on the Mount functions within Matthew's Gospel as a covenant renewal speech.[1] In a clear echo of Moses on Mount Sinai (see Matt. 5:1), Jesus initiates a re-

1. Richard A. Horsley, *Covenant Economics: A Biblical Vision of Justice for All* (Louisville: Westminster John Knox, 2009), 99-114 and 149-64. For another study that is focused specifically on economic issues in the Sermon on the Mount, see Leif E. Vaage, "The Sermon on the Mount: An Economic Proposal," in *God's Economy: Biblical Studies from Latin America*, ed. Ross Kinsler and Gloria Kinsler (Maryknoll, NY: Orbis, 2005), 127-51.

newed covenant, inviting his auditors to imagine and live into a new kingdom that is committed to and reflective of God's will, economically and
otherwise. The Sermon's covenantal character is critical for understanding its formative function with respect to Matthew's reading communities
and, in particular, its import with respect to economic justice, especially
for those who read Matthew 5–7 today in the context of unremitting market
imperialism and the increasingly libertarian character of Western moral
reasoning.

Jesus's teaching as presented in these three chapters harks back to a
theological and legal framework for communal life articulated in Exodus,
Deuteronomy, and Leviticus. The covenantal laws in those documents,
which are *presupposed* in the Sermon on the Mount (see, e.g., Matt 5:17–20),
defined the terms by which the Israelite community was to demonstrate
covenantal faithfulness in its relationship with God. Justice and righteousness required healthy and whole relationships—*shalom*—in all contexts. In
that sense, economic justice was the responsibility of the entire community. Indeed, as we have already seen, Israel's covenantal laws pertaining
to poverty and economic justice revealed that the people were to consider,
first and foremost, how its most vulnerable members were faring in order
to determine whether or not the community was adequately embodying
the character and quality of justice demanded by God according to the
terms of the covenant.

The Israelite legal provisions were often hortatory and aspirational;
that is, they were fundamentally formative, seeking to engender a particular type of just community, and they did so in at least two ways: first, they
informed the Israelites about how they were to conduct themselves; specific kinds of behavior were expected; and second, the laws were designed
to form the very ways in which the Israelites thought about their conduct
and communal responsibilities. That is, covenantal laws did not merely
command specific behaviors—as if a list of acceptable and unacceptable
practices would have been sufficient. Rather, the laws reflected God's character and highlighted what God considered most important—and, often,
why. Thus, the legal traditions were aimed at forming the very ways in
which the Israelites reasoned, shaping their moral imaginations or mental
paradigms, we might say, with respect to economic justice and how the
poor were to be treated. To be clear, covenantal perspectives, rather than
any other economic assumptions or cultural values, were to guide how the
Israelites reasoned through issues regarding appropriate behavior within
the communal context of the covenant.

In a similar fashion, Jesus's Sermon on the Mount seeks to (trans)-form his followers' reasoning as well as their conduct—theologically, morally, and economically. Interestingly enough, whatever the precise character of Matthew's original readership may have been, several factors would have contributed to their understanding of the Sermon and its significance for their economic conduct, including—among many things that could be mentioned—the dyadic or group-first orientation of first-century Mediterranean cultures; the effects of Roman cultural, political, and economic imperialism, including urbanization and the attendant pressures exerted upon traditional kinship structures and support systems; military occupation; heavy taxation and tribute; onerous debt; increasingly inadequate access to land (see, e.g., Matt. 21:33-41) or sufficient employment (see, e.g., Matt. 20:1-16); the continual need to foster patronage relationships and maintain social honor; and, for Matthew's readership specifically, the experience of marginalization as a faith community constituted around a prophet crucified by the Romans, a community that now—following a devastating war with Rome (66-73 CE) and the destruction of the Jerusalem Temple (70 CE)—found itself at odds, theologically and otherwise, with other Judean religious factions regarding matters of tradition, law, and conduct.[2]

Then, as now, achieving economic justice requires (trans)formation—especially in the context of economic and other forms of empire. The Sermon transforms Jesus's followers so that they can better see what is really going on around them, and it reminds them that *every* imperial system *can* be resisted. Matthew 6:19-34 provides an especially vivid example of such formation for renewed reasoning, and we will focus on that passage within the context of a brief survey of economic dynamics in the broader Sermon.[3]

2. Horsley, in *Covenant Economics*, for example, notes a number of the phenomena described in this paragraph. For a more general study of the socioeconomic conditions in the first century, see Samuel L. Adams, *Social and Economic Life in Second Temple Judea* (Louisville: Westminster John Knox, 2014).

3. Charles H. Talbert, in *Reading the Sermon on the Mount: Character Formation and Ethical Decision Making in Matthew 5-7* (Grand Rapids: Baker, 2004), 29, contends that the Sermon on the Mount "functions as a catalyst for the formation of character." Talbert's helpful approach could be extended to emphasize the "formation of the character of the renewed covenantal community," which would highlight the irreducibly communal nature of biblical economic justice in the Israelite covenant and similar dynamics found in the Sermon on the Mount.

The Blessings: Envisioning Kingdom Realities

Matthew 5:1-12. The Sermon on the Mount begins with a series of blessings (or "Beatitudes") that we considered briefly in Chapter 3. These blessings reflect a covenantal worldview entirely different from most imperial Roman or twenty-first-century perspectives. The first four blessings paint a picture of a strange—and yet, according to Jesus—entirely real, divine economy, one in which those who recognize their need to rely on God in the face of potential or real economic hardship (Matt.5:3), or who sorrow at the unjust state of the world (5:4), or who "take refuge in the Lord" despite loss of land and employment (5:5), or have an insatiable desire for justice (5:6)—will indeed experience all that has heretofore eluded them.[4] These blessings assure Matthew's communities that familiar economic and political institutions are functionally bankrupt, presently and eschatologically, and that standard indicators of economic realities do not apply in God's reign. From the beginning Matthew invites his communities to renew their covenantal relationship with the "heavenly emperor," whose rule belies the traditional characteristics and trappings of empire. Readers are invited to see a different, *more real,* reality, and to reason about their communal conduct from that perspective.

In concert with Israel's covenantal laws, the latter blessings (5:7-11) indicate that the divine economy is characterized by mercy rather than domination (5:7). It honors those whose hearts are pure (5:8), whose efforts are devoted to fostering economic wholeness and shalom (5:9). And Matthew's readers learn that the various forms of mistreatment and marginalization that they have experienced, which surely had economic impacts on their lives, place them firmly on the right side of history (5:10-11).

It is worth noting that the only imperatives in the Beatitudes ("rejoice" and "be glad") appear in verse 12. Jesus's prior blessings did not command people to *do* anything. Rather, the earlier statements enabled his followers to see and understand the counterintuitive, divine framework within which their conduct could be shaped and entirely transformed. To act appropriately, communities must reason adequately; to reason adequately, communities must be able to see and name reality accurately.

---

4. See Frank J. Matera, *The Sermon on the Mount: The Perfect Measure of the Christian Life* (Collegeville, MN: Liturgical, 2013), 36.

Salt and Light

Matthew 5:13-16. Immediately following the Beatitudes, Matthew challenges his readers to see the true contours of their covenantal identity and missional vocation within the wider divine economy. According to Jesus, they are together "the salt of the earth" (5:13) and "the light of the world" (5:14-15), whose "good works"—which, given the content and context of the Sermon, would certainly include economically oriented behaviors—are to be seen by all (5:16). Jesus's followers are being invited to live consciously and conspicuously as a community characterized by a renewed covenant.

"I Have Come Not to Abolish But to Fulfill"

Matthew 5:17-20. Lest readers wonder whether Jesus's effort to transform their economic reasoning represents a break from their Israelite roots, he stipulates emphatically that the law remains entirely in effect (see Matt. 5:17-20). In other words, for Matthew's Jesus, divine assumptions and commitments revealed in Israel's covenantal economic provisions have not been abrogated in any way. Indeed, Jesus has come "to fulfill" the law, to enable his followers to see themselves as a covenant community faithful to the God of past, present, and future justice. The kind and quality of justice evidenced in such a community will exceed anything seen in "the scribes and Pharisees."

"You Have Heard That It Was Said . . . . But I Say to You"

Matthew 5:21-48. Next, Jesus heightens the motivational quotient of previous covenantal expectations, further seeking to transform the reasoning of the renewed covenant community. Murder, adultery, divorce, and swearing oaths all had, among other things, economic dynamics and implications. And mere behavioral compliance was not to be equated with covenantal righteousness. Jesus seeks to form a community whose economic and moral reasoning would embody an unshakable commitment to reconciling love, especially given that debtors' prison and economically oriented lawsuits were familiar (5:21-26). Jesus calls for a radically single-minded commitment to purity of heart, mind, and conduct, as illustrated in his comments about adultery, divorce, and oaths (5:27-37).

Verses 38-42 correspond to covenantal legal traditions. Anyone can retaliate against injustice, but Jesus's covenant community will think outside the box, embodying the kind of creative resistance to economic and social injustice that can bring down powerful—albeit ultimately doomed—empires. Extraordinary compassion and radical generosity must characterize individual and communal economic reasoning (5:42). The instruction to love enemies, even those (e.g., tax collectors) whose conduct is at odds with the economic well-being of Jesus's followers (5:43-48), is designed to form a community that reasons with extreme creativity, endless compassion, and uncalculating generosity. Actions rooted in such reasoning will begin to reflect the wholeness and "devotion to God" that Jesus's followers are to embody (5:48).[5]

"Your Father Who Sees in Secret Will Reward You"

Matthew 6:1-18. Jesus continues to emphasize motivational factors in Matthew 6. For example, in his discussion of almsgiving, prayer, and fasting, he reorients his followers' understanding of worthwhile rewards—or wages, as we might translate the Greek word *misthos*—and who actually "pays" them (6:1-8, 16-18). Merely giving alms, for example, is inadequate from the perspective of a renewed covenant; for Jesus, truly just almsgiving, prayer, and fasting are rooted in appropriate reasoning and motivation.

At the heart of the Sermon on the Mount, the "Lord's Prayer" (6:9-13) reflects concrete economic issues, including food provision (6:11),[6] economic debt (6:12),[7] and, according to Douglas Oakman, "trials in rigged courts before evil judges" (6:13).[8] The prayer is explicitly formational: Jesus says, "Pray, then, in this way." Praise is directed not toward Caesar, the Roman imperial lord, but rather to the ultimate ruler, "our Father in heaven," with whom the community has a relationship (v. 9). Those who

---

5. Matera, *Sermon on the Mount*, 64.

6. See Warren Carter, *Matthew and the Margins: A Sociopolitical and Religious Reading* (Maryknoll, NY: Orbis, 2000), 167.

7. Carter, *Matthew and the Margins*, 167, notes the link between this petition and the covenantal command to forgive debts every seventh (sabbatical) year in Deuteronomy 15:1-11.

8. Douglas E. Oakman, *Jesus, Debt, and the Lord's Prayer: First-Century Debt and Jesus' Intentions* (Eugene, OR: Cascade, 2014), 84. Oakman highlights other economic dynamics in the prayer as well.

pray "in this way" recognize that contemporary economic empires and forces are impermanent, and are as subject to the power of God as was the Egyptian Pharaoh.

Verse 10 identifies, through third-person imperatives, what covenantal community members most desire: "Your kingdom come. Your will be done, on earth as it is in heaven." In effect, Jesus teaches them to call on God to act: "Bring *your* empire to fruition, God! We are ready! Make things here work as they do in your realm, where you are in charge!" They eagerly anticipate the arrival of the kingdom's complete justice and shalom, presaged in both Israelite covenantal law and the Sermon itself, when God's rule is fully manifest.

"Store Up for Yourselves Treasures in Heaven"

Let us now turn to the primary passage from the Sermon under consideration in this chapter, Matthew 6:19-34. We will first consider verses 19-24, before turning to the rest of the passage. The first section consists of three short segments that, despite how they may appear at first glance, are tightly linked within Matthew's presentation of Jesus' teaching. Let us turn to verses 19-21.

Whatever Jesus means, specifically, by storing up "treasures in heaven," the contrast between earthly and heavenly storage is obviously significant; in one realm, treasures come to naught, whereas in the other, they endure. In the previous section of the Sermon on the Mount (Matt. 6:1-18), Jesus has just cautioned his audience not to participate in traditional forms of Jewish piety—giving alms to the poor (verses 2-4), praying (verses 5-15), and fasting (verses 16-18)—simply for the sake of human approval. Those who do such things in order to be "seen" and "praised by others" (see 6:2, 5) will receive nothing more than whatever human admiration and honor they obtain in the moment. Their actions are effectively self-referential, and their rewards (or "wages") are fleeting. Jesus tells his followers to operate out of the limelight in order to garner honor and praise from God, whose approval is ultimately all that matters. Those who participate in pious activities for God's benefit will actually be rewarded. This is the context for verses 6:19-21. Those who act appropriately in 6:1-18 are laying "up treasures in heaven" rather than "on earth" (vv. 19-20).

Recent research by Gary Anderson demonstrates that storing up "treasures in heaven" in 6:19-21 is particularly linked to almsgiving in the relevant Jewish literature.[9] The Sermon is thus forming a community of people whose hearts are oriented toward God's perspectives, as their treasures, reckoned in terms of a divine economy, are stored in the divine realm, where standard economic and social reasoning do not apply. In verse 21, Jesus explains the formative function of treasures in human life: "Where your treasure is, there your heart will be also." It is important that readers pay close attention to the way in which Jesus frames this statement: He does not say, "Where your heart is, there your treasure will be," though that would better reflect how we tend to reason within our market-driven, choice-oriented economic milieu. If Jesus *were* to have said, "Where your heart is, there your treasure will be," the sense would have been that his followers should devote their treasure to what their hearts desire. While that sentiment might make sense, and would cohere quite well with contemporary consumer-oriented logic, that is not, in fact, what Jesus says. He does not instruct his followers—as if he were a skilled advertising or marketing director—to be willing to part with their treasure for what they love.

Jesus's actual statement—"where your treasure is, there your heart will be also"—clearly suggests that human beings do not make unencumbered choices nearly to the extent that we think we do. Despite the common economic assumption that we have complete and unhindered freedom of choice, Jesus's imagery suggests that we are not entirely free: our hearts *follow* our treasure. This is not a proconsumerism statement masquerading as faith; rather, Jesus indicates, among other things, that our financial priorities shape and form the desires of our hearts. In this case, idolatry lies close at hand, which helps to explain the statement about God and wealth that Jesus will soon make (v. 24).

Readers of Jesus's statements in Matthew 6 are encouraged to ponder whether our religious behavior is oriented toward this-worldly reward rather than divine approval (vv. 1–18) and whether our hearts are effectively coopted by material treasure (vv. 19–21). Notice, in each case, that Jesus's comments are designed not merely to foster specific religious behaviors but also to demonstrate that it is crucial for his followers to reason appropriately about their behavioral choices in the first place.

Although, at first glance, the next paragraph (vv. 22–23) appears to have little in common with the surrounding material (vv. 19–21, 24), economic concerns remain in view. Jesus reminds his audience of the de-

---

9. Gary A. Anderson, *Charity: The Place of the Poor in the Biblical Tradition* (New Haven, CT: Yale University Press, 2013), esp. 124-26.

structiveness of inappropriate attachment to wealth—and covetousness—through an allusion to what was known in the Mediterranean world as the "evil eye." Though the exact sense of Jesus's statement is not entirely clear, at least some in the ancient world seem to have understood the eye to be the source of light for seeing, reflective of the light within a person (e.g., in the sense of someone's character). In that case, accurate, healthy vision would depend on having light within. A person with an unhealthy eye—if the eye shines the light from within—would have significant darkness within. Greed and envy are likely in view here, given that the reference to an unhealthy eye is likely an allusion to the notion of "the evil eye."[10]

"No One Can Serve Two Masters"

In Matthew 6:24, we find one of the most memorable and confounding statements in all of Jesus's teaching, one that functions as the climax of the Sermon's formation with regard to economic reasoning, identifying in the starkest terms what the stakes really are. It is worth reflecting on the fact that Jesus does not view slavery as an optional phenomenon. Rather, he assumes that everyone is mastered—enslaved—by something, but only one master can have our ultimate loyalty. Jesus's statement effectively rejects the notion that humans have completely unfettered freedom to make choices for themselves. On the contrary, he implies that slavery is the operative and appropriate rubric for human life. There are only two options: God or wealth (Greek: *mammon*). It is fascinating to note that among all the masters that might potentially usurp God's rightful place in ruling over human beings, Jesus places wealth in direct opposition to God. In short, Matthew 6:24 suggests that the most pervasive and pernicious type of idolatry may be economic in nature.

Clearly, the statement "you cannot serve God and wealth" represents an explicitly conceptual type of formation, providing the basis for economic reasoning rather than offering concrete behavioral instruction. In other words, verse 24 is framed in a general and open-ended way, lacking any contextual or situational specificity. Thus, it serves to reorient and shape readers' moral imaginations, not so much telling Jesus's followers what to *do* as forming who and how they are to *be*. The potential implications of "you cannot serve God and wealth" for actual economic conduct

10. See Malina and Rohrbaugh, *Social-Science Commentary*, 50 and 357-59.

are left unspecified and thus prove to be nearly endless. Ultimately, given the human tendency to serve mammon rather than God, Jesus challenges his followers to examine, to question, and—as it becomes necessary—to resist the hallmark assumptions, values, and priorities of any human economic system (see, e.g., Matt. 22:15-22).

Many North Americans imagine that our market-oriented economic system and the presumably rational choices that contemporary market logic encourages and engenders are, in a fundamental sense, morally neutral, and furthermore, that eager and loyal support of a system that often glorifies self-interested competition is entirely consonant with Christian faith. Matthew 6:24 suggests the need for transformed reasoning on both counts.

In the Context of God's Abundance, Why Worry?

Let us turn now to Matthew 6:25-34. Integrally linked to all that has come before, these verses suggest that within the covenantal economy of God's kingdom, worry is unnecessary, fundamentally illogical, and perhaps even a sign of idolatry. The opening "therefore" in verse 25 suggests that one legitimate way to understand Jesus's statement about God and wealth in verse 24 is to view it from the perspective of what follows in verses 25-34: the latter section reflects on at least one of the implications of verse 24. Those who serve God have no reason for inordinate worry, a condition that clearly reflects the ruling power of mammon. Anxiety about securing the basic necessities of life need not "master" Jesus's followers.

Unlike the kingdom community, "Gentiles," according to Jesus, strive for things that are typical objects of worry and catalysts for anxiety. We should understand Jesus's reference to the Gentiles here as an indication that those outside of the covenantal community have an inadequate and misguided approach to reasoning about daily needs and economic realities. In effect, the Gentiles serve mammon inasmuch as they are not shaped and formed by the economic logic and transformed reasoning characteristic of God's reign: the result is worry.

God's care is all-encompassing and addresses the most basic of needs. Those who serve God, as opposed to wealth, look to God as the supplier of their needs rather than worrying about the necessities of life, or about how to accumulate more than is necessary. To serve God rather than wealth is to live without undue anxiety and worry, given that the Creator of all things knows and provides what humans need (v. 32).

According to Jesus, God will provide what humans need for life, but not whatever excess beyond basic necessities humans might desire. Many of us have much more than we need for basic survival, and yet our anxiety and worry persist; meanwhile, billions struggle to have even their basic needs met. Glaring and growing gaps exist between those of us who are overly sated, with more than we need, or can even use, and those who lack even the rudimentary necessities of sustainable nutrition, clean water, adequate shelter, and clothing. Such inequities presumably reflect what happens when human beings serve wealth rather than God. Perhaps our anxieties are symptomatic of our deeply rooted economic idolatries: that is, being consumed with worry and anxiety is a sure sign of being mastered by mammon. Of course, Jesus does not suggest that life's necessities will simply appear without any struggle or toil. He invokes commonplace imagery of "the birds of the air" as an illustration of God's care (v. 26). God provides for the birds, which "neither sow nor reap nor gather into barns," and by implication God can satisfy the needs of people as well.

Individualistic readings of Matthew 6:25-34 have raised theodicy questions. In a world of radical inequities and chronic poverty, many people in our world do *not* receive everything they need. Where, then, is God's justice? One individualistic interpretive strategy in the West has been to move tangible signs of justice into the future, understanding Matthew 6:25-34 as an argument that those suffering from material deprivation should wait patiently for an otherworldly and future kingdom in which their needs—material and spiritual alike—will finally be met. Indeed, the history of Christianity is replete with examples in which the marginalized and downtrodden have been encouraged to wait, in faithful silence, for God's eventual rescue to come in the heavenly by-and-by. Needless to say, such an approach to the passage tends to absolve the wealthy and comfortable of any sense of responsibility to respond to the real, contemporary pain and suffering experienced by those around them.

There are good reasons for assuming that Matthew's earliest readers would not have understood the text in a primarily individualistic way. First, the culture in which Jesus spoke (and in which Matthew wrote) was not characterized by the kind of thoroughgoing individualism that we in the modern West are familiar with. Ancient people in the first-century Mediterranean world were individuals, to be sure, but they understood themselves as deeply and inextricably connected to wider kinship and community networks, and they relied on those connections (e.g., families, patrons, benefactors, almsgiving) to navigate the worst vicissitudes of their economic and social situations.

Second, as I have already noted with respect to the Sermon on the Mount as a whole, Matthew's Gospel presents Jesus's teaching as formation for his followers' mission in the world in the context of a renewed covenant. Given the Sermon's formative function for appropriate economic reasoning and behavior in the community of Jesus's followers, the implication of verses 25–34 may be that God will supply concrete economic necessities *through* the kind of communal economy called for in the Torah and by Jesus (e.g., via sharing, generosity, debt forgiveness, mercy, and nonexploitation). That is, when a community strives together for the "justice" of God's reign, amazing economic things can happen (v. 33). If some do not find their basic needs for food, water, shelter, and clothing met, the implication of verses 25–34 is not that God has failed to provide—or that Jesus has lied about divine care of and protection for birds and humans—but that the community of faith charged with putting its complete trust in God (v. 24) has apparently failed to be the kind of covenantal community that they are called to be.

Jesus's teaching encourages his followers to recognize that the only thing worthy of human striving is the reign of God and the justice that it embodies (v. 33). Indeed, God's people have the opportunity to experience a real foretaste—albeit messy and radically incomplete—of the soon-to-be-revealed fullness of God's power and justice, in which compassion and generosity can overcome the self-interested hoarding of resources. Worry and anxiety in such a kingdom community reflect entirely unnecessary, illogical, and perhaps even idolatrous responses to concrete, everyday need in view of the abundance and mutual support that is possible in authentic covenantal community.

Matthew 6:25–34 is a powerful reflection on what it can mean to serve God rather than wealth (6:24). Contemporary Christian communities would do well to consider the extent to which, economically, they actually function according to idolatrous "Gentile" reasoning and conduct, as opposed to Jesus's kingdom vision. The presence of anxiety and worry may prove to be a helpful diagnostic in this regard.

By challenging us to reflect on the true nature of "treasures" and the critical difference between serving God and wealth, Matthew 6:19–34 thoroughly recasts the ways communities of faith must reason through economic situations of all kinds. In that sense, faith communities that engage this passage in a serious and sustained way will find themselves formed—and potentially transformed—for their missional witness in the world.

"In Everything, Do to Others As You Would Have Them Do to You"

Matthew 7:1-29. Given the economic dynamics presupposed in Jesus's Sermon, perhaps the admonition against judging at the outset of Matthew 7 should be understood in connection with Matthew 6:22-23. Both paragraphs deal with eye problems, and in light of evil-eye imagery and the fact that all of the intervening material in 6:24-34 is of an explicitly economic character, perhaps the prohibition against judging others should be understood, at least in part, in economic terms. In effect, the Sermon demands that judgment regarding economic matters be left to God; none of Christ's followers are to take God's place in judging how other community members work out the particular implications of serving God rather than wealth (6:24), or how they deal with daily economic concerns (6:25-34). Everyone has personal "eye problems" with which to deal.

Matthew 7 closes with three reminders: God gives "good things to those who ask" (7:7-11); scriptural expectations for conduct are met when covenant members treat others—economically and in every way—as they themselves wish to be treated (7:12); and the will of God must ultimately be enacted through concrete obedience (7:13-27). A shift to singular pronouns in 7:24-27 emphasizes that, while the Sermon on the Mount (Matthew 5:1-7:29) is communally directed, it has radical and concrete implications for individuals. Actual obedience is required—communally and individually. True community requires that all actually participate.

In addition to forming the covenant community's moral reasoning with respect to economic matters, the Sermon also engenders some specific behaviors that are to characterize Jesus's followers' communal life and vocation in the world. Contrary to many interpretive approaches to the Sermon on the Mount, neither Jesus nor Matthew understood the Israelite covenantal legal tradition as mere exhortation to theological or ethical ideals.

Community members are to conduct themselves in particular ways in light of how their economic reasoning has been formed by Jesus's teaching in the Sermon: specifically, they are formed to rejoice in the face of persecution (e.g., 5:10-12), praying for their persecutors (5:44); to seek to practice radical forgiveness (e.g., 6:12, 14-15) and participate in active processes of reconciliation (e.g., 5:23-32), whatever the situation; to release debts (6:12) or refrain from reckoning indebtedness in the first place, as communities meet the needs of every beggar and borrower (5:42). Community members seek to love their enemies (5:43), including economic ones, and refuse to retaliate violently against injustice, consciously and proactively seeking ways to resist any abuse with genuine creativity (see 5:38-42). In the covenantal economy, followers of Jesus give alms (6:2-4; cf. 6:19-21), pray (6:5-13), and fast (6:16-18) without fanfare. They repudiate greed (e.g., 6:22-23) and the idolatry of wealth, and they reject all other gods, whether "foreign" or economic (6:24). The covenant faithful seek God's rule and justice above all else, recognizing that worrying gets them nowhere (6:25-34; cf. 7:7-11). And they leave judgments to God, attending to their own economic and other blind spots before calling out others' impairments (7:1-5).

Ultimately, community members seek to treat others with the same compassion, mercy, and economic justice that they would hope to be afforded themselves (7:12a), in effect, practicing the kinds of economic relationships that Israel's covenantal legal tradition sought to foster. Such conduct fulfills the expectations of Torah and the prophetic tradition (7:12b) and begins to reflect God's will—on earth, as it is in heaven (7:13-14, 21-27).

The Sermon on the Mount seeks to form readers so that, from the perspective of God's larger economy, they will recognize and understand what is really going on in the world. In the abiding presence of the king (Matt. 1:23; 28:20), equipped with such a transformed vision, believers will be empowered to resist all ideologies and idolatries—personal and systemic—with radical faithfulness. Covenantal resistance will, of course, have to be multifaceted and unstintingly creative; believers must be prepared to suffer indignity, abuse, and persecution. Deference to the demonic forces of injustice—economic and otherwise—is not an option.

The covenantal character of the Sermon reminds us that economic justice is a communal responsibility. Together, Jesus's followers *can* inhabit and embody specific covenantal practices, by both thinking differently and acting differently. Uncalculating generosity, unremitting compassion, and thoroughgoing forgiveness, including debt release, are possible and necessary. As the Sermon reminds us, we must, in the end, act with both creativity and obedience. This is a covenantal economics that is meant to be lived: justice necessitates that we actually embody the expectations of law and the prophets, treating everyone—including the poor and marginalized—as family, as we ourselves would like to be treated (7:12). Covenantal laws and assumptions in the Old Testament pointed the way. Deuteronomy indicates that choosing obedience is "choos[ing] life." In Acts, the earliest believers embodied a life-giving form of covenantal economics (Acts 2:43-47; 4:32-35), and Matthew expects the Sermon on the Mount to (trans)form Jesus's followers into that kind of community. May we today also "choose life."

Matthew 25:31–46: The Sheep and the Goats

In Matthew's Gospel, Jesus demonstrates time and again that those who oppose him (perhaps especially the scribes [e.g., 9:3; 16:21; 20:18] and Pharisees [e.g., 9:34; 12:14, 24; 16:1; 21:45–46; 22:15]) do not have the power to derail God's purposes at work in Jesus's ministry. In fact, by the end of chapter 22, Matthew indicates that everyone has stopped asking Jesus questions, unable to best him rhetorically or theologically. Chapters 23–25 then consist of extensive teaching by Jesus; he is the only character who speaks directly until chapter 26. This large block of instruction is the fifth major section of teaching that Matthew has woven into the action-dominated plotline of Mark's Gospel, which served as the narrative framework for Matthew's own retelling of Jesus's story. As is typical in Matthew's Gospel, the ending of the present block of teaching concludes at 26:1 with the narrator's literary marker, "When Jesus had finished . . ." (see also 7:28; 11:1; 13:53; 19:1).

In chapter 23, Jesus teaches "the crowds and his disciples" and speaks in harsh terms about the misguided priorities, instruction, and conduct of the "scribes and Pharisees." Most scholars recognize that at least some of the verve reflected in this chapter is attributable to a conflict (after Jesus's death and resurrection) between scribal and Pharisaic (e.g., early rabbinic) groups and Matthew's own community of faith, which was itself largely, if not exclusively, Jewish. That is, in the decades following the destruction of the Temple in 70 CE, Matthew's Jewish-Christian community seems to have been engaged in a struggle with other Jewish groups over what it meant to be the authentic and faithful heirs of the larger Jewish tradition (including appropriate interpretation of Scripture).

So, while we should take Matthew's depiction of Jesus's teaching seriously, we should also keep in mind that the author is intentionally highlighting points of disagreement between Jesus and the Pharisees (perhaps especially reflective of conflicts and tensions in his own day). It is important to acknowledge that it is unlikely, historically speaking, that Matthew's narrative reflects an entirely nuanced and objective portrayal of all Pharisees in Jesus's day. Certainly, some of these Pharisees—and perhaps many—may have been as conniving, power-hungry, and self-righteous as Matthew's narrative suggests. But we must remember that the general populace would have recognized the Pharisees in Jesus's day as being deeply committed to putting what they understood to be God's will into action in daily life. By comparison with the aristocratic, politically connected, and theologically conservative Sadducees, the Pharisees were a relatively well-regarded and theologically reflective group at that time. (Note that, according to Matthew 5:20, Jesus does not seem to assume that the scribes and Pharisees are devoid of righteousness; he simply points out that the reign of heaven requires even more righteousness than what they were widely known for.) In fact, it is likely that Jesus is described in Matthew (and in the other Gospels) as having more conflicts with the scribes and Pharisees than he did with the Sadducees in large part because the former groups actually shared more perspectives in common with Jesus than he did with the Sadducees.

As is evident in our own families—and perhaps in various religious and political contexts—we tend to argue more vigorously over the fine details of theology or politics with those whose views are actually closer to our own than we do with those whose views we find completely objectionable or irrelevant. Jesus's arguments with and pronouncements against the scribes and Pharisees in Matthew's Gospel should be understood as an intrafamilial fight (given that all of the participants are Jews). Jesus does not regard his opponents as intrinsically evil, and it is highly unlikely that Matthew intends to suggest that either. Jesus argues vigorously with his opponents in this Gospel because he has much in common with them; at the same time, he has especially harsh words for them inasmuch as he believes that their teachings and examples can be profoundly misleading for God's people.

After Jesus's especially strong words in Matthew 23 against the scribes and Pharisees, his teaching turns in chapters 24–25 to a range of eschatological pronouncements and parables, statements that are directed toward his disciples "privately" on the Mount of Olives (24:3). The so-called parable of the sheep and the goats, our focus text, appears at the end of this strikingly intense portion of Jesus's teaching. From then on (beginning in Matt. 26), the plot of the narrative emphasizes action and suffering as it moves quickly toward the cross.

The Sheep and the Goats as Communal Formation

Matthew 25:31-46 is often described as a "parable," but that is not an entirely appropriate designation. Matthew himself does not introduce the passage as a parable, as he often does (e.g., throughout Matt. 13); moreover, this text does not present a simple comparison between two things (e.g., X is like Y; see Matt. 22:2; 25:1) that is so typical of Jesus's parables, but rather a description of a coming eschatological event (v. 31: "When the Son of Man comes . . .").

Nevertheless, Jesus's description of future judgment here has a certain parabolic quality. The use of relatively common elements (such as everyday livestock) places issues of faithful conduct into sharp relief; furthermore, the passage fosters—perhaps we should say, demands—new ways of seeing reality among Matthew's readers, both ancient and contemporary. That is, Matthew 25:31-46 represents a clear example of the kind of communal formation that parables represent with regard to both appropriate conduct and the kind of moral reasoning that supports and engenders such behavior. Indeed, more specifically, Jesus's account of the sheep and the goats illuminates and clarifies the Christian community's vocation and missional calling, functioning as missional formation for Christian readers communally located in a world of poverty, pain, and suffering.

The scene in Matthew 25:31-46 takes place in an eschatological context—that is, at some point in the future. Jesus says: "When the Son of Man comes in his glory, and all the angels with him, then he will sit on the throne of his glory" (v. 31). The imagery is of the final judgment, when the ultimate authority of the "Son of Man" (a title drawn from Daniel 7, and often recognized as Jesus's most common self-designation in the synoptic Gospels) is to be fully manifested. The description here is overtly royal and messianic. Angels attend the "Son of Man," he sits upon a "glorious throne," and he is explicitly called "the king" in verses 34 and 40.

Once enthroned, the king initiates a process of welcoming into his presence those who will "inherit the kingdom prepared for [them] from the foundation of the world" (v. 34), even as he will banish those unworthy of a kingdom inheritance ("depart from me into the eternal fire prepared for the devil and his angels" [v. 41]). The picture painted at the outset is stark and arresting: readers are witnesses to an ultimate reckoning, a moment of full and complete accountability. Of course, what makes this reckoning so poignant is that the text seems to imply that everyone, including Matthew's readers, are implicated in this visionary account. According to verse 32, "All the nations will be gathered before" the king, who is to be understood as Jesus (now revealed as the victorious and reigning Son of Man).

The King "Will Separate People One from Another"

The king is described as a "shepherd" in Matthew 25: 31–46 (compare similar imagery in 2 Sam. 5:2; Ps. 78:70–71), invoking imagery of royal care, management, and complete authority. He "separates" the nations "as a shepherd separates the sheep from the goats" (v. 32), placing the sheep on his right, with the goats to his left (v. 33). There has been significant discussion about the images of sheep and goats, and what leads Jesus to refer specifically to them. Precise distinctions that we may make between sheep and goats, culturally or otherwise, are probably of less importance than the fact that Jesus invokes one type of animal to represent those "nations" who would be welcomed as inheritors of the kingdom and another to represent those who would not. Most likely, questions about specific distinctions and characteristics between sheep and goats are less critical than the implication (yet to come in the passage) that the fundamentally crucial distinction in the passage is between those who treated the poor with compassion and mercy and those who did not.

After welcoming "those on his right" into their inheritance—a "kingdom prepared for [them] from the foundation of the world" (v. 34)—the king proceeds to explain why they will now be entering this realm. There are six reasons, each one referring to an unfortunate situation that the king had experienced in the past (e.g., "I was hungry")—each one rooted in the behavior of the sheep (vv. 35–36). Each of the six situations is paired with a corresponding response that the sheep ("you," always in the plural) provided to the king. They alleviated hunger with food, and thirst with something to drink; when the king was a stranger, the sheep welcomed him; when he was naked, they clothed him; when he was sick, they visited him—in prison and they "came" to him. Again, in each situation in which the king was suffering, the sheep responded in a concrete and appropriate way.

Notice that, in a strict sense, there is nothing particularly surprising or especially heroic about how the sheep responded to the king's suffering. That is, they met a specific need by appropriately addressing what the king lacked—whether food, or drink, or clothing, or the like. The sheep did not go "above and beyond the call of duty" (as we might be tempted to assume when reading the passage) in terms of meeting the king's need; they simply provided a fitting response to the situations in which the king found himself. This point can be easily overlooked, as evidenced by the way the actions of the sheep have become reified within the Christian tradition as especially noteworthy forms of merciful service—as "acts of mercy," as they are often known. (The Roman Catholic tradition typically speaks of seven such acts, adding burial of the dead to the six delineated in this passage.)

The conduct of the sheep was, to be sure, merciful and compassionate. But we should not miss the fact that they simply behaved in ways that were in direct response to existing and specific needs. In effect, for example, they treated the king as if he were a member of their own families. Would we make a special point of lauding a parent simply for providing food or clothing for her own child, or would we view the provision of such things as a normal and appropriate part of one's role as a parent? What the sheep did met concrete human needs in a manner analogous to the way humans care for each other when they already share a familial or friendly relationship. The king is not rewarding the sheep for saving the world; that's not what they did. Rather, the king rewards them for having met his basic human needs.

"You Did It to Me"

Perhaps most surprising, of course, is the king's claim that the sheep have done anything for him at all. The imagery is startling. How many kings have trouble finding food or water or clothing? What king would ever permit members of "the nations" to attend to him during an illness? Incredulous, the sheep themselves are stunned by the king's welcome and his recitation of their actions. In verses 37-39, they exclaim, "Lord, when was it that we saw you hungry and gave you food, or thirsty and gave you something to drink? And when was it that we saw you a stranger and welcomed you, or naked and gave you clothing? And when was it that we saw you sick or in prison and visited you?"

The sheep are perplexed for at least two reasons: first, they don't remember doing any of these things for the king; second, we may assume that they are astonished that the figure on the throne would have ever been in need in the first place. As the narrative proceeds, we readers who observe the scene from the outside share the latter confusion concerning the neediness of the king. Destitute, helpless kings are uncommon. And, with regard to the first point of confusion, readers are unaware of what has taken place prior to this scene and are thus unable at this point to evaluate what it may mean for the king to claim that the sheep have done all these things for him.

After the inquiries from the sheep in verses 37–39, the king immediately responds, giving the reason he has welcomed them into their kingdom inheritance—even as he clears up the remaining points of confusion: "Truly I tell you, just as you did it to one of the least of these who are members of my family, you did it to me" (v. 40). The sheep are rewarded for their actions, though most striking is the king's comment that the conduct in question was manifested in a direct way toward others, and specifically toward the least of those in his family. The king, as it turns out, was not literally hungry, or thirsty, or naked; rather, what was done for those who were experiencing literal hunger or thirst, or nakedness, was done, albeit indirectly, for him. The king views something done for others as having been done for him. Note that he does not say that the sheep acted mercifully and compassionately toward others *as if* to the king. He says that those actions were, in fact, done *to him*. This is powerful imagery.

The king so identifies with and cares for these destitute and marginalized "family members" (the Greek term here, literally "brothers," is inclusive of men and women) that any action by the sheep toward them is something that the king regards as something that is done, in point of fact, to himself. To put the matter another way, the sheep engaged with and ministered to the king whenever they served these "least" ones. Therefore, in the context of Matthew's Gospel, the sheep did not introduce those who were suffering to the compassion and merciful treatment that the king would have otherwise provided them, bringing relief on his behalf, so to speak. Rather, the sheep actually found, albeit unwittingly, the king in the suffering ones.

This imagery has tremendous implications for how we understand the divine mission into which the Christian community has been caught up and called. The gospel is not merely what the church takes *to* the world; rather, the gospel also involves what the church *receives* as it faithfully engages the world. The sheep actually met the king, the "Lord," in the marginalized and destitute. In effect, we might say that salvation comes to the faithful more than the faithful bring it to others.

There has been significant scholarly discussion regarding the precise meaning of "the least of these who are members of my family." Most scholars assume that Jesus's statement about "the least of my brothers [and sisters]" is best understood as referring to those in the Christian community, and perhaps even more specifically to early Christian missionaries. The implication, then, would have something to do with how "the nations" treat those Christians. While this may be true in a strictly exegetical sense, Frederick Dale Bruner's comments are probably more on target:

> Elsewhere this family name described other Christians (most notably in chap. 18; cf. 12:46-50); thus, as we have seen, many interpreters believe that Jesus speaks here of loving deeds done to Christians, Christian missionaries, or Christian workers of all kinds. But the universal setting of the scene ("all angels," "all nations," "Last Judgment"), the absence of reference to sufferings experienced "in my name," the presence of universal sufferings of all humankind, the unconsciousness of the righteous that they had served the Lord (which they might have assumed if they had served the Lord's messengers, 10:41), and the ultimate judgments of eternal punishment or eternal life—all these tilt interpretation in a universal, worldwide direction. Jesus in his final sermon is talking about everyone and about how each person in every nation will be assessed at the Last Judgment.[11]

Ultimately, even if Matthew may have been thinking here in terms of members of the Christian community narrowly, it is likely that the wider implications of the passage, as Bruner suggests, are more universal in nature.

"You Did Not Do It to Me"

The tone of the narrative shifts dramatically in verses 41-43, when the king turns to the goats on his left and says, "You that are accursed, depart from me into the eternal fire prepared for the devil and his angels; for I was hungry and you gave me no food, I was thirsty and you gave me nothing to drink, I was a stranger and you did not welcome me, naked and you did not give me clothing, sick and in prison and you did not visit me." The king details the same situations in which "he" had been found, but in none of

---

11. Frederick Dale Bruner, *Matthew: A Commentary,* Volume 2: *The Churchbook, Matthew 13-28,* rev. and exp. ed. (Grand Rapids: Eerdmans, 2004), 574.

these cases did the goats respond. They provided no food when the king was hungry, offered no drink when he was thirsty, and so on. We should again emphasize the fact that the positive responses by the sheep were not so much heroic as they were appropriate: they simply did for others what was needed. By contrast, the goats' responses to the suffering of others were simply inappropriate. Real needs went unaddressed; the suffering continued to suffer. Note that the text does not attribute negative *motives* to the goats, as if the problem were with their attitudes; it doesn't even say that they ignored or shunned or otherwise mistreated the destitute and marginalized. The passage simply says that they did not meet the needs they encountered, but their omissions would have eternally negative implications.

It is worth noting that the goats are just as confused and surprised by the king's curse as the sheep were to receive the king's welcome. In verse 44, the goats protest: "Lord, when was it that we saw you hungry or thirsty or a stranger or naked or sick or in prison, and did not take care of you?" The sheep had not known that they were ministering to the king, and the goats did not know that they had failed to do so. How could the king now hold them accountable when they had not even known that they were over-looking the king's needs, not to mention that they had been unaware of the stakes involved? The wording of the goats' query highlights not only their nervousness in the face of the king's judgment but also their dismissiveness of "the least," whom they failed to help. Unlike the sheep, who expressed their confusion and surprise in a way that matched the king's careful and deliberate recitation of each situation and its response (e.g., "Lord, when was it that we saw you hungry, and gave you food?"), the goats respond with a laundry list, in a quick flurry of words ("hungry or thirsty or a stranger or naked") that demonstrates little interest in focusing carefully on each need, and on each person in need.

The king answers the goats, perhaps not surprisingly at this point, with the same explanation that he gave earlier to the sheep, albeit this time cast in a negative way: "Truly I tell you, just as you did not do it to one of the least of these, you did not do it to me" (v. 45). After a relatively lengthy drama punctuated with direct statements, questions, and responses be-tween the participants, the final verse of the passage is noteworthy in that it consists of a sweeping and yet almost understated summary by Jesus (or perhaps Matthew, as the narrator): "And these will go away into eternal punishment, but the righteous into eternal life" (v. 46). The conclusion to which the entire passage had been moving arrives: the conduct of the sheep and the goats has eternal consequences. The stakes could not have been higher.

The Sheep and the Goats: Reflecting on Beliefs and Surprise

As we explore the implications of this passage, it is crucial to note that the diverging fates of the sheep and the goats seem to have had little or nothing to do with what they believed. The text does not say that the sheep, for example, were to inherit the kingdom because of their orthodox theological perspectives, as if the question of their eternal situation were rooted primarily in one or more "theologically correct" propositional statements of faith. The king does not quiz either the sheep or the goats about whether they believed in him, or in the right things about him. Belief—at least in the sense of a propositional, theological statement that someone could affirm or reject—seems irrelevant in the case of the sheep and goats. What they believed was apparently not as important to the king as what they did with whatever beliefs they may have had. That is, the sheep apparently lived out the implications of whatever they believed, and so did the goats. Their specific beliefs remain implicit in the narrative. We can only infer what they may have believed based on what they ended up doing in their lives. The sheep and goats alike clearly showed what they believed about what was most important and needful in the way they lived. In effect, the actions of the sheep (and, by contrast, the inaction of the goats) spoke louder than any of their words, which seems to echo well what the New Testament document known as James says about the necessary relationship between faith and works (James 2:14-26). (See the discussion in chap. 12 below.)

In what ways may the Christian community today be fixated on the particulars of belief to the exclusion of how such beliefs are enacted and embodied in a needy world? Christian history is, of course, replete with examples of how beliefs have been used as weapons or wedges, rather than as the inspiration for faithful, compassionate, merciful action. What would the king have to say to us today? Are we so consumed by what we or others believe that we fail to act for those who suffer? Or, to put matters another way, does our inaction in this world of pain and marginalization highlight what is, in fact, our unbelief? James will remind us that "the demons believe—and shudder." If the demons can believe and, at the same time, directly oppose God, then belief is presumably not the singular thing that we tend to make it. Belief divorced from appropriate conduct is worthless, according to James—and apparently in Matthew 25:31-46 as well. Perhaps it is we who should shudder.

The sheep were surprised that they *had* addressed the king's needs, and the goats were surprised that they *hadn't* done so; this aspect of the narrative merits thoughtful reflection by those of us who read it today. The sheep did what was necessary for those who were suffering, and yet they were unaware that they were doing anything for the king. Neither were they aware that, in effect, they had been encountering the king in their interactions with those for whom they provided care ("you did it to me," v. 40). What is striking here is that the sheep's surprise and righteous behavior suggest that they were merely doing what they knew needed to be done; people needed help, and they simply provided it. It appears that the sheep were not calculatedly seeking a reward, nor were they spending their energies debating about whether the marginalized and destitute were worthy recipients for aid. The sheep simply stepped up. In that sense, their conduct was not especially radical in itself: the things they did were relatively unremarkable things to do—feeding, visiting, and providing care. What was radical was that the sheep actually *did* these simple things—simply because they were needed. How striking that showing straightforward kindness, mercy, and compassion so often seems radical to us.

Whatever their motivation, the sheep were operating within an economy of merciful service that contrasted sharply with what we as humans find to be normal, whether in the first century or today. The sheep had not calculated what they had to gain or what they had to lose. They did not evaluate the worthiness of those who needed help. They engaged in the needs of others despite any discomfort that might be involved for them. And they apparently did not expect or even anticipate anything in return. The sheep did not act from the perspective of typical economic exchanges or reciprocity. They were not concerned about questions of market efficiency or appropriate incentives. They responded to a need just because it was a need. If we let go of our quid-pro-quo economic reasoning, the behavior of the sheep seems quite logical and uncontroversial.

Why do we find this passage so striking, so challenging, so radical? Perhaps we, like the goats, have been formed more by values, priorities, and systems that encourage and "reward" calculated, reciprocal, self-interested conduct than we wish to admit. It is certainly easier not to get involved in suffering. But is responding concretely to fundamental human needs really all that radical? Why are so many readers surprised by Jesus's pronouncements in this passage?

The goats, for their part, were also surprised by what Jesus said. Everything the sheep *did*—serving the needy in specific, concrete ways—the goats *did not do*; and everything the sheep *did not do*—such as calculating the worthiness of the needy, considering possibilities for reciprocity, or evaluating potential personal costs of getting involved—those were the things the goats presumably *did*. The surprise the goats feel is particularly striking given that they seem to have been unaware that their inactivity with regard to the suffering was effectively an affront to the king. They are surprised that they missed the king in the form of the needy and, by extension, that they have been banished from the king's eternal realm. By implication, it would seem that the goats assumed they were actually living appropriately with respect to the king's expectations, and thus their surprise.

How might the Christian community today be similar to the goats? Perhaps we assume too readily that what we do is exactly what God wants. Is the mission we believe we are carrying out the mission of the now-enthroned king, or is it largely something of our own conception? Will we be surprised, like the goats, to find that we have not actually been tracking faithfully with God after all? These are the kinds of crucial questions—located, missional questions—that the church must ask in every age, which is to say, in whatever age the readers of Matthew 25:31-46 find themselves. What would the king say? Are we sheep or goats?

Much more could be said about this passage, but the foregoing discussion should suffice to suggest that the contemporary Christian community would do well to reflect thoughtfully and carefully on the missional implications of Matthew 25:31-46. While the specific actions of the sheep were not particularly radical, given that they merely attended to some real and basic needs, the passage suggests that the inaction on the part of the goats was, in fact, radical—radically disobedient—with eternal implications. What would need to change in our lives for us to be found radically obedient—like the sheep? The implication of the passage is that what the king demands is neither crazy nor radical. All that is required is simple, straightforward mercy and compassion, attending to real people with real needs, just as we would with those whom we love. Come to think of it, that is what Matthew 25:31-46 is calling for: fundamental and concrete love for all.

Concluding Reflections on Material from Matthew's Gospel

Matthew 5:1–7:29 and 25:31–46 merit renewed and extensive reflection within the contemporary North American Christian community. The Sermon on the Mount is rooted more concretely in economic matters than is typically recognized, and the account of the sheep and the goats provides a radical vision of what participating with Christ in God's kingdom economy looks like. Each of these texts has a crucial role to play in helping to transform our economic reasoning and behavior for the sake of the church's faithfulness to the mission of God into which it has been called and caught up.

There are, of course, other Matthean passages that incorporate economic imagery and are relevant for the renewing of our reasoning—even if such imagery most likely functions to address other matters. For example, in response to a question from Peter about forgiveness (Matt. 18:21–22), Jesus tells a parable that draws extensively, if hyperbolically, on ancient familiarity with indebtedness (18:23–35). Then, after a conversation with a "wealthy young man" who departed grieving instead of accepting the encouragement to "sell [his] possessions, and give the money to the poor" (Matt. 19:16–30; cf. Mark 10:17–31; Luke 18:18–30), Jesus declares that "many who are first will be last, and the last will be first" (19:30). Matthew immediately follows that account with a unique parable about vineyard workers who work different amounts of time but are paid the same wage. Jesus's only comment on the story is to reverse the components of his earlier statement (19:30): "So the last will be first, and the first will be last" (20:16). Some would also highlight Matthew 25:14–30, in which investment imagery plays a major role. Though much more could be said with regard to these three texts, space limitations permit me to note only how they underscore the difficulty for many of us of embracing and reasoning on the basis of a divine economy characterized by radical abundance and generosity, whether in terms of forgiveness (18:23–35), salvation (19:16–20:16), or even furthering the purposes of the master (25:14–30).

FOR FURTHER REFLECTION

▶ I have suggested that the Sermon on the Mount (Matthew 5–7) is appropriately understood as a speech by Jesus that calls his followers to participate in a renewed covenant with God. Does thinking about the Sermon in this way affect how you understand its contents?

▶ Jesus says: "Where your treasure is, there your heart will be also" (Matt. 6:21). Can you think of examples in which our hearts effectively end up "following" our treasures?

▶ Why does Jesus, in Matthew 6:24, place God and wealth in such sharp contrast?

▶ Are we enslaved to the wrong master? What does our tendency to worry and fixate on money matters say about who (or what) truly functions as our master?

▶ What would it look like to live more fully into the abundance of the kingdom?

▶ Would your economic reasoning and behavior change if you realized that in encountering "the least of these" you were also meeting Jesus?

▶ We have noted that the sheep simply responded directly and appropriately to the needs of those whom they had encountered. So why do most of us find the account of the sheep and goats to be so striking and challenging?

CHAPTER 11

Kingdom Reversals and Economic Reasoning in Luke

The Gospel of Luke is especially important for missional reflections on matters of economic justice and poverty. Throughout the narrative, Luke emphasizes the fact that the kingdom of God both represents and enacts a thoroughgoing reversal of the status quo. In the very first chapter, a young girl destined to be the mother of the messianic prophet Jesus praises the actions of God in phrases that would warm the hearts of many sociopolitical and economic revolutionaries: Mary declares that God "has brought down the powerful from their thrones and lifted up the lowly; he has filled the hungry with good things, and sent the rich away empty" (Luke 1:52-53). From that point on, the Gospel seldom relents, highlighting again and again how every form of human reckoning with regard to status, possessions, and wealth warrants reappraisal in light of God's values, concerns, and priorities. I have already highlighted in chapter 3 how Jesus's comments in Luke 4:14-30 and 6:17-26 fit within this larger narrative scheme; in this chapter I wish to explore a few Lukan texts that demonstrate the need for Jesus's followers to have their reasoning transformed, specifically with regard to economic phenomena. First, we turn to a famous passage in Luke 15.

The Parable of the Two Lost Sons and Their Father

Although it appears only in Luke's Gospel (15:11-32), the parable of the so-called "prodigal son" is one of Christianity's most beloved stories. It is the story of a lost young man who rejects his father—essentially telling him, "I wish you were dead"— before squandering his inheritance. His father, though, never loses hope that his younger son will return. When he realizes that his son is coming back, he forfeits all of his dignity by hiking up his tunic and running down the road to greet the wayward young man. Many have recognized that this is the story of the gospel in a nutshell: a loving father who actively seeks a restored relationship with the lost son, someone who never stops showing mercy to the undeserving. Yet this parable is typically known by an inadequate and somewhat ironic title. It is worth noting that Jesus did not call it the parable of the "prodigal son," nor does Luke. That now-common moniker refers, of course, to the younger son. It's true that the younger son *was* lost and then found. But the story does not end when the younger son is found. Indeed, the parable is as much, or more, about the older son than about the younger son.

The actual biblical parable concludes with a scene involving the older son, who despises his younger brother and grumbles about the attention their father is paying to him. Moreover, he *also* rejects the father, even as he claims that he has remained with him and has been loyal to him for all the years since his brother's disappearance. The older son will not come in to join the dinner party that his father is throwing to celebrate the return home of his formerly lost younger son. He balks at showing any welcome or hospitality at all to his brother or to his father's guests, which would have been the special role and task of the eldest son in that culture. The shame he heaps on his father at this moment rivals the shame the family has already suffered due to the younger son's prior behavior. The older son remains lost; indeed, *he* remains the truly prodigal son. How will he respond to his father's plea to welcome his brother? Will he change his mind and finally attend and host the party? The parable ends in an open-ended way, leaving readers to wonder whether the older son will remain lost.

A Response to Grumbling by the Pharisees and Scribes

When we refer to Luke 15:11–32 as the parable of the prodigal son, we have at least partially misunderstood Jesus's reasons for telling the story in the first place. At the beginning of Luke 15, before Jesus had even told this parable about the two lost brothers, Luke informs us that "all the tax collectors and sinners were coming near to listen to" Jesus (v. 1); he also tells us that "the Pharisees and the scribes were grumbling and saying, 'This fellow welcomes sinners and eats with them'" (v. 2). These religious leaders, with status, power, and privilege—obvious insiders within the Jewish community—were irritated by Jesus's hospitality toward outsiders, namely, tax collectors and others whose reputations made them seem worthy of derision and exclusion.

According to Luke, Jesus's oblique yet pointed response to the grumbling Pharisees and scribes was simply to tell "them this parable" (15:3). In fact, Luke then portrays Jesus telling not merely one but *three* parables: all three focus on the theme of things that were lost and then found. In the first parable (vv. 4-7), one sheep, out of a flock of a hundred, becomes lost, and then later is found. In response, the shepherd throws a party. In the second parable (vv. 8-10), a woman finds a coin she had lost, and she throws a party. The third parable (vv. 11-32) is about a young son who has lost his way—but who ultimately finds himself and returns home. Not surprisingly, his return leads to a party! Readers of this last parable are left—along with the grumbling Pharisees and scribes (15:1)—to ponder whether the elder lost brother will be found.

We will return to the story of the two sons and their father later in the chapter. In the meantime, we turn to another famous Lukan parable.

The Rich Man and Lazarus

Jesus's parable about an unnamed rich man and a poor man named Lazarus, which appears only in Luke's Gospel (16:19-31), is a text that portrays the eternal significance of the compassion and mercy that Christ calls his followers to exhibit in their missional engagement in and with the world at large. The imagery and implications of this parable are fascinating, even arresting, and it has been used for centuries by Christian leaders to illustrate the perils of indifference to the poor and the selfish use of wealth. On October 2, 1979, during his first papal visit to the United States, John Paul II preached from this text to 80,000 people in Yankee Stadium, calling attention to those in the contemporary world who, like Lazarus, have needs that continue to go unaddressed. The challenge was clear: Christians in the United States must be vigilantly aware of the temptation to ignore the Lazaruses in their midst and around the world.

What's in a Name?

There are many facets of this text that we could reflect on; the following paragraphs highlight but a few of its interesting exegetical characteristics and theological dynamics. First, Jesus introduces his hearers to an un-named "rich man." This nameless designation is interesting, especially since Jesus also introduces an extremely "poor man." Ironically, the destitute man has a name—Lazarus. It is noteworthy that such a poor man, who is ignored and shunned by most elements of society, would be named in Jesus's story. Today, most of us would simply refer to him as "a homeless guy"; few would bother to speak with him directly or inquire further about his identity.

As an alternative form of the Hebrew name Eleazar, Lazarus seems to mean "God helps," which is worth some reflection. Despite the fact that no one else seems to pay attention to him—least of all the rich man—Lazarus is known and helped *by God*. (This deep connection with God is highlighted in verse 23, where we find Lazarus "in the bosom of Abraham," cared for by the ancestor of God's own people.) As one who suffers and dies without assistance from those in his community who could, in fact, offer help, Lazarus represents the poor everyman. And yet the parable suggests that, no matter how other human beings treat the marginalized, oppressed, and destitute, *every* poor man and woman is known by name and helped by God. Such people are not forgotten or ignored in the divine realm, as is so often the case in the human realm. Lazarus is not nameless, nor faceless—not just anyone anymore. Lazarus is named. Lazarus is God's beloved.

Despite the fact that few people who were following Jesus around would have been of comparable economic standing, and thus it seems odd to describe the rich man in the parable as something of an "everyman" figure, he is ironically anonymous, nameless, and depersonalized. He serves as a generic stand-in for ungenerous wealthy elites. In the Roman Catholic tradition, the rich man in this parable has effectively become named: he is known as Dives, which is Latin for "rich." But even with this "name" designation, his generic and impersonal identity is simply something like "rich guy."

We must not miss the irony here. In our own time, just as in Jesus's world, we remember the names of the wealthy and powerful. But Jesus's parable turns that on its head. As we have already noted, the kingdom of God as portrayed in Luke's Gospel represents a complete reversal of the status quo. All traditional human expectations are thrown aside where God's values, assumptions, priorities, and will hold sway. This Lukan theme of reversal is seldom illustrated more poignantly than in this parable of the rich man and Lazarus: the rich man is the no-name placeholder, while the poor man is beloved, remembered, and cared for.

"Good Things" and "Evil Things"

Also noteworthy is the parable's description of "the rich man": though brief, it emphasizes his wealth and particularly the ostentatious character of his lifestyle. The rich man dressed himself in purple, the color of royalty, and in fine linen, which would have made it obvious to everyone that he was a man of significant means. The rich man wants to be noticed and flaunts his wealth. Moreover, he "celebrates" extravagantly—we might say that he parties—on a daily basis. The NRSV appropriately renders the Greek phrasing as "feasted sumptuously every day," particularly in light of the comment (in v. 21) that Lazarus "longed to satisfy himself with the crumbs [literally, 'the droppings'] from the rich man's table." Every day, the rich man ate so well that Lazarus could have satisfied his hunger simply by eating what accidentally ended up on the floor. Jesus has painted a stark picture of contrast: never-ending, lavish opulence in the face of glaring nutritional insufficiency and suffering.

Lazarus is in a bad state. Not only is he perpetually hungry, but he is also "covered in sores" (v. 20). Moreover, we are told that dogs, animals that were known as unclean (both literally and, for Jews, in a religious sense), "would come and lick his sores" (v. 21)—adding further insult to injury.

We should be honest with ourselves: the portrait of Lazarus in this parable is of a repulsive figure. Few of us would be drawn to engage such a person up close and personally. Perhaps his physical sores carried contagious infection. Prudence might well have convinced Jesus's contemporaries to steer clear of Lazarus. Perhaps we have encountered and avoided people like Lazarus in analogous circumstances in our own time.

Death and Beyond

The tone of the parable shifts dramatically in verse 22. In a disarmingly abrupt tone, Luke informs his readers that Lazarus and the rich man both died; but he describes their deaths in radically different ways. Lazarus, we're told, "died and was carried away by the angels to be with Abraham." Forgotten, ignored, and shunned during his life of constant suffering, he ends up—as his name implies—being "helped by God." The angels gather him up and take him into the loving embrace of his ancestor and father,

Abraham, which, as we discern in the rest of the parable, represents a heavenly and eternal afterlife of comfort and joy.

In stark contrast to his celebratory lifestyle, the rich man "died and was buried." He is placed unceremoniously in the ground, and his death is as unnoticed as was Lazarus's life. At this point in the narrative, we witness the supreme irony of his moniker, "rich man." How inconsequential now are his riches. In death, this unnamed character's "name" (i.e., rich guy) is rendered meaningless and brutally worthless. As the parable truly reminds us, you can't take it with you.

Immediately (v. 23), we find the formerly rich man "in Hades." Now being tormented, the man "looked up and saw Abraham far away with Lazarus by his side" (literally, "at his bosom"). Across the expanse, he appeals to his "Father Abraham," begging for mercy and requesting that Lazarus be sent to "dip the tip of his finger in water that he might cool my tongue, for I am in agony in these flames" (v. 24). Here, even in death and despite his suffering, we glimpse the deeply entrenched character of the "rich man": even in his current state he assumes that he maintains some status and superiority with respect to Lazarus, and that he may direct Lazarus's activity—as if the (formerly) poor man were his waiter or servant—even in the afterlife.

Notice that at no point in the parable does Lazarus actually speak. He is an entirely passive and mute character over whom even the dogs once had power. By contrast, the rich man never stops, even during his torment, viewing himself as one with privilege, power, and personal agency.

Reversal of the Status Quo

It is worth reflecting on the fact that this parable shows no interest in what Lazarus or the rich man believed, religiously or theologically, during their mortal lives. What they may have 'believed' about God, for example, does not seem relevant to the story. So why did the rich man end up in Hades? Could he be faulted for keeping his distance from such an off-putting character as Lazarus? Remember, the rich man had apparently been generous enough not to kick Lazarus away from his gate. What was his offense? A strong hint may appear in v. 24. The now-tormented, formerly rich man *knows Lazarus's name*. This small detail is actually of enormous significance: it suggests that the rich man had known Lazarus while they were both still alive, but that he had chosen to ignore him. The implication is that the rich man is being held accountable in death for not paying attention to Lazarus and his needs while they were both alive. The rich man is now suffering not simply because he committed a particular sin, but more precisely because he failed to respond to a need when it was presented to him. His guilt concerns an act of omission rather than one of commission. During his life, the rich man had enjoyed his privilege, power, and personal agency, but he had not made use of any of that for Lazarus's benefit. Rather than exploiting his ample means in order to provide a tangible Abrahamic embrace for his Jewish brother, Lazarus, the rich man ignored him completely. And the consequences could not have been more horrific and all-encompassing.

Why, though, was Lazarus rewarded? Had he done something to merit God's favor? In truth, the parable does not tell us anything specific. The implication is that (again, as his name suggests) Lazarus was cared for and helped by God, not because he believed or did anything in particular, but rather because, unlike the rich man, God is a God of mercy and compassion.

The rich man had daily opportunities to show mercy to Lazarus, but he neglected to do so. And when he cried out for Abraham's mercy (v. 24), he discovered that it was too late. Indeed, Abraham indicates that even as the father of God's people, his hands are effectively tied. Given the chasm between Abraham's embrace and Hades, there can be no movement or interaction between Lazarus and the rich man. Again, we find a deep irony here. While a mere gate separated the two during their lifetimes, it might as well have been a cosmic chasm for all the good it did Lazarus. The rich man did not have any interest in crossing over to Lazarus in those days. Now, in death, all he wants is to have Lazarus come to him. But alas, even if Lazarus were willing to do so, he cannot.

We need not interpret this passage as if it presents a literal description of the afterlife. The parable is just that—a parable. It does not intend to provide an exact description of how salvation and judgment are related geographically, or precisely what suffering in the afterlife is like. The parable paints a picture and seeks to illustrate how crucial our choices in life really are.

Despite the fact that the formerly rich man remains Abraham's descendant, the reversal of the status quo that we expect to see in Luke's portrayal of the reign of God is complete: "Child, remember that during your lifetime you received your good things, and Lazarus in like manner evil things; but now he is comforted here, and you are in agony" (v. 25). What the rich man had in life, Lazarus now has in death; and Lazarus's suffering in life is mirrored by the rich man's situation in death.

The words of John the Baptist as he preached to those coming for baptism (Luke 3:8) are poignant in this regard: "Bear fruits worthy of repentance. Do not begin to say to yourselves, 'We have Abraham as our ancestor'; for I tell you, God is able from these stones to raise up children to Abraham." It is not enough that the rich man is a child of Abraham, as wonderful as that status may be. By failing to bear the kind of fruit expected from those of such lineage, the rich man in Jesus's parable has effectively rendered his Abrahamic family ties moot.

Realizing that his own situation is beyond redemption, the rich guy does something centered on someone other than himself for the first time in the parable. Continuing to appeal to his relationship with Abraham, he asks that help be provided for his brothers—in the form of a warning: "Then, father, I beg you to send [Lazarus] to my father's house—for I have five brothers—that he may warn them, so that they will not also come into this place of torment" (vv. 27-28). The desperate, formerly rich man turns to consider his family members, now that he is aware, in light of his own fate, that their conduct will eventually bring them to the same eternal suffering. Once again, he assumes that Lazarus should be sent to do his bidding, but Abraham quickly rejects that idea, reminding him that his brothers already have all of the information they need to make appropriate choices in life: "They have Moses and the prophets; they should listen to them" (v. 29). There is nothing mysterious here, says Abraham. Scripture makes amply clear what it looks like to live authentically and obediently before God as Abraham's children, as children of the covenant. Just as God cares for the widow, the orphan, and the alien, so God's people are to embody the same care for the forgotten, abused, and marginalized. The rich man's brothers don't need a visit from Lazarus's ghost in order to know what kind of lives they are to lead in the midst of human suffering, poverty, and pain. They have the scriptures already, Abraham says, and they should pay attention to them.

Perhaps not surprisingly, given his consistent temerity up to this point in the story, the rich man has one final objection to offer: this time he essentially tells Father Abraham that he is wrong. He insists that his brothers will repent and change their ways "if someone goes to them from the dead" (v. 30). The rich man's brash persistence has no effect, however, as Abraham gets the last word: "If they do not listen to Moses and the prophets, neither will they be convinced even if someone rises from the dead" (v. 31).

The parable thus concludes with an unmistakable foreshadowing of Jesus's eventual resurrection.

In effect, Abraham is telling the rich man—and indeed those in the contemporary world who know that Jesus has risen from the dead—that the message of the Hebrew Scriptures ("Moses and the prophets") closely coheres with the message delivered by the now-risen Jesus. What Abraham's children need to know in order to keep from ending up like the rich man is already contained in the Torah and the prophets. They do not need to see anyone rise from the dead to be convinced; if the scriptures do not convince them, nothing else will. Luke may be implicitly critiquing those in the Jewish community of his day who have rejected the risen Jesus, but his message here also implicates, from a different direction, those in the Christian community. Those who claim belief in the risen Jesus must recognize that the Messiah's message about covenantal mercy and justice, and the reversals entailed in God's in-breaking kingdom (e.g., Luke 4:18-21; 6:17-26), are already amply articulated in the scriptures of the people of Abraham. The rich man and his brothers may have been oblivious, but they had already been warned. The same is true for those of us who read this parable today.

For the Christian community, the point of the parable seems sufficiently clear: God is to be found with the poor and suffering, and unlike the rich man, we are to be found there—with those for whom God's heart aches. As for the rich man, so for us: being part of God's people does not mean much if we do not bear fruit worthy of true repentance, mercy, compassion, and justice. May we not be like the rich man whenever, wherever, and however we encounter "Lazarus" today. Rather, may we be God's hands and feet, participating in the help God seeks to provide through us in the life of every Lazarus, the ones whom "God helps." May we thus be found playing an active and eager role in the grand reversal of the status quo that the reign of God represents.

Zacchaeus, the Tax Collector

I have noted earlier that Luke 15 begins with the tax collectors and sinners coming near to see Jesus; meanwhile, the Pharisees and scribes grumbled because Jesus had a habit of not only welcoming those people, but even worse, eating with them. Indeed, earlier in Luke's Gospel, Jesus indicates that some had called him "a glutton and a drunkard, a friend of tax collectors and sinners"! Obviously, there are two ways to get a reputation for being a glutton and a drunkard: either eat and drink too much, or associate with those who do. Either way, Jesus had a reputation for being friends with the wrong people. What a scandal! The religious elites could not tolerate that Jesus partied with such outsiders and, in addition, seemed to enjoy their company.

The Literary Context: Things Lost and Found

In relating the three parables about things lost and found (15:3–32), Jesus indicates that the grumbling scribes and Pharisees—symbolized by the older son in the story of the two lost sons—were really as much or more lost than the tax collectors and sinners were. We see similar concerns in the account of Zacchaeus (Luke 19:1–10), a guy whose story resonates in a number of ways with the account of the two prodigal sons.

Just like the tax collectors and sinners in 15:1, Zacchaeus wants to *see* Jesus. And just as the scribes and Pharisees had grumbled against the tax collectors and sinners, they now grumble against Zacchaeus. Luke portrays these religious elites as being concerned with status, power, and privilege. Who should be considered an insider? Who are the outsiders? Who deserves to be welcomed? Who merits respect?

Getting to Know Zacchaeus

Let us consider Zacchaeus. What is his status? In short, it's a mixed bag: on the one hand, he is a chief tax collector—and he is rich. Therefore, professionally and economically speaking, Zacchaeus has attained quite a high status. But socially, religiously, and in terms of his personal stature, he has a very low status: not only is Zacchaeus a despised tax collector, but he is noteworthy for being a short one. Zacchaeus's connections within the taxation system of the Roman Empire make him an important figure, something of an insider. His wealth may well have come from his willingness and ability to exploit and take advantage of his own people through taxation. By colluding with the Romans, a foreign occupational force, Zacchaeus has helped fleece his fellow Jews.

Everything that makes Zacchaeus important and privileged also leads his Jewish community to regard him as an outsider—a sinner worthy of exclusion. Zacchaeus would have been shunned by his fellow Jews, leaders and laity alike, who would have considered him a sellout to the Romans—the worst of the worst. His status as a despised outsider is rooted in his own behavior, and it is seemingly well deserved. When we first encounter Zacchaeus, he wants to see Jesus. But comically, he is so short that in order to see him, he needs to run ahead and climb a sycamore tree like a little child. Neither running nor climbing trees was particularly dignified for grown Jewish men.

Zacchaeus actively seeks Jesus with the enthusiasm of a little kid. It is noteworthy that in Luke 18:16-17, Jesus had said, "Let the little children come to me . . . for it is to such as these that the kingdom of God belongs . . . . Whoever does not receive the kingdom of God as a little child will never enter it." Seeking Jesus with childlike enthusiasm may well be the one thing that this reviled insider-outsider has going for him.

A Necessary Invitation

As the story of Zacchaeus (Luke 19:1-10) begins, Jesus is "passing through" Jericho, continuing a lengthy journey toward Jerusalem that was initiated back in Luke 9:51. It is worth noting that, despite merely passing through Jericho, Jesus seems to make a beeline for the diminutive tax collector. He looks up into the tree and tells Zacchaeus to hurry down. In fact, Jesus says that it is *necessary* for him to stay at Zacchaeus's home today (v. 5): he *must* stay with him. (The Greek verb used here indicates that this is a God-ordained meeting.) According to Luke, it is quite literally a matter of divine necessity for Jesus to come to the tax collector's house. While many first-century Jews would have excluded and avoided tax collectors, Jesus initiates an invitation to stay at Zacchaeus's home; in effect, he invites himself over. From Luke's perspective, this visit is an integral part of Jesus's mission of salvation. It is as necessary that Jesus stay with Zacchaeus as it is that the latter change his ways.

Zacchaeus immediately clambers down the tree. He is ready for this invitation—to *his own house*—and he responds right away, welcoming Jesus and rejoicing (v. 6). Remember that the finding of the lost sheep, coin, and son were the occasions for parties in Luke 15. Zacchaeus now eagerly throws a dinner party when Jesus finds *him*.

More Grumbling As Another Lost One Is Found

Luke reports that everyone grumbled when they saw Jesus interacting with Zacchaeus (v. 7). The evangelist uses the same word for grumbling here that he used at the beginning of chapter 15 to describe the scribes and Pharisees. Now everyone gripes and gossips about how Jesus is partying with Zacchaeus, a tax collector and a sinner. Everyone is intent on excluding the latter, even though, as a Jewish descendant of Abraham, Zacchaeus is really their own brother.

Was Zacchaeus, then, lost prior to his encounter with Jesus? In short, yes. Luke's narrative suggests that the theme of being "lost" initiated in chapter 15 continues through the story of Zacchaeus. Several passages in Luke 15–19 arguably highlight lost characters. Following the parables about the lost sheep (15:4-7), the lost coin (15:8-10), and the two lost brothers (15:11-32), Luke goes on to tell of a lost manager (16:1-9); lost Pharisees (16:14-16); a lost rich man (16:19-31); nine lost former lepers (17:11-19); a lost judge (18:1-8); a self-righteously lost Pharisee (18:9-14); lost disciples (18:15-17, 31-34); a lost ruler (18:18-25); lost crowds (18:35-39); and, finally, a lost chief tax collector of short stature (19:1-10).

It is striking that the first three examples of things lost—the sheep, the coin, and the younger son—end up being "found." Subsequently, though, *none* of the lost persons—from the older son (15:25-32) to the crowds (18:35-39)—is definitively found. In Luke's narrative, Zacchaeus is noteworthy for being the first formerly lost person to be found since the lost younger son in chapter 15. Indeed, Jesus's closing statement to Zacchaeus demonstrates as much: he declares that "the Son of Man came to seek out and to save the lost" (19:10). Luke's narrative artistry is on full display here: parallel grumblings (in chap. 15, by scribes and Pharisees and the older son; in chap. 19, by "all") as well as parallel findings of what was formerly lost (in chap. 15, a sheep, a coin, and a younger son; in chap. 19, Zacchaeus) create a theologically rich narrative echo, what scholars call an "inclusion."

How is Zacchaeus found? Luke seems to suggest that Zacchaeus participated actively in the process. Both he and Jesus were seeking each other. Zacchaeus, acting like a child, eagerly awaited his chance to see Jesus (19:3-4). Ultimately, Jesus—on a mission as the Son of Man "to seek out and to save the lost"—*found* the childlike Zacchaeus in a sycamore tree (19:5). Zacchaeus's reaction to being found by Jesus is as eager and enthusiastic as his initial effort to see Jesus had been. In the face of widespread grumbling, Zacchaeus enthusiastically declares that he will give half of his wealth to the poor and four times more if he has defrauded anyone (v. 8). In response (v. 9), Jesus announces that "salvation has come to [his] house!"

Zacchaeus has been found! He is liberated. He belongs. The publicly derided outsider is now, in kingdom terms, an insider. Zacchaeus has truly become what he is—a son of Abraham, a member of God's family. Notice how different Jesus's analysis of Zacchaeus's situation was from the crowd's perspective. Those grumbling saw themselves as insiders and Zacchaeus as an outsider. But from Jesus's perspective, the situation is reversed. Ironically, the ones who exclude the outsider end up making themselves outsiders!

"Then Who Can Be Saved?"

At this point, attentive readers may want to say, "Wait a minute!" In Luke 18, shortly before the account of Zacchaeus, Luke describes "a certain ruler" (v. 18) whom Jesus encourages to "sell all that [he] owns and distribute the money to the poor" (v. 22; cf. Mark 10:17-31, treated in chap. 9 above). According to Luke, the ruler "became sad" because "he was very rich" (v. 23). Jesus responds to this incident by saying that it would be "easier for a camel to go through the eye of a needle than for someone who is rich to enter the kingdom of God" (v. 25). The disciples were incredulous and asked: "Then who can be saved?" Jesus acknowledges the impossibility of salvation but observes that "what is impossible for mortals is possible for God" (vv. 26-27).

Why, readers may understandably ask, was the ruler in Luke 18 required to sell everything he owned, when Zacchaeus did not renounce everything and nevertheless experienced salvation? And further, what are the implications of these two stories for contemporary Christians? Does the story of the ruler indicate that we must divest ourselves of everything? Or may Jesus's followers retain a portion of possessions and wealth, as the story of Zacchaeus suggests?

Remember that Jesus makes some fairly radical comments in Luke's Gospel about matters of wealth and status. For example, in his so-called Sermon on the Plain (6:17-49), while blessing the poor and hungry, Jesus levels prophetic "woes"—in effect, curses—against the rich and satisfied: "Woe to you who are rich." "Woe to you who are full now" (vv. 24-25). Jesus once told a parable to warn against greed, insisting that no people would keep their possessions after death (12:13-21). Later, Jesus said, "When you give a luncheon or a dinner, do not invite your friends or your brothers or your relatives or rich neighbors . . . . But when you give a banquet, invite the poor, the crippled, the lame, and the blind" (14:12-13). Jesus also declared that "No slave can serve two masters . . . . You cannot serve God and wealth" (16:13). And, as we have already explored, he told a vivid parable about the rich man who suffers for eternity in Hades because he ignored the plight of Lazarus in this life (16:19-31).

So, again, what is Luke's perspective regarding the appropriateness of wealth, possessions, power, and status in the lives of Jesus's followers? Is everything to be renounced? Or is partial divestment sufficient, as it seems to have been in the case of Zacchaeus?

The truth is that Luke's Gospel does not seem to provide a simple answer. Zacchaeus's situation is not unique. Luke tells, for example, of "many" women "who provided for [Jesus and the disciples] out of their resources" (8:3); likewise, in Acts, Luke describes generous individuals who apparently did not entirely divest themselves of their wealth (e.g., 4:36-37). From Luke's perspective, then, there does not appear to be an easy, one-size-fits-all approach to wealth and possessions.[1] Come to think of it, a simple, straightforward policy may have been what the sad ruler in Luke 18 was seeking. He wanted Jesus to tell him what he needed to "do to inherit eternal life," undoubtedly hoping for a response from the "good teacher" (v. 18) that would allow him to keep the comfortable lifestyle to which he had become accustomed.

According to Luke, Jesus provided a three-point plan that was as straightforward as it was simple: first, "sell" everything; second, "distribute the money to the poor"; and third, "follow me" (Luke 18:22). This plan required nothing mystical or mysterious, nothing particularly confusing or ambiguous. For the ruler, there could be no doubt regarding the next steps. Jesus had given him a clear roadmap to eternal life. Ironically, though, the man found this simple and straightforward plan impossibly difficult (see vv. 24-25). He stood there, consumed by sadness, pondering Jesus's words. Why did Jesus indicate that the ruler needed to do something that he did not end up requiring of Zacchaeus? And why did the ruler become so sad, finding Jesus's guidance so impossible to follow?

---

1. See, e.g., John T. Carroll, *Luke: A Commentary* (Louisville: Westminster John Knox, 2012), 374-77.

Lacking a Vision of Abundance

It appears that the ruler was looking out for himself. In his reaction to Jesus's comments, he was, like many of us, thinking individualistically—about Number One. Remember how Jesus had responded when the ruler asked what he needed to do in order to inherit eternal life: "There is still one thing lacking. Sell all that you own and distribute the money to the poor, and you will have treasure in heaven; then come, follow me" (v. 22). The ruler became sad because he realized that in following Jesus he would lose something. He would have to surrender his fortune. In short, he was thinking in terms of scarcity. He was fixated on what he would lose if he gave up his wealth.

Ironically, Jesus said that the ruler "lacked" something *with* all of his wealth (v. 22). What he lacked was a vision of abundance, and by implication, generosity. Notice that Jesus had encouraged him not merely to get rid of his wealth as such, but rather to give his resources for the sake of the common good, for the benefit of the poor. The ruler's sadness reveals that the plight of the poor was not, for him, a high priority. Although he had the power to do good for others by sharing, he cared mostly about himself. He knew how to "store up treasures" for himself, but he was "not rich toward God" (see 12:21).

"If I give something up," he thought, "I lose." That is also how we tend to think. Indeed, contemporary economic reasoning is rooted in the notion that resources are scarce, and that self-interested competition for those resources is both natural and necessary. We perform cost-benefit analyses dozens of times per day, seeking to maximize time, pleasure, and resources. We are as used to thinking about what we might lose as what we might gain. Like us, the ruler was sad because he was unsure whether the cost of loss was worth the benefit of potential gain.

By contrast, when Zacchaeus encounters the real ruler, the Lord, he suddenly *sees* something radically new. He sees and begins to reason not in terms of scarcity, but in terms of abundance. He realizes that he is part of a larger community, and that he can choose to behave differently than he has. Instead of cheating and extorting the community around him, Zacchaeus can show hospitality and generosity toward them. He can stop calculating in cost-benefit terms, and assessing every moment what he, personally, may lose or gain. When he encounters Jesus, Zacchaeus gains a new imagination—a kingdom imagination. This is exactly what happens when, in the book of Acts, the earliest apostles start sharing everything because the Spirit of God is in their midst (see Acts 2:43-47; 4:32-37; see also my treatment of these texts in chap. 12 below).

Zacchaeus suddenly sees life, for the first time, not in terms of scarcity, but rather in terms of the radical abundance that characterized the Garden of Eden at creation. When he is *found* by Jesus, he realizes that he does not have to choose to see life in terms of his possessions, or in terms of what he might lose. He can live with a new kingdom vision, one characterized by generosity, one in which repentance bears real fruit (v. 8), and in which formerly broken relationships (e.g., with those he cheated) can be restored.

Zacchaeus eagerly sought Jesus. And he really saw him. In so doing, Zacchaeus was transformed; indeed, his very imagination was transformed. Abundance suddenly replaced scarcity as the rubric of his life. Zacchaeus was liberated from self-interest, greed, and fear, freed to live in restored relationships with God and neighbor (cf. 12:22-34). Truly, liberation and salvation came to Zacchaeus's house the day that Jesus found him. In the end, Zacchaeus experienced the miracle of what God can do with what is impossible for humans. He discovered that, with God, camels actually can go through the eyes of needles (18:24-27).

Concluding Reflections

Let us return briefly to the so-called parable of the prodigal son. While the older brother refuses to go in to the party in honor of his brother's return (15:28), there is an open-ended quality to the parable: it ends with the father earnestly articulating to his elder son why it is necessary to have a party. Readers are left to ponder: Was the father able to convince him to change his mind? Will the older son remain lost, or will he, in effect, be found?

It is also fascinating to note that Luke's account of the rich ruler (18:18-30) differs curiously from Matthew's (19:16-30) and Mark's (10:17-31) versions of the same story. In those two Gospels, the rich young man *leaves sadly* when Jesus instructs him to sell his possessions and to give the proceeds to the poor. In Luke's story, however, the man *remains* with Jesus; he is deeply sad, but he does not depart (18:23). As in the case of the lost older brother (Luke 15), readers are left to ponder the ruler's future. What does he do next? Presumably, as in Matthew and Mark, he departs. But Luke does not say so explicitly. In fact, while the rich ruler may be sad, he still has a chance to choose to reason and behave on the basis of abundance rather than scarcity. The outsider could choose to become an insider. Luke leaves the story unfinished, encouraging us to imagine that the rich man's sadness could still turn to joy.

We see that joy in the story of Zacchaeus. Unlike the older brother and the rich ruler, Zacchaeus chooses to change. He reverses course. He opens himself up to the abundance of the kingdom rather than staying self-protected against what he might lose. And his choice to reason in terms of abundance and generosity promises to bear fruit for others.

Luke leaves readers to ponder how lost characters—the older son and the rich ruler, in particular—might still be found. And in the story of Zacchaeus, he shows us what being found by Jesus looks like. Will we, like the scribes and Pharisees, choose to grumble and to remain lost, or will we choose to seek Jesus with the childlike eagerness and enthusiasm of Zacchaeus? Like the chief tax collector—the despised sinner—we, too, can have our imaginations and our reasoning transformed. We can choose to live in terms of abundance and generosity toward others, in true community, rather than continuing to reason in terms of what we might lack. In so doing, we will join Jesus in rejoicing with seeming outsiders, instead of renouncing our own insider status by grumbling about the status of others. Luke's Gospel encourages his readers to party with Jesus and the outsiders with whom he is so regularly found, surrendering to abundance and generosity. As the story of Zacchaeus suggests, abundant salvation—our own salvation—is at hand!

FOR FURTHER REFLECTION

▶ One of the primary themes in Luke's Gospel is the idea that the in-breaking kingdom of God entails reversals of the status quo. Where do you see examples of such reversals in Luke?

▶ How do images of the "lost" and "found" in the stories discussed in this chapter function to transform the readers of Luke's Gospel?

▶ How, if at all, has your understanding of the story in Luke 15:11-32 (i.e., the so-called parable of the prodigal son) changed after reading this chapter?

▶ Are there ways in which we, like the rich man (Luke 16:19-31), may be guilty of serious sins of omission?

▶ I have suggested that Zacchaeus's life was transformed when, in socializing with Jesus, he suddenly began to see the reality of the world in terms of the abundance of the kingdom of God. What would happen in your life and in your community of faith if your reasoning—economically and otherwise—were to be transformed as Zacchaeus's was?

▶ In various places in Luke's Gospel, religious "insiders" grumble about Jesus's interactions with "outsiders." Are there contexts in which contemporary Christians also participate in such grumbling?

▶ In what ways do the Lukan stories examined in this chapter function to transform the economic reasoning and behavior of God's people for faithful participation in the larger mission of God in the world?

▶ Sometimes Luke leaves the ending of a story ambiguous and unresolved (see, e.g., the older brother in 15:25-32 and the rich ruler in 18:18-30). Readers are left to wonder how things played out beyond Luke's narrative. How will your own story of potential transformation end?

CHAPTER 12

Economic Reasoning and Faith
in the Context of Divine Abundance

In this chapter I will briefly examine four more passages that are especially relevant as we reflect on the church's mission with respect to matters of economic justice. Other New Testament texts could be highlighted, of course, but space limitations necessitate that we restrict our reflections to a few representative texts. We will pay attention to Acts 2:43-47; Acts 4:32-37; 2 Corinthians 8-9; and James 2.

"All Things in Common":
Unity and Covenantal Abundance in Acts

In Acts 2:43-47, we find a remarkable description of the earliest Christian community and its economic behavior. Luke describes a remarkably dynamic and generous ethos within the believing community, in which more than three thousand people remained together, holding "all things in common" (v. 44) and selling what they owned and distributing "the proceeds to all, as any had need" (v. 45). Acts 4:32-37 also testifies to the community's collective and charitable behavior. Unity among the believers was a matter of paramount importance in those early days. Although these passages presuppose the legitimacy of private ownership and property rights, Luke indicates that the needs of those in the community took precedence over personal prerogative. Individual and communal need trumped every other economic rationale or calculus. The presence of God's Spirit in the midst of the community seems to have inspired generosity, compassion, and other-centered goodwill. No coercion was involved, and Luke does not suggest the need for incentives in order to foster such a remarkable gift-sharing economy among the early followers of Christ.

"Not a Needy Person among Them"

Attentive readers may recognize the resonance between Acts 4:34 and Deuteronomy 15:4 in the claim that "there was not a needy person among them." Luke seems to view the community's conduct as a demonstration of the kind of covenantal obedience required in Deuteronomy 15:4-5, understanding the absence of need among the believers as an indication of the faithfulness of the new covenant community now gathered in the Spirit and focused on the risen Jesus. As we have already seen in chapter 6, Deuteronomy 15 predicated its assurance that there would be no needy people in Israel on covenantal obedience: "There will . . . be no one in need among you, because the LORD is sure to bless you in the land that the LORD your God is giving you as a possession to occupy, *if only* you will obey the LORD your God by diligently observing this entire commandment that I command you today" (vv. 4-5).

The absence of needy people among the earliest believers apparently indicated to Luke that the promise of Deuteronomy 15:4-5, previously unfulfilled, was not only possible but was now coming to pass. Moreover, given that Jesus had been raised by God to reign as Lord, and the believers' economic needs were being met internally through Spirit-inspired communal generosity, the assurance of Deuteronomy 15:6 must have sounded more realistic than it would have during Israel's tumultuous history: "When the LORD your God has blessed you, as he promised you, you will lend to many nations, but you will not borrow; you will rule over many nations, but they will not rule over you." The community was now experiencing, in Scripture-fulfilling ways, God's blessing. They would have little need to borrow from outsiders, given that they were pooling their resources, and they knew that their master (rather than any other human ruler) was indeed in charge.

Luke's narrative suggests that the earliest believers were practicing the kind of economic relations that Deuteronomy 15:6-11 demanded of the covenant community: they were ready to "open [their] hand[s], willingly lending enough to meet the need." In fact, it seems that they went beyond Deuteronomy 15 with regard to lending and debt remission: they did not merely lend their money or possessions to the needy, but they actually pooled whatever resources they had—so that, in effect, the "haves" had no more than did the "have-nots"—and the "have nots" were now as much "haves" as any other members of the community. Although there would always be poor people "on the earth," according to Deuteronomy 15:11, Luke suggests that the early Christians concretely obeyed that verse's command to "open your hand to the poor and needy neighbor in your land." Indeed, given how they were choosing to conduct themselves, no one within their community was, in fact, needy (see 15:4). The early Christians were tangibly putting Deuteronomy 15 into action.

The community's economic behavior reflects a strikingly collaborative approach to addressing human needs—again, without any form of coercion. The community of believers, in the presence and power of the Holy Spirit, seem spontaneously to have developed a creative and countercultural economic model: the needs of individuals and the health of the collective group took precedence over private ownership or personal prerogative. They sold their possessions—including, according to Luke, both "lands" and "houses," and "brought the proceeds of what was sold" to the apostles for redistribution (Acts 4:34–35).

In contemporary North American discourse, resource and wealth redistribution is often viewed with suspicion, perhaps primarily because it regularly requires some form of coercion (e.g., taxation). In the Spirit-infused context of the earliest Christian community, voluntary redistribution within the community—for the good of the entire community—seems to have been understood as a reasonable and commonsense phenomenon, something that grew out of the love and grace experienced and shared by the group. Every member of the community, as an intrinsically valuable human being and follower of the risen Jesus, mattered within the group as a whole. As a logical implication, the burgeoning community quickly began to engage in economic conduct that met any financial needs that arose, without coercion.

The contrast between this model and the kinds of economic reasoning and behavior with which most of us are familiar today is stark. *Need*—rather than wealth, talent, effort, status, moral desert, or any other characteristic or mode of economic calculus—became the criterion that drove the allocation of the early Christian community's resources. The health of the community, individually and as a whole, trumped personal autonomy, desire, prerogative, and ambition. For those of us who live in a context brimming with the influence of libertarian individualism, Luke's description of the early Christian community appears quite foreign indeed.

An Idealized Image of Christian Community?

It is important at this point to acknowledge that Luke's description of the early church in Acts 2:43–47 and 4:32–37 is often described, sometimes quite dismissively, as an overly idealized picture of the early Christian community. And there is some truth in that claim. The harrowing story of Ananias and Sapphira (Acts 5:1–11) demonstrates that complete unanimity of purpose and behavior eluded the community. And Luke's account of inequitable distribution of food among the widows of the Hebrews and Hellenists (Acts 6:1–6) indicates that the early communitarian ethos was not easy to maintain. Resources were not always distributed fairly and equitably, and the egalitarian behavior of the community was not necessarily sustained over the long haul.

Acts 2:43–47 and 4:32–37 are, in part, theologically driven descriptions of the community (e.g., in light of texts such as Deuteronomy 15:1–11). Those who view these passages in Acts as idealized pictures of the early Christian community are thus essentially correct. As a consequence, many contemporary believers find these passages to be functionally irrelevant as a guide to Christian conduct today, assuming that secular economic norms offer the only reasonable behavioral options—for Christians and non-Christians alike. But perhaps, rather than simply dismissing Acts 2:43–47 and 4:32–37 as idealized glosses on the actual historical record, readers should *embrace* the idealistic quality of Luke's descriptions. Indeed, that may be the point.

Perhaps, rather than bemoaning the idealized nature of Luke's descriptions, we should interpret his comments as statements of goal and purpose, as illustrations of what is indeed possible in authentic Christian communities. That is, these two passages may offer contemporary, missionally located Christian communities a vision of what communal and covenantal faithfulness looks like. What would happen if contemporary Christian communities were to begin to read these texts, not as idealized exaggerations of earliest Christian history, but as pointers to what the church is called and actually empowered to do and be through the Spirit of God?

Acts 2:43–47 and 4:32–37 may even be able to help us better understand Jesus's statements to his disciples following the departure of the rich man who could not give up his possessions (see Mark 10:17–31). After lamenting that it is "more difficult for a rich person to enter the kingdom of God than for a camel to pass through the eye of a needle," Jesus says that those who have given up possessions will reap even more in this age. Generally, readers in North America focus on what the story seems to say about how much they must renounce. In our individualistic and often privileged context, Jesus's promise in Mark 10:29-30 of a massive this-worldly return on his followers' kingdom investment (i.e., what they would forsake to follow Jesus) seems strange and unrealistic.

Acts 2:43-47 and 4:32-37 may well illustrate exactly what Jesus meant. By giving up their ownership of possessions to the larger community of disciples, the early Christians actually gained many more brothers and sisters and houses and fields than they would otherwise have had. Luke's accounts of the early believers' economic conduct may be idealized, but rather than dismiss them as pie-in-the-sky images without significant import for believers today, the Christian community in every age should embrace and seek to embody them as realistic and reasonable descriptions of what it *can* look like to live together in the power of the Spirit of God.

The Pauline Collection and the Corinthians

In general, Paul does not emphasize economic justice; but he does occasionally weigh in on such matters. For example, in Galatians 2:9-10, Paul notes that when James, Cephas (Peter), and John acknowledged his calling to the Gentiles, they urged him to "remember the poor," presumably referring to at least some of the Judeans in and around Jerusalem, since the area was experiencing severe agricultural and economic difficulties. Paul emphasized that he "was . . . eager to do" so. For him, providing support and care for the poor was an intrinsic facet of Jewish faith in the God who created and sustained everything.

In 1 Corinthians 11:17-22, the apostle castigates the community for allowing factions to develop in their midst, factions that appear to reflect economic and class distinctions: some of the Corinthian Christians, presumably those who were wealthy enough not to be involved in daily labor, gather early enough to eat and celebrate among themselves before other community members (from among the working and enslaved classes) are able to join them. Paul's disgust with such economic marginalization is readily evident in verses 20-22.

Note that, according to Paul, those meals—where attendance was divided largely along social and class lines—*could not* be considered celebrations of the Lord's Supper. It is not difficult to understand why. Paul sees such marginalization and divisions as evidence that these meals are not truly oriented toward the Lord; if they were, they would be marked by love and unity.

One of the primary ways in which Paul demonstrated his commitment to meeting the needs of the poor was through his lengthy project of collecting funds for the poor Jewish Christians in and around Jerusalem. While he doubtless did other things in his daily life and work to express his compassion for the marginalized and economically insecure (consider Gal. 6:2, 10), the large undertaking in which he sought to gather resources for the needy is noteworthy for the way in which Paul, through the collection, concretely linked his largely Gentile churches with the Jewish Christians in Judea. Paul describes the collection in a few places, such as 1 Corinthians 16:1-4, where he describes how the Corinthians should begin to gather funds for the contribution; in Romans 15:25-27, Paul refers to the participation in the collection of the churches of Macedonia and Achaia; and in 2 Corinthians 8-9, which we will explore briefly below, he offers both social and theological rationales for generosity among the Corinthians.

Paul's Appeal in 2 Corinthians 8-9

It is notoriously difficult to pin down exactly what took place—and when—following the time during which Paul wrote 1 Corinthians. Second Corinthians has some rather sharp changes of tone and subject that have led many, perhaps the majority, of scholars to conclude that it actually represents at least two—and perhaps several—letters written in response to different situations between Paul and the Corinthian Christians. Despite the uncertainty that surrounds 2 Corinthians, however, the social and theological reasoning Paul uses to urge Corinthian support for the collection is sufficiently clear for our purposes.

Paul opens his appeal in chapter 8 by describing the difficult situation facing the Macedonian Christians, who, despite "a severe ordeal of affliction" (2 Cor. 8:2), were remarkably generous in contributing to the collection for their spiritual brothers and sisters in Judea. Paul attributes this generosity to "the grace of God . . . granted" to them (v. 1), reporting that the Macedonians' "abundant joy and their extreme poverty . . . overflowed in a wealth of generosity on their part" (v. 2). It seems clear that the apostle's rhetorical strategy involves highlighting what happened in Macedonia as a means to goad the Corinthian Christians into exhibiting a similar kind of largesse. He emphasizes that those in Macedonia "voluntarily gave according to their means, and even beyond their means" (v. 3), and that apparently, unlike the Corinthian group, they pleaded with Paul and his colleagues "for the privilege of sharing in this ministry" (v. 4). It should be easy to see that the apostle is challenging the Corinthians by honoring their fellow Christians in Macedonia; in their first-century Mediterranean cultural context, which sees honor as a limited good, meaning that there is only so much to go around, Paul is threatening shame on the Corinthian Christians. The Macedonian situation is presumably more difficult than what his current readers are experiencing, and so there is no reason why the Corinthians cannot give. If the Macedonians gave "even beyond their means," the Corinthians should be able to give something—and not merely desire to do so.

Having made that comparative move, Paul then turns to a more positive (though no less rhetorically persuasive) approach: playing to the Corinthians' self-perception, Paul reminds them that, even "as [they] excel in everything—in faith, in speech, in knowledge, in utmost eagerness, and in our love for you"—he expects them "to excel also in this generous undertaking" (v. 7). Even here, there is a certain irony in the praise Paul offers. In 1 Corinthians 1:7, he had emphasized their spiritual giftedness, even though much of the letter itself suggests that they do not always "excel" in living out the implications of their faith and knowledge. Their eagerness is positive, and they do not lack love from Paul and his co-workers, but despite the apostle's kind words, they have not abounded in everything, particularly not in love (see, e.g., 1 Cor. 12–14).

Beginning in 2 Cor. 8:8, Paul assures the community that he is not ordering them to participate in the collection; at the same time, he continues to challenge them by comparing them to the Macedonians. The Corinthians would have undoubtedly wanted to maintain whatever honor and reputation they had with Paul and among the other Christian communities. The apostle's clarification that he was "testing the genuineness of [their] love against the earnestness of others" (v. 8) would have presumably carried significant rhetorical weight. In other words, Paul was not prepared to allow good Corinthian intentions to suffice; he wanted to see them follow through.

"You Know the Generous Act of Our Lord Jesus Christ"

Paul backs up his comparative arguments with a powerful and deeply theological rationale for the kind of Corinthian generosity he wants to see: the apostle reminds his readers of "the generous act of our Lord Jesus Christ, that though he was rich, yet for your sakes he became poor, so that by his poverty you might become rich" (v. 9). Paul does here what he does often in 1 Corinthians: he reframes the basis for Christian moral and behavioral reasoning in light of Christ's own conduct. When, for example, some of the Corinthian Christians argue that they are justified in eating meat that had been used in sacrificial rituals dedicated to other gods, Paul reframes the situation (1 Cor. 8:1–11:1). Whereas those Corinthians had emphasized their knowledge that such meat was fundamentally harmless, Paul—despite agreeing with them—counters that the self-giving love embodied by Christ, rather than knowledge, is the operative Christian criterion for conduct in such situations. The apostle had sought in that context to reorient the entire debate in light of Christ's own actions, and he again does something similar in 2 Corinthians 8:9.

In effect, Paul points out that Christ, who, as God's chosen one, effectively had access to and power over everything, gave up all of that in order that others might benefit. Jesus used his "riches" for the sake of others, allowing himself to "become poor," in order that others, including the Corinthian Christians, "might become rich." The obvious implication of this theological observation, of course, is that the community in Corinth has a similar—though, compared with Christ's experience, much less deadly—opportunity at hand. The generosity the Corinthians have the opportunity to demonstrate had already been modeled, for their own benefit, by the Lord they claim to serve. How could they not participate in something like the collection, given what Christ had done for them? Christ's example, including his willingness to give up everything for others, serves for Paul as the fundamental consideration in behavioral questions. In this case, Christ's obedience to God provides the appropriate and definitive lens through which to think about giving and generosity.

We should not miss the fact that Paul focuses on Jesus's death in order to reflect theologically on matters of economic import. Then, as now, opportunities for showing generosity typically involve some form of economic calculation: How much generosity is appropriate? When and to whom must we be generous? On what basis do we make such decisions?

Paul suggests that Christ's generosity knew no limits. Although the apostle does not therefore assume that the Corinthian Christians should give up everything for the Judean Christians (on the analogy of Christ giving up everything for others), it would seem that Paul is trying to press the Corinthian believers to reorient their reasoning. In 1 Corinthians, he tells the community to imitate Christ, who, like Paul, acted for the sake of others (10:31–11:1).[1] Doing so will not necessarily require giving up their lives. Rather, to imitate Christ is, at least in part, to reason as Christ reasoned, and then to act accordingly. Christ chose to act for the sake of others; Paul wants the Corinthians to act for the same reasons in this current situation.[2] As contemporary followers of Christ, we are to reason about any potential action in light of the needs and interests of others, not primarily on the basis of what we might lose, or how our own economic security might be affected.

Reasoning and Acting on the Basis of Abundance

Paul is seeking to form the Corinthians' moral reasoning so that they might operate on the basis of abundance rather than scarcity. Even the Macedonians believers, who were apparently mired in a deeper state of scarcity than the Corinthian Christians were, abounded in generosity. They focused not on what they lacked, but rather on what they *did* possess—and on what others might gain through their generosity. According to Paul, the Macedonians gave beyond what any seemingly rational calculus would have deemed reasonable or possible. Reasoning from the standpoint of abundance, their generosity overflowed. Ultimately, Paul urges his Corinthian readers to allow Christ's own approach to behavior to become their own, just as the Macedonians had done—everything for the sake of others.

1. On the missional significance of 1 Cor. 10:31–11:1, see Michael Barram, *Mission and Moral Reflection in Paul*, Studies in Biblical Literature 75 (New York: Peter Lang, 2006); Michael Barram, "The Bible, Mission, and Social Location: Toward a Missional Hermeneutic," *Interpretation* 43 (2007); and Michael Barram, "Pauline Mission as Salvific Intentionality: Fostering a Missional Consciousness in 1 Corinthians 9:19–23 and 10:31–11:1," in Trevor Burke and Brian S. Rosner, eds., *Paul as Missionary: Identity, Activity, Theology, and Practice*, Library of New Testament Studies (London; New York: T. & T. Clark International, 2011).

2. For a broader study of Paul's attempt to reorient Corinthian missional reasoning, see Michael Barram, "'Fools for the Sake of Christ': Missional Hermeneutics and Praxis in the Corinthian Correspondence," *Missiology: An International Review* 43 (2015): 195-207.

In 2 Corinthian 8:10-11, Paul explicitly gives his own advice to the Corinthian Christians, drawing out the obvious implications of what he has already written. He wants them to complete the process of the collection that they had begun eagerly "last year . . . according to [their] means." Again, Paul is not asking them to give up everything for the Judean Christians. But he does assume that they can give an appropriate gift in view of what they do have. In verse 12, Paul explains that the desire to give according to one's means makes a gift acceptable. In other words, acting on the desire is important, and the size of the gift does not, in itself, make it acceptable. Those with less can give generously even though the size of their gift may be smaller than one given by those of greater means.

Paul assures the Corinthians in verse 13 that his intention is not that others (e.g., the Macedonians) should have it easy while the Corinthians should be under pressure to provide large gifts. But at the same time, Paul tells them that this is a matter of "equality" (or, as the NRSV translates, "balance") between "your abundance" and their need or lack (v. 13). The purpose of this reasoning, according to Paul, is "so that their abundance may be for your need, in order that there may be a fair balance" (or "equality," v. 14).

Paul realizes that, while the Macedonians are currently worse off than the Corinthians are, economic situations can change. The Macedonians could one day be in the position of having an abundance that would allow them to make up for whatever the Corinthians might eventually lack. Paul has in view the idea that "balance," or "equality," should lead the two communities to levels of generosity that might, in view of their situations, differ in a given moment, but that would, on the whole, provide equity with regard to how they might serve others over the long haul. (In this sense, the NRSV's use of "fair balance" is probably an appropriate translation of the Greek term that might otherwise be rendered "equality.") Paul seeks to engender economic behavior that appropriately harnesses the means of each community, recognizing that those with greater abundance can and should contribute a larger gift. Ultimately, each community should contribute according to its means in such a way that they both share in meeting the overall need.

Paul concludes his primary theological argument in 2 Corinthians 8 by referring to the situation the Israelites faced in the wilderness when God provided them with manna to eat (v. 15). According to Exodus 16:17-18, everyone ended up with enough—neither too much nor too little. Manna seems to provide, for Paul, a theological metaphor of sufficiency rooted in the abundance of God's provision. As they were in the wilderness, the faith communities in Paul's day (and in our own) have every opportunity to trust in God's sufficient provision and to give generously in light of their means. Needs could be met when the faithful would come together in equitable ways to respond. Those with greater resources, according to Paul, have an opportunity—and ultimately a responsibility—to bear a larger portion of the need than those who have fewer resources at their disposal. The point is not to arrive at a strict mathematical level of equality between groups but to embody a reasonable and appropriate balance given the means available. The key concern, as Paul's reference to the book of Exodus suggests, is that all of this must be rooted in trust. God's provision of manna occurred daily; hoarding and saving was not allowed. The people had to learn in the gathering of manna to trust in divine provision for their current needs. The same basic orientation was necessary with regard to meeting the concrete needs of those in Judea. Chapter 8 closes with a recommendation of Titus, who would facilitate the collection among the Corinthians (vv. 16-24).

"So That It May Be Ready as a Voluntary Gift and Not as an Extortion"

The transition between 2 Corinthians 8 and 9 is a bit abrupt, and some scholars believe that the two chapters may reflect separate stages in Paul's Corinthian correspondence. Whatever the precise situation, the apostle encourages the Corinthians to bring the collection project to a close, particularly with an eye to assuring that neither he nor they will be shamed by a failure on their part to follow through, given the praise he has heaped on the Corinthians among the Macedonians (9:1-4).

In order to help bring the project to completion, Paul sends Christian "brothers" (apparently distinct from Titus's visit) to Corinth. No doubt, doing that would have had the effect of forcing the community's hand, pushing them to finalize the collection. In a rhetorically subtle but powerful way, Paul assures his readers that he is taking this step so that their "promised" contribution would "be ready as a voluntary gift and not as an extortion" (v. 5). In other words, the apostle is putting significant pressure on the Corinthians (in light of the possibility of "humiliation," v. 4), even as he is trying to remind them that they are the ones who have freely chosen to give a gift of their own accord. While the anticipated gift is indeed, in the strictest sense, voluntary, Paul's reminder of potential shame effectively serves as a form of rhetorical "extortion."

Abundance for the Purpose of Generosity

In 2 Corinthians 9:6-14, Paul articulates his primary concern, and he situates his previous comments (9:1-5) in their appropriate theological context. The Corinthian Christians can give freely because they have already received an abundance from God (v. 8). Once again, divine provision in the form of radical abundance serves as the framework for appropriate economic reasoning—in this context, with respect to generosity.

As the stories of the forbidden fruit in the Garden of Eden (Gen. 2) and the appearance of manna in the desert (Exod. 16) suggest, we humans have always known how to reason economically on the basis of scarcity. Although nothing necessary was lacking in those two contexts, those involved chose to act—that is, they reasoned and conducted themselves—on the basis of what they did not have. In the garden, Adam and Eve wanted the fruit of the *only* tree from which they were not to eat: a lack of access to that particular tree proved more problematic and disconcerting to them than the complete abundance of the rest of the garden was comforting and reassuring. From a biblical perspective at least, scarcity thus became a critical frame of reference for discernment from the very outset of human existence. In the desert, some Israelites inevitably found it easier to trust in their ability to gather excess manna than in the promises of God's provision for later need. Whereas the story of the garden suggests that humans often snatch scarcity from the jaws of abundance, the story of manna highlights the human tendency to doubt and distrust God's generosity as we reason from the vantage point of fear and self-interest, hoarding as many available resources as possible. How much would change if, having had our reasoning transformed, we could simply and fully live into God's unlimited abundance!

For Paul, God has already provided and will continue to provide—*always*: "God is able to provide you with every blessing in abundance, so that by always having enough of everything, you may share abundantly in every good work" (2 Cor. 9:8). Again, this abundance serves as the foundation for Paul's final appeal in verses 6-14 that the Corinthian Christians bring their generous intentions to fruition.

Using a familiar agricultural metaphor, the apostle assures them that, within a context of divine abundance, the extent of their generosity matters, and not just for the recipients of their liberality: "The one who sows sparingly will also reap sparingly, and the one who sows bountifully will also reap bountifully" (v. 6). Stinginess will do little in terms of protecting or blessing the stingy person, but there is much to "reap" from generous sharing. Paul indicates that individual believers must give in accord with what they have decided in their minds (literally "hearts"), willingly and freely, because "cheerful" giving is pleasing to God (v. 7).

Notice how the apostle's comments presuppose the necessity of discernment and appropriate economic reasoning; there is no simple, one-size-fits-all calculus or amount for giving that applies to every member of the community. Each person must make decisions in view of the Lord's abundance, trusting God to meet the needs of both giver and receiver. Such trust, particularly in the context of traditional human economies, requires transformation.

In this portion of the letter, Paul is attempting to form his readers so that they will reason in a transformed way—beginning with abundance—for the sake of generosity. He assures the Corinthians that God can and will multiply their generosity and increase the results of their "righteousness" (or "justice," v. 10); indeed, they will be "enriched in every way" because of their openhandedness, and God will receive great thanksgiving (vv. 11-12) and glory (v. 13). Ultimately, Corinthian generosity will foster relational connections with those whom they help ("they long for you"), even as the givers are repaid through the recipients' prayers (v. 14). In other words, according to Paul, abundance begets abundance.

Scarcity is an unknown construct in the kingdom of God; in the divine economy there is no such thing as a "limited good." When abundance is shared, no one loses; in fact, everyone gains. It is important, of course, that we not interpret Paul's words to mean that Christians should practice generosity merely in order to get something in return. He is not advocating here a kind of prosperity theology, in which Christians give simply because they want to receive. Rather, from Paul's perspective, the benefits of true generosity represent a natural outgrowth of Christian reasoning that has been transformed by divine abundance. To place significant focus on what a giver may receive is actually a form of reasoning in terms of scarcity, and an insidious one at that. True generosity does not emerge because of what will return to the giver; true generosity emerges from a transformed vision of God's economy of abundance. Are we ready to participate in what God is doing abundantly in the world? Are we willing to have our reasoning transformed so that abundance, rather than scarcity, becomes the framework for all of our economic conduct, from the ways we produce and consume to the ways and extent to which we express generosity? Those are questions of deep missional significance.

Faith and Works

James 2:1–26 is an appropriate text with which to conclude our reflections inasmuch as it explores the link between faith (what we claim to believe) and good works (how we are called to live). The epistle of James has a checkered history, particularly in Protestant biblical interpretation. According to Martin Luther, the message of James conflicted with the apostle Paul's emphasis on the importance of "faith," in comparison to "works"; thus Luther found James to be of little value for Christian thought and practice. Recall that in Galatians, Paul wrote:

> . . . we know that a person is justified not by the works of the law but through faith in Jesus Christ. And we have come to believe in Christ Jesus, so that we might be justified by faith in Christ, and not by doing the works of the law, because no one will be justified by the works of the law. (Gal. 2:16)

Luther assumed that, by "works of the law," Paul was referring to human attempts to achieve justification and salvation through individual merit (i.e., good works). He viewed James as essentially refuting Paul's seminal and pivotal insight that justification is a matter of grace (the unmerited favor and mercy God shows to human sinners), which was, in Luther's understanding, the crux of Christian faith.

Many scholars now take issue with Luther's interpretation of Paul, arguing that the apostle's reference to "works of the law" was likely a socioreligious designation for distinctive Jewish practices (such as observance of the Sabbath, kosher food laws, and circumcision) that demarcated their special status as God's people. From this perspective, Paul's problem with "works of the law" may have been less a concern with the futility of "works-righteousness" per se—that is, human efforts to earn salvation—than with an assumption that Jewish socioreligious identity markers confirmed one's righteous status before God.

Whatever contextualized nuances may have been at play in Paul's thinking, it seems fair to say that Luther at least partially misunderstood the exact context and force of the apostle's argument. In any event, James 2 is not a refutation of Paul's thought. James's discussion of faith and works is best understood as a vigorous argument that faith and works cannot be separated, something with which Paul would have undoubtedly agreed. Most likely, some early Christians had begun to invoke Paul's emphasis on faith over works as a simplistic meme or slogan, understanding faith as largely, if not entirely, distinct from works. Matters of belief thus trumped concrete behavior, threatening to render appropriate conduct superfluous for Christians. In response, James seeks not so much to refute Paul, but rather to condemn any such sloganeering misrepresentations of Paul's theology. And James does so in strong terms.

"Do You ... Really Believe in Our Glorious Lord Jesus Christ?"

James 2:1 begins with a pointed rhetorical question: "My brothers and sisters, do you with your acts of favoritism really believe in our glorious Lord Jesus Christ?" The Greek grammar anticipates only one adequate response: No. The content of Christian faith and the conduct of Christians must cohere. There is an inextricable relationship between faith and works.

The Greek word for "favoritism" here merits brief attention. The term literally means a "receiver of faces." Those who show favoritism receive or accept the faces of certain individuals, thereby honoring them, while they ignore or denigrate—and thus shame—(the faces of) others. The imagery is explicitly relational in nature: to show favoritism involves concretely engaging some human beings (in effect, "paying attention to their faces") while marginalizing others. James asks how anyone can really claim to be oriented to the God who refuses to show partiality (see Deut. 10:17-18; Acts 10:34; Rom. 2:11; Gal. 2:6; Eph. 6:9) while discriminating between people. Christians, who are called to love both God and neighbors, are not to play favorites—even though, in practice, they all too often do.

In verses 2-4, James describes the situation that seems to have inspired the question in verse 1. The proposed scenario was probably not entirely hypothetical. A stranger with relatively high social status would have received a warmer welcome into the community than would someone whose presence could not elevate—and might potentially diminish—the status of the group. The unexpected arrival of a bedraggled, smelly stranger might make members of the community uncomfortable, as would undoubtedly be the case in many churches today. Notice that James does not envision the poor visitor being rejected outright by the community; the Christians at least tolerate this individual. Nevertheless, as far as James is concerned, to make even subtle distinctions between guests would amount to showing favoritism.

James minces no words: those who would shun a poor person while welcoming someone of wealth and status "have . . . become judges with evil thoughts" (v. 4). In the Torah, judges, who are appointed to serve with God's blessing, are prohibited from showing partiality (e.g., Lev. 19:15 and Deut. 1:17). By contrast, James refers to self-appointed judges rendering judgments without divine authority. It is noteworthy that the basis of favoritism itself, for James, is "evil," and that the Greek word translated "thoughts" (in the phrase "evil thoughts") can also connote "reasoning." It is intriguing in the context of this study, which emphasizes biblical formation for appropriate economic reasoning, to recognize James's point as a warning against those who might become self-appointed "judges with evil reasoning."

"Has Not God Chosen the Poor . . . ?"

Verse 5 introduces another rhetorical question: "Has not God chosen the poor in the world to be rich in faith and to be heirs of the kingdom that he has promised to those who love him?" This time the grammar suggests to the readers that the only appropriate response is Yes. Rhetorically, James's question is more assertion than question. There is ample precedent in Jesus's own teaching for the idea that "the poor" would be "rich in faith" and "heirs of the kingdom" (e.g., Matt. 5:1-12; Luke 4:14-30; 6:17-26; 14:15-24). Significantly, the question implies that James assumes that his readers also affirm such understandings about the place and status of the poor in the kingdom. Those whom society—and all too often people in the church—perceives to be dispensable, inconsequential, and unworthy of attention are actually those whom God views as having powerful faith and as "heirs of the kingdom."

The relevance of the scenario sketched in verses 1-5 becomes clear in verse 6, as readers are told that they "have dishonored the poor." Given the central role of honor and shame in Mediterranean cultures—and James's affirmation regarding the status of the poor in the divine economy— the accusation that the Christians have brought shame upon the poor is an especially poignant one. Since honor was understood to be a limited good, the gain of honor by one party necessitated the loss of honor by another.

In an effort to bolster their status, those dishonored members have then resorted to denigrating poorer individuals. Rather than address the situation directly with their rich adversaries, the believers have turned upon others weaker than themselves. The questions in verses 6 and 7 express James's incredulity: "Is it not the rich who oppress you? Is it not they who drag you into court? Is it not they who blaspheme the excellent name that was invoked over you?" The Greek syntax of each rhetorical question anticipates an affirmative response. James is rhetorically exposing the radical incoherence and inconsistency at work in the favoritism that the Christians are showing to the rich.

Note that the rich "drag [Christians] into court." Although the precise context of such court cases is not clear, the economic dynamics of the larger argument suggest that James has matters of poverty and especially debt in mind. Even though the wealthy apparently have no qualms about taking less fortunate people to court, James finds his readers eager to shower them with honor.

The ultimate irony is that the Christians honor the very same people who dishonor (literally "blaspheme") the name of Christ, into which they were each baptized (v. 7). Such behavior amounts to disloyalty and a dangerous flirtation with idolatry. Ultimately, the believers hurt others and the reputation of their Lord—even as they themselves are hurt. Only the wealthy emerge unscathed, indeed, more highly honored. The Christians who show favoritism are thus nothing more than pawns in a game that ends badly and shamefully for them.

"Mercy Triumphs over Judgment"

In verses 8–13, the argument takes a more theoretical and textually oriented turn. First, James reminds his readers that doing "well" means loving one's neighbor as oneself, as opposed to currying favor from those who exploit them. He calls such neighbor-love "the royal law according to the scripture" (v. 8), implying that Jesus Christ affirmed this law as characteristic of the reign of God. To "show partiality" is to break this royal law, and those who do so are reckoned as "transgressors" (v. 9).

For James, to break part of the law is not a minor thing: "Whoever keeps the whole law but fails in one point has become accountable for all of it" (v. 10). According to James, Christians cannot pick and choose which aspects of the law they will observe, since all of the law comes from God (v. 11). Again, in order to fulfill the law, believers are to love neighbors as they love themselves (v. 8). Loving neighbors with this kind of unconditional love and mercy is rooted in a law not of judgment but of freedom and "liberty."

James wants his readers to live—in speech and conduct—with un-calculating mercy, the kind by which they will be "judged," according to "the law of liberty," by God. And lest his audience miss the point, James declares that "judgment will be without mercy to anyone who has shown no mercy; mercy triumphs over judgment" (v. 13). In other words, those who show no mercy will be shown no mercy. Showing favoritism to the rich is, in effect, to judge (v. 4) without mercy. According to James, God will not treat such a transgression lightly.

Ultimately, this passage asserts that mercy is both more powerful and more desirable—to humans *and* to God—than is judgment. Even a momentary demonstration of favoritism is a major problem, especially in light of a divine economy characterized by mercy more than judgment. It is striking that those who fail to embody such mercy will experience the judgment that they mete out to others. Favoritism is exposed as a transgression with truly stark and enduring ramifications. What would happen socially and economically if we were to live completely into the reality that in God's kingdom "mercy triumphs over judgment"?

Faith without Works Is Dead

The argument thus arrives at the chapter's overarching concern: to oppose any suggestion that having faith renders appropriate conduct irrelevant. At least some of James's readers "say [that they] have faith [even though they] do not have works" (v. 14). Yet James has already demonstrated that those who show favoritism while claiming to have faith are transgressors (vv. 8-11). Therefore, James poses two obvious rhetorical questions: "What good is it, my brothers and sisters, if you say you have faith but do not have works? Can faith save you?" The logical and appropriate response to the first question is to acknowledge that there is no merit or sense in the idea of faith apart from works. And, to the second rhetorical question, the correct answer (indicated in Greek) should be obvious: "No, faith cannot save you."

James's conclusion that "faith cannot save" (v. 14) may appear to place him at loggerheads with Paul, who argues vigorously, emphatically, and at great length—especially in Galatians and Romans—that through God's grace, faith is the only thing that can save. Yet James and Paul are not actually in opposition here. James's point is that a person's *claim* to have faith must be backed up by concrete actions, by works. The proof is in the pudding, as it were. A claim to have faith that is not borne out by demonstrable behavior is just that—a claim. If there is no appropriate behavior, there is no authentic faith (see below, v. 17).

Paul's contention is that works alone do not save (no matter how "works of the law" is best interpreted). Faith is necessary, pivotal. And Paul would not spend so much time in his letters exhorting his communities to conduct themselves appropriately if concrete behaviors were irrelevant for Christians. Essentially, James and Paul are emphasizing different sides of the same coin: Faith that is true faith bears fruit in good works. And faith that does *not* become embodied in good works is *not* true faith. James and Paul would agree that that kind of faith (which is, in reality, nonfaith) cannot save. True faith is demonstrated by appropriate conduct.

Moving toward his conclusion, James reiterates the point with a final illustration: "If a brother or sister is naked and lacks daily food, and one of you says to [him or her], 'Go in peace; keep warm and eat your fill,' and yet you do not supply their bodily needs, what is the good of that?" Words unaccompanied by action have little meaning in the face of human suffering. Do not be mistaken, James concludes in v. 17, "faith by itself, if it has no works, is dead."

Dead—that's a strong word. Dead things are inanimate; they cannot breathe, or move, or act. Faith that cannot—that does not—act is dead. Dead faith, by implication, merely awaits burial. It is worthless in the face of real, *live* situations in which God calls human beings to act decisively, often in support of the poor, suffering, and marginalized.

Using a form of Greco-Roman diatribe, in which an interlocutor interjects a statement or question in order to further the author's instructional purposes, James 2:18-26 drives home the conclusion that "faith without works is . . . dead" (v. 26). For James, true faith is not about propositional affirmations: "Even the demons believe" that "God is one"—and [it makes them] shudder" (v. 19). The demons know who God is and what God is doing in the world through Christ. They know what they are doing when they oppose the God of the universe. So belief alone is worth nothing. Even the demons have that, and they are freaked out. How much more proof, James asks, do we need in order to grasp the fact that belief apart from works cannot save us? The demons, who have belief down pat, continue to fight God. How much different is it when Christians claim to believe and yet do not act on their beliefs in concrete ways that cohere with God's purposes in the world? True faith, true belief, includes and requires action.

James concludes with two more illustrations (vv. 21-25) drawn from

Hebrew Scripture—Abraham and Rahab—to demonstrate that true faith includes works. The passage ends at verse 26 with an analogy that harks back to verse 17: "For just as the body without the spirit is dead, so faith without works is also dead." In effect, James indicates that works are to faith what the spirit is to the body. Dead bodies (without spirit) do not act; the same is true of faith that is dead—because it is not accompanied by works.

Missional Reasoning in Light of James 2

James 2:1-26 is an especially relevant passage for missionally located reasoning about economic justice and discipleship. While many of us are unaccustomed to thinking about our economic behavior in biblical and theological categories, James seems to suggest that we are in danger of dead faith when we fail to act in the face of economic suffering. Our economic behavior is thus a biblical and theological concern of the highest degree.

Each of us has been tempted at one point or another to treat people differently—with favoritism or dismissively. Indeed, we often value and honor those with wealth and status over others, and it is common within our society today to assume that economic disadvantage points to a failure on the part of poor or otherwise marginalized persons. James 2 serves as a bracing reminder to those who claim to follow Jesus that such distinctions have no place in the kingdom of God. Have we "become judges with evil thoughts"?

James reminds us that our behavior toward our fellow human beings must be rooted in appropriate and just moral reasoning, reasoning cognizant of the biblical perspective that the poor are "rich in faith" and poised to inherit God's kingdom. The place of the poor and marginalized in God's eyes should serve as the starting point for all considerations of what appropriate behavior toward such people might look like. And, given that God's eye is on all who suffer at the margins, the same reasoning would no doubt apply with regard to our wider social relationships, priorities, and policies. Contemporary economic values such as competitiveness, effectiveness, efficiency, self-reliance, success, and the like must take a back seat to the flesh-and-blood needs of those God so deeply cares about.

Ultimately, showing favoritism is a symptom of a much deeper problem, namely, that we do not actually value the poor and marginalized as God does. To treat the wealthy and powerful better than others is the natural result of a radically inadequate theological anthropology, in which we fail to value human beings according to their intrinsic worth as those created in the image of God. In this sense, James 2:1-26 seeks not merely to stop the phenomenon of favoritism and partiality, as if the text were only concerned with outward behaviors; rather, the passage tries to get at the deeper issue that leads to such discriminatory conduct, namely, the faulty reasoning and logic rooted in an inappropriate valuation of those who are poor and marginalized. James seeks to reform the economic reasoning of its readers so that their treatment of others, whether wealthy or poor, coheres not with traditional sociocultural values and categories but with the perspectives of the God whom they claim to serve. James challenges the Christian community to reason appropriately and, when the situation warrants, he indicts believers for failing to do so.

Understood in this way, James 2:1-26 functions as a deeply missional text. Although the passage is not primarily about outreach per se, it does seek to reorient the community's economic reasoning and logic so that God's people will be more fully prepared to live appropriately and concretely in their located vocation as a people caught up in God's creative purposes. As with other passages we have explored, this one can help contemporary Christian communities reflect on the ways we may need to be transformed in order to become more faithful to the mission we have been given by God, both in terms of our economic reasoning and the concrete behavior that appropriate missional reasoning will increasingly inspire.

FOR FURTHER REFLECTION

► What would happen if, like the earliest Christian community (see Acts 2:43-47; 4:32-37), we were to reason and behave entirely in terms of the needs of others?

► Christians celebrate and announce the unmerited gift of Christ's death and resurrection that they have received. Why is it often difficult for those of us who have experienced such grace to offer tangible mercy, compassion, and financial assistance to others without calculating whether they deserve it or not?

► What would complete trust in God's abundance do for our attempts to show generosity?

▶ Are we willing to have our reasoning transformed by God so that divine abundance, rather than scarcity, becomes the framework for all of our economic conduct?

▶ Do our reasoning and behavior as Christians indicate that we really believe in Jesus Christ (see James 2:1)?

▶ Are there contexts in which we act as "judges with evil thoughts" (James 2:4)? Discuss.

▶ What would happen if "abundance" and "mercy" were to become the primary economic criteria for our economic reasoning and behavior?

▶ To what extent might our economic conduct ("works") suggest that our faith is, in effect, largely dead?

CHAPTER 13

Missional Hermeneutics,
Transformed Reasoning, and Choosing Life

The purposes and purposiveness of God as revealed in Scripture, more than the church's historical or contemporary practice, must determine how we understand mission, and thus what it means to approach the biblical text from the vantage point of a missional hermeneutic. If *mission* is primarily understood in terms of evangelism or outreach or the like, then much of the biblical text is manifestly not about mission. But if we understand mission in terms of the purposiveness of God, a purposiveness into which the interpreting community has been caught up and called, then mission becomes a relevant, crucial, and inherently appropriate interpretive rubric for every verse in the Bible—including the passages that we have explored in this book.

Mission is about being sent: God sends the Son, Spirit, and a people into the world to bear witness to divine purposes. Evangelism, as traditionally understood, is surely and undoubtedly an important facet of that mission, but the divine purposiveness that is reflected in the Bible is both a broader and deeper category, embracing the totality of the reign of God. The mission of the church, to the extent that it is to reflect and bear witness to the purposiveness of God, includes—but is not to be equated with or limited to—evangelism or outreach per se. Everything relating to the reign of God, including economic justice (which, unfortunately, is often understood to be different from or even at odds with evangelistic concerns), is a missional matter.

The value of "missional hermeneutics," properly understood, is not that we imagine every biblical text to be about, or even reflective of, evangelism or outreach. Rather, the benefit of such a hermeneutical approach is that it helps remind us that even what we might think of as "nonevangelistic" texts are deeply missional in character and function to the extent that they are reflective of the divine—and, by extension and calling, the church's—mission. To engage in missional hermeneutics is to approach the biblical text with the conviction that the Bible reveals to readers a God of mission—a purposive, sending God. In fact, to read Scripture responsibly is therefore to read it missionally, privileging the very character of a thoroughgoing missional text that reveals this purposive God. In that sense, missional hermeneutics encourages us to pay closer and more faithful attention to the holistic mission of the God who calls and sends Jesus's followers as a community of faith into the world. That mission is reflected, at least to some degree, in specific biblical texts—including the passages we have explored in this book. Therefore, it is both appropriate and imperative to reflect on discrete texts missionally.

The biblical text does not merely contain snippets of mission (qua evangelism) and it does much more than portray a narrative of mission; it is, in whole and in part, both a product of (as reflected, for example, in Paul's Epistles) and tool for mission (e.g., in terms of its formative and transformative function). If we understand it properly, we do not so much find mission in the Bible as we find a missional Bible. This more comprehensive understanding of mission has the benefit of shifting our interpretive focus beyond typical descriptive analyses of the biblical metanarrative toward more complex and contextually located hermeneutical issues, including the missional function of biblical texts themselves in relationship to their readers.

A robust missional hermeneutic does not represent a weakening of or a retreat from the rigorous discipline of critical biblical scholarship; rather, a missional hermeneutic reflects the best of critical analysis and methodology, coupled with a deep commitment to interpretive honesty, given that we read as those who are located within the context of a comprehensive, divine mission—and that we are reading texts that are tools and products of that larger mission.

A missional reading, properly understood, maintains a critically analytical posture even as it resists the kind of detachment at arm's length that is so often characteristic of traditional historical-critical interpretation. Missional interpretation both frees us and challenges us to take seriously, and even to prioritize, the contemporary, located contexts in which readers approach discrete texts, including those pertaining to money, wealth, poverty, economic justice, and so forth. In that sense, a missional hermeneutic encourages us to wrestle with such passages in light of contemporary situations "on the ground" and not merely in terms of overarching theoretical, methodological, or theological principles. We read and are read by biblical texts, in specific contexts—and those contexts matter. We interpret as those who are—in the very process of reading and interpretation—being formed and transformed for located and concrete witness as contemporary communities of faith.

Throughout this book I have emphasized that the Bible does not merely command or prohibit particular behaviors with regard to economic matters. Rather, it seeks in many ways and in many contexts to shape and to form—indeed, to transform—both readers' behaviors and also the very ways in which they reason economically. Paul's moral exhortation to the Roman Christians, "Do not be conformed to this world, but be transformed by the renewing of your minds" (Rom. 12:2), captures this dual formation in a vivid manner. The apostle's epistolary call for the believers to allow God to "transform" them "by the renewing of" their "minds" immediately precedes a four-chapter section of concrete and contextual moral instruction (Rom. 12–15). Paul is not simply concerned with their behavior; he wants their conduct to be rooted in appropriate gospel-shaped reasoning.

My primary emphasis in this book has been to highlight how some illustrative biblical texts related to matters of money, wealth, poverty, and economic justice function to transform the economic reasoning of their readers. We have noted again and again that these biblical passages are not merely, or even primarily, concerned with guiding readers toward narrowly specific economic choices or behaviors. Throughout, we have discovered that biblical texts tend to focus on the formation of human reasoning, seeking to shape readers' moral imaginations so that they will not merely act differently than human beings typically do, but so that they will actually think and reason differently about why and how they might choose to behave in the first place. In other words, the Bible is intent on transforming the entire mental framework ("by the renewing of [our] minds," Rom. 12:2) within which Christians even contemplate and make sense of their behavioral opportunities and choices, rooting our actions in an entirely different moral universe and calculus.

In Deuteronomy 30:15, as Moses concludes his review of the terms of the covenant between God and the people, he says, "I have set before you today life and prosperity, death and adversity." In other words, Moses declares that he has made it clear to them how to experience full and abundant life in relationship with both God and one another. Faithful observation of the covenant is thus not about mere legal compliance; rather, it is actually what brings true, full life. Failure to observe the terms of the covenant is to miss out on real life and thus to deal in the realm of death. This is not because God is vindictive and punitive; rather, it is because God knows how human beings are made, how we are wired, and what leads us to flourish. An engine that is given the wrong fuel develops problems. Similarly, God's people do not thrive when they seek to operate apart from the love, wisdom, guidance, mercy, justice, and grace of God. Moses says, in effect, "I have given you the options—how to live and how to die." And in Deuteronomy 30:19, he urges the Israelites to "choose life."

Choosing life—that is what this book is about. In our contemporary economic environment, we are constantly encouraged, in effect, to choose death. We are told that we should give our respect and homage to the mysterious wisdom of markets, trusting that a providential "invisible hand" will guide us to security, prosperity, and freedom. We are taught to use utilitarian or libertarian reasoning as if there were no other options. On the one hand, we view every economic choice in light of its potential results or consequences, thereby rendering human beings, the environment, and the entire created order subject to objectification and use as means to an end. On the other hand, we assert our individual rights and autonomy, clinging to an ideological construct that effectively liberates us from a sense of responsibility for the well-being of others. Our values, priorities, and policies indicate that we are deeply committed to death-dealing forms of economic reasoning: we find self-interest, competition, and profit-seeking more natural and intellectually defensible than generosity, cooperation, and mutuality; we laud those who horde wealth and status, and we eschew those who suffer from poverty and exclusion. Books could easily be filled with examples of the explicit and implicit ways that we choose death on a daily basis. What might it look like to "choose life" today with respect to money, wealth, possessions, poverty, and economic justice?

In this book, we have inductively explored a number of illustrative biblical passages as we reflected on that kind of question.[1] Reflecting on

---

1. Readers are also encouraged to explore other studies that have addressed, in a range of ways, economic matters in biblical and theological perspective. Among many book-length works are, for example, Helen Alford et al., eds., *Rediscovering Abundance: Interdisciplinary Essays on Wealth, Income, and Their Distribution in the Catholic Social Tradition* (Notre Dame, IN: University of Notre Dame Press, 2006); Albino Barrera, *Biblical Economic Ethics: Sacred Scripture's Teachings on Economic Life* (Lanham, MD: Lexington, 2013); Craig L. Blomberg, *Neither Poverty nor Riches: A Biblical Theology of Possessions* (Downers Grove, IL: InterVarsity, 1999); Walter Brueggemann, *Money and*

these texts from the vantage point of a missional hermeneutic, particularly in light of the second and third streams within George Hunsberger's typology, I have emphasized how they seek to form and transform the economic reasoning and behavior of God's people, for the sake of individual and communal faithfulness to the *missio Dei*. [2] I would like to close this study by noting, very briefly, four especially important themes among the many that have come up for us to reflect on. These are but a few of those issues related to our economic reasoning that God's Spirit seeks to transform in us "by the renewing of our minds, so that we will know what is the will of God—what is good and acceptable and perfect" (Rom. 12:2).

A Covenantal Context

The God of the Bible seeks out not merely individuals, but a people, a community that earnestly desires to initiate and maintain a relationship of covenantal faithfulness and mutuality with God. A covenant is established, one with stipulations designed to foster health and wholeness—indeed, life. Obedience to the covenant does not earn divine love; rather, the covenant itself is predicated on the fact that the people already have God's favor. Both parties are expected to remain faithful to the terms of

Possessions (Louisville: Westminster John Knox, 2016); John R. Donahue, *What Does the Lord Require? A Bibliographical Essay on the Bible and Social Justice*, rev. and exp. ed. (St. Louis: Institute of Jesuit Resources, 2000); Daniel K. Finn, *Christian Economic Ethics: History and Implications* (Minneapolis: Fortress, 2013); Justo L. González, *Faith and Wealth: A History of Early Christian Ideas on the Origin, Significance, and Use of Money* (Eugene, OR: Wipf and Stock, 2002); Roelf Haan, *The Economics of Honor: Biblical Reflections on Money and Property*, trans. Bert Hielema (Grand Rapids: Eerdmans, 2009); Leslie J. Hoppe, *There Shall Be No Poor among You: Poverty in the Bible* (Nashville: Abingdon, 2004); Walter J. Houston, *Justice—The Biblical Challenge* (Oakville, CT: Equinox, 2010); Richard Horsley, *Covenant Economics: A Biblical Vision of Justice for All* (Louisville: Westminster John Knox, 2009); Bruce W. Longenecker and Kelly D. Liebengood, eds., *Engaging Economics: New Testament Scenarios and Early Christian Reception* (Grand Rapids: Eerdmans, 2009); Bruce V. Malchow, *Social Justice in the Hebrew Bible: What Is New and What Is Old* (Collegeville, MN: Liturgical, 1996); J. David Pleins, *The Social Visions of the Hebrew Bible: A Theological Introduction* (Louisville: Westminster John Knox, 2001); Joerg Rieger, *No Rising Tide: Theology, Politics, and the Future* (Minneapolis: Fortress, 2009); Ronald J. Sider, *Rich Christians in an Age of Hunger*, 5th ed. (Nashville: W Publishing Group, 2005 [1997]); Sondra Ely Wheeler, *Wealth as Peril and Obligation: The New Testament on Possessions* (Grand Rapids: Eerdmans, 1995).

2. See chap. 2 above.

the covenant as a means by which they can maintain healthy human and divine relationships.

Within the terms of the covenant, God's people are enjoined and formed to care for each other and to foster the well-being of the weakest and the most marginalized. The biblical vision of a faithful covenant community is clear: justice starts at the bottom—again, with the economically and socially vulnerable, such as the widows, orphans, and aliens. If those at the lowest rungs of society are suffering, something is very wrong, and the terms of the covenant have been broken. The biblical prophets responded harshly in such contexts. They indicate that God does not stay neutral in situations of injustice.

Generosity, impartiality, and fair dealing are pivotal covenantal justice concerns. Charitable works, while crucial and necessary, are insufficient. Debt relief and wealth redistribution (e.g., the Jubilee) are strikingly consonant with biblical values. And the biblical imagery of the Sabbath is crucial, both for its implications regarding the needs and rights of laborers and for its theological import as a vision for a sustainable balance of work and rest.

Human Dignity

Human beings, created in the very image of God, are to be treated as those who have intrinsic and inestimable value. They must not be objectified, commodified, exploited, or viewed as means to any other ends—no matter how much doing so might reflect market utility. To protect human life and to foster well-being requires not merely passive avoidance of unjust behavior; rather, biblical justice envisions proactive, just treatment toward all people. We are interdependent, interrelated, and inherently social. We need each other. Mistreatment of one of us hurts all of us.

Liberation for the Oppressed

Jesus's own mission statement in Luke 4 indicates that he understands his mission in terms of liberation, not merely in a spiritual sense, but also in terms of economic and social forms of bondage. He understands his vocation to embody and fulfill (Luke 4:21) the Isaianic calling to "bring good news to the poor . . . to proclaim release to the captives and recovery of sight to the blind, to let the oppressed go free" and "to proclaim the year of the Lord's favor" (4:18-19). Jesus's ministry enacts Isaiah's vision, continuing and ultimately—in his death and resurrection—fulfilling the divine mission to liberate human beings from all that enslaves them and alienates them from God and from one another.

God reveals Godself as the divine liberator in the story of the Exodus, a narrative that, in testifying to the liberating character and activity of Yahweh, reminds us that injustice is the result of human choices—individually and in the aggregate. As a rule, God is not to be blamed for economic injustice, poverty, or oppression. From the Exodus forward, the biblical canon reminds readers not to shirk their responsibility for and complicity in the situations of injustice that continue to play out before our eyes.

Further, we are reminded again and again that the story of the Exodus is, for Christians, our story. By extension, we, too, are expected to know the experience of oppression and of living in a vulnerable state in a strange land. We should thus know instinctively how to treat everyone appropriately, including those who today represent the biblical poor—the widows, orphans, and aliens. If we claim the God of the Exodus, we must also claim the implications of what it means to serve such a God, one who hears the cries of the oppressed and crushes the systems that create and foster economic and social injustice. Any economic behavior that capitalizes on the misfortunes of the downtrodden is thoroughly suspect.

Living into the Abundance of the Kingdom

Over and over again, we have seen that biblical imagery emphasizes the abundance of God's provision for humans—in the created order, in the Exodus, in the community of God's people, and so forth. The Bible seeks to transform our moral imaginations so that we will reason economically from the perspective of abundance and gratitude as opposed to scarcity and fear. Too often we reason with sclerotic hearts and minds, focusing on what we lack or may lose. We are called to catch and live into the vision of the abundance of God's kingdom, reasoning and acting in accordance with that vision. We need not accept today's economic orthodoxies, which urge us to assume that self-interest and profit, for example, are the only ways in which to make logical sense of our world. Abundance, generosity, cooperation, sustainability, compassion, mercy, love, and justice—these need not (indeed, they must not) remain oddly spiritualized, idealistic terms for

Christians. We serve the God who can and will make these realities. Are we ready for the radically alternative kind of economic logic that characterizes abundant kingdom living?

Many Christians assume that there is a radical difference between the Hebrew Bible, or Old Testament, on the one hand, and the New Testament, on the other. They find the God of the Old Testament to be quite at odds with what they find in Jesus. While there are certainly some differences between the two Testaments, the remarkable thing—especially evident when we focus on matters of economic reasoning—is how similar they actually are. The covenantal framework of the Old Testament is present in the New, albeit in a renewed form. And Jesus clearly draws extensively on Old Testament covenantal and prophetic perspectives as he teaches. In short, although there is manifest diversity in the biblical record with regard to matters of wealth, poverty, money, economic justice, and so forth, there is at the same time a remarkable amount of agreement.

Jesus's call for covenant renewal (see esp. Matt. 5-7 and Luke 6:17-49) presupposes deep interdependency and mutuality within the covenant community. And many of the New Testament passages we explored highlight the way divine abundance provides space for new kinds of economic reasoning and conduct. While slavery to wealth is true slavery, slavery in service to God brings true life. We cannot serve life and death at the same time. Luke, in particular, emphasizes the extent to which the reign of God is characterized by present and coming reversals of the status quo as we know it. Matthew also emphasizes that Christ is found in service to the poor and marginalized (especially in 25:31-46). Ultimately, as we open ourselves and our economic reasoning up to be transformed by the power of the Spirit of God, we are assured that we will begin to bear the tangible fruit of faithful economic conduct (see James 2). Divine abundance is real. Our reasoning must be transformed. May we not continue to succumb to the idolatries of traditional human economic reasoning. What seems impossible for us is possible for God (see Mark 10:27). Let us choose life!

Bibliographic Citations

Adams, Samuel L. *Social and Economic Life in Second Temple Judea*. Louisville: Westminster John Knox, 2014.

Alford, Helen, et al., eds. *Rediscovering Abundance: Interdisciplinary Essays on Wealth, Income, and Their Distribution in the Catholic Social Tradition*. Notre Dame, IN: University of Notre Dame Press, 2006.

Anderson, Gary A. *Charity: The Place of the Poor in the Biblical Tradition*. New Haven, CT: Yale University Press, 2013.

Barram, Michael. "The Bible, Mission, and Social Location: Toward a Missional Hermeneutic." *Interpretation* 43 (2007): 42-58.

———. "'Fools for the Sake of Christ': Missional Hermeneutics and Praxis in the Corinthian Correspondence." *Missiology: An International Review* 43 (2015): 195-207.

———. *Mission and Moral Reflection in Paul*. Studies in Biblical Literature 75. New York: Peter Lang, 2006.

———. "'Occupying' Genesis 1-3: Missionally Located Reflections on Biblical Values and Economic Justice." *Missiology* 42 (2014): 386-98.

———. "Pauline Mission as Salvific Intentionality: Fostering a Missional Consciousness in 1 Corinthians 9.19-23 and 10.31-11.1." In *Paul as Missionary: Identity, Activity, Theology, and Practice*, edited by Trevor Burke and Brian S. Rosner, 234-46. Library of New Testament Studies. London; New York: T. & T. Clark International, 2011.

Barrera, Albino. *Biblical Economic Ethics: Sacred Scripture's Teachings on Economic Life*. Lanham, MD: Lexington, 2013.

Blomberg, Craig L. *Neither Poverty nor Riches: A Biblical Theology of Possessions*. Downers Grove, IL: InterVarsity, 1999.

Brueggemann, Walter. *Money and Possessions*. Louisville: Westminster John Knox, 2016.

Bruner, Frederick Dale. *Matthew: A Commentary,* Volume 2: *The Churchbook, Matthew 13-28.* Revised and expanded edition. Grand Rapids: Eerdmans, 2004.

Carroll, John T. *Luke: A Commentary.* Louisville: Westminster John Knox, 2012.

Carter, Warren. *Matthew and the Margins: A Sociopolitical and Religious Reading.* Maryknoll: Orbis, 2000.

Cavanaugh, William T. *Being Consumed: Economics and Christian Desire.* Grand Rapids: Eerdmans, 2008.

Clark, Charles M. A. "The Challenge of Catholic Social Thought to Economic Theory." *The Journal for Peace and Justice Studies* 12 (2002): 163–77.

Donahue, John R. *What Does the Lord Require? A Bibliographical Essay on the Bible and Social Justice.* Revised and expanded edition. St. Louis: Institute of Jesuit Resources, 2000.

Goheen, Michael W. *Reading the Bible Missionally.* Grand Rapids: Eerdmans, 2016.

González, Justo L. *Faith and Wealth: A History of Early Christian Ideas on the Origin, Significance, and Use of Money.* Eugene, OR: Wipf and Stock, 2002.

Guder, Darrell L., ed. *Missional Church: A Vision for the Sending of the Church in North America.* Gospel and Culture Series. Grand Rapids: Eerdmans, 1998.

Haan, Roelf. *The Economics of Honor: Biblical Reflections on Money and Property.* Translated by Bert Hielema. Grand Rapids: Eerdmans, 2009.

Hoppe, Leslie J. *There Shall Be No Poor among You: Poverty in the Bible.* Nashville: Abingdon, 2004.

Horsley, Richard A. *Covenant Economics: A Biblical Vision of Justice for All.* Louisville: Westminster John Knox, 2009.

Houston, Walter J. *Justice—The Biblical Challenge.* Oakville, CT: Equinox, 2010.

Hunsberger, George R. "Mapping the Missional Hermeneutics Conversation." In *Reading the Bible Missionally,* edited by Michael W. Goheen, 45–67. Grand Rapids: Eerdmans, 2016.

———. "Proposals for a Missional Hermeneutic: Mapping a Conversation." *Missiology* 39 (2011): 309–21.

Kling, David W. *The Bible in History: How the Texts Have Shaped the Times.* New York: Oxford University Press, 2004.

Knight, Douglas A. *Law, Power, and Justice in Ancient Israel.* Louisville: Westminster John Knox, 2011.

Longenecker, Bruce W., and Kelly D. Liebengood, eds. *Engaging Economics: New Testament Scenarios and Early Christian Reception.* Grand Rapids: Eerdmans, 2009.

Malchow, Bruce V. *Social Justice in the Hebrew Bible: What Is New and What Is Old.* Collegeville, MN: Liturgical, 1996.

Malina, Bruce J., and Richard L. Rohrbaugh. *Social-Science Commentary on the Synoptic Gospels.* 2d ed. Minneapolis: Fortress, 2003.

Matera, Frank J. *The Sermon on the Mount: The Perfect Measure of the Christian Life.* Collegeville, MN: Liturgical, 2013.

Meyers, Carol. *Exodus*. New Cambridge Bible Commentary. New York: Cambridge University Press, 2005.

Oakman, Douglas E. *Jesus, Debt, and the Lord's Prayer: First-Century Debt and Jesus' Intentions*. Eugene, OR: Cascade, 2014.

Pleins, J. David. *The Social Visions of the Hebrew Bible: A Theological Introduction*. Louisville: Westminster John Knox, 2001.

Rieger, Joerg. *No Rising Tide: Theology, Politics, and the Future*. Minneapolis: Fortress, 2009.

Sandel, Michael J. *Justice: What's the Right Thing to Do?* New York: Farrar, Straus and Giroux, 2009.

Sider, Ronald J. *Rich Christians in an Age of Hunger*. 5th ed. Nashville: W Publishing Group, 2005 [1997].

Talbert, Charles H. *Reading the Sermon on the Mount: Character Formation and Ethical Decision Making in Matthew 5–7*. Grand Rapids: Baker, 2004.

Vaage, Leif E. "The Sermon on the Mount: An Economic Proposal." In *God's Economy: Biblical Studies from Latin America*, edited by Ross Kinsler and Gloria Kinsler, 127–51. Maryknoll, NY: Orbis, 2005.

Van Houten, Christina. *Alien in Israelite Law: A Study of the Changing Legal Status of Strangers in Ancient Israel*. JSOTSS 107. Sheffield, UK: JSOT Press, 1991.

Wheeler, Sondra Ely. *Wealth as Peril and Obligation: The New Testament on Possessions*. Grand Rapids: Eerdmans, 1995.

Index of Names and Subjects

words," 72; two versions of (in
Exodus and Deuteronomy), 72, 78;
use of the second-person plural
pronoun in, 73; "you shall not bear
false witness against your neighbor," 83–84; "you shall not commit
adultery," 83; "you shall not covet,"
84–85; "you shall not make for
yourself an idol," 74–76; "you shall
not make wrongful use of the name
of the LORD your God," 77–78; "you
shall not murder," 82; "you shall
not steal," 83
deities, in the Ancient Near East, 74;
Israelites' worship of, 74; swearing
of oaths to, 78
dignity, human, 243; Roman Catholi-
cism on, 144–45
dikaiosynē (Greek: righteousness,
justice), 46
discernment, 7; of the will of God,
7–8, 19
Donahue, John R., 242n1

eisegesis, 33
elderly, the, honor and respect for,
81–82
Enuma Elish, 141–46, 152; and authorization of the exploitation of the
Babylonian labor force, 142; and inspiration of a competitive and warlike perspective on other human
communities, 142–43; as a myth,
141–42; narrative of, 141; social
hierarchies in, 142; and validation
of the Babylonian Empire, 142
evangelism, 22, 238; and mission, 22,
238
"evil eye," 179
Exodus, the, 54–59, 60–61, 63–64, 137,
244; African slaves' interpretation
of, 59–60; as Christians' own story,
80; etiology of the word "exodus"
(Greek *ex* and *hodos*), 54; and God's
personal name (YHWH), 54–55;
and the hardening of Pharaoh's
heart, 57–58; and the identity and
purpose of the Israelites, 60–61;
Latin American Christian leaders'
interpretation of, 60; narrative of,

54–55; the Puritans' interpretation
of, 59; as a reminder that God does
not attempt to reform the system,
but destroys it, 58–59; as a reminder
that injustice and oppression result
from human choices, 56–58; as a
reminder that oppression and injustice are fundamentally human creations, 55–56; the role of Moses and
Aaron in, 59; social location and the
interpretation of the Exodus story,
59–60; and Yahweh as a liberator of
the oppressed, 55, 56, 64, 244

faith: James on, 193, 233–34; Paul on,
233–34; view of as cognitive assent
to a belief structure, 52; view of as
existential engagement in a humble
journey of authentic discovery of
God in relationship, 52
false witness, 83–84
favoritism, 230–31, 235–36; the Greek
word for "favoritism" ("receiver of
faces"), 230
Finn, Daniel K., 242n1
1 Corinthians, reframing of the basis
for Christian and moral behavioral
reasoning in light of Jesus's own
conduct in, 223
formation, 5; formation by economic
dynamics (see also *Homo economicus*), 14; formation by life, 10,
11, 14; moral formation, 7. *See also*
Bible, the, as both a tool for and a
product of formation
freedom: biblical notion of (freedom
for), 68; as a fundamental theme in
the Bible, 56–57; libertarian notion
of (freedom *from*), 68, 68–69

Genesis, first creation story in, 140,
141, 143–46; affirmation of the
created order as "good," 143; date
of, 141; God's bringing order out of
the watery chaos, 143; humans as
created in the image of God (*imago
Dei*), 143–45; humans as God's representatives, 145; human work as a
extension of divine work, 143; literary style of, 140; as myth, 140–41,

Index of Scripture

Titles Published in

THE GOSPEL AND OUR CULTURE SERIES

Michael Barram, *Missional Economics: Biblical Justice and Christian Formation* (2018)

Lois Y. Barrett et al., *Treasure in Clay Jars: Patterns in Missional Faithfulness* (2004)

James V. Brownson et al., *StormFront: The Good News of God* (2003)

Michael W. Goheen, ed., *Reading the Bible Missionally* (2016)

Michael J. Gorman, *Becoming the Gospel: Paul, Participation, and Mission* (2015)

Darrell L. Guder, *Called to Witness: Doing Missional Theology* (2015)

Darrell L. Guder, *The Continuing Conversion of the Church* (2000)

Darrell L. Guder, ed., *Missional Church: A Vision for the Sending of the Church in North America* (1998)

George R. Hunsberger, *Bearing the Witness of the Spirit: Lesslie Newbigin's Theology of Cultural Plurality* (1998)

George R. Hunsberger, *The Story That Chooses Us: A Tapestry of Missional Vision* (2015)

George R. Hunsberger and Craig Van Gelder, eds., *The Church between Gospel and Culture: The Emerging Mission in North America* (1996)

Stefan Paas, *Church Planting in the Secular West: Learning from the European Experience* (2016)

Craig Van Gelder, ed., *Confident Witness — Changing World: Rediscovering the Gospel in North America* (1999)

Craig Van Gelder and Dwight J. Zscheile, *Participating in God's Mission: A Theological Missiology for the Church in America* (2018)

Made in the USA
Las Vegas, NV
18 August 2021